A PHENOMENOLOGY OF INDIGENOUS RELIGIONS

Bloomsbury Advances in Religious Studies

Series Editors: Bettina E. Schmidt, Steven Sutcliffe and Will Sweetman
Founding Editors: James Cox and Peggy Morgan

Bloomsbury Advances in Religious Studies publishes cutting-edge research
in the Study of Religion/s. The series draws on anthropological,
ethnographical, historical, sociological and textual methods amongst
others. Topics are diverse, but each publication integrates theoretical
analysis with empirical data. The series aims to refresh the interdisciplinary
agenda in new evidence-based studies of 'religion'.

American Evangelicals, Ashlee Quosigk
Appropriation of Native American Spirituality, Suzanne Owen
Becoming Buddhist, Glenys Eddy
Community and Worldview among Paraiyars of South India,
Anderson H. M. Jeremiah
Conceptions of the Afterlife in Early Civilizations, Gregory Shushan
Contemporary Western Ethnography and the Definition of Religion,
Martin D. Stringer
Cultural Blending in Korean Death Rites, Chang- Won Park
Free Zone Scientology, Aled Thomas
Globalization of Hesychasm and the Jesus Prayer, Christopher D. L. Johnson
Individualized Religion, Claire Wanless
Innateness of Myth, Ritske Rensma
Levinas, Messianism and Parody, Terence Holden
New Paradigm of Spirituality and Religion, Mary Catherine Burgess
Orthodox Christianity, New Age Spirituality and Vernacular Religion,
Eugenia Roussou
Post- Materialist Religion, Mika T. Lassander
Redefining Shamanisms, David Gordon Wilson
Reform, Identity and Narratives of Belonging, Arkotong Longkumer
Religion and the Discourse on Modernity, Paul- François Tremlett
Religion as a Conversation Starter, Ina Merdjanova and Patrice Brodeur
Religion, Material Culture and Archaeology, Julian Droogan

A PHENOMENOLOGY OF INDIGENOUS RELIGIONS

Theory and Practice

James L. Cox

BLOOMSBURY ACADEMIC
LONDON · NEW YORK · OXFORD · NEW DELHI · SYDNEY

BLOOMSBURY ACADEMIC
Bloomsbury Publishing Plc
50 Bedford Square, London, WC1B 3DP, UK
1385 Broadway, New York, NY 10018, USA
29 Earlsfort Terrace, Dublin 2, Ireland

BLOOMSBURY, BLOOMSBURY ACADEMIC and the Diana logo are trademarks of
Bloomsbury Publishing Plc

First published in Great Britain 2022
This paperback edition published 2023

A catalogue record for this book is available from the British Library.

Library of Congress Control Number: 2021949398

ISBN: HB: 978-1-3502-5072-7
          PB: 978-1-3502-5076-5
          ePDF: 978-1-3502-5073-4
          eBook: 978-1-3502-5074-1

Series: Bloomsbury Advances in Religious Studies

Typeset by Integra Software Services Pvt. Ltd.

To find out more about our authors and books visit www.bloomsbury.com
and sign up for our newsletters

CONTENTS

FOREWORD

As a co-editor of the *Advances in Religious Studies* series, and as a long-standing colleague of Professor James Cox at the University of Edinburgh and in the British Association for the Study of Religions, I am delighted to write the Foreword to this impressive collection of essays. These texts are drawn from a distinguished career in Religious Studies and are gathered together here for the first time to form an integrated argument for the value of using a phenomenological method in the study of Indigenous Religions. James Cox has been the leading English-language proponent of phenomenological methodology for the study of religions over the last twenty-five years. Under the rubric of phenomenology, he has continued to affirm the positive value of ethnographically thick 'description' and the nuanced interpretation of primary sources during a period when others have turned entirely to deconstruction and post-structuralist critique. Jim (as he is known informally to his colleagues and friends) has preferred to refine and adapt (and where necessary, of course, critique) the phenomenological framework as a productive continuing method. I would argue that his great achievement has been to bring phenomenology 'down to earth', as it were, recrafting it from a recondite hermeneutic into an accessible, practical method for describing and explaining human behaviour and social interaction. In two groundbreaking publications – *Expressing the Sacred*, first published in 1992 and revised in 2010 as *Introduction to the Phenomenology of Religion*, and *Guide to the Phenomenology of Religion: Key Figures, Formative Influences and Subsequent Debates* in 2006 – Jim set out the theory and practice of what we might call a 'new phenomenology': comparative, empirical, scientific in the best sense, no longer focused on detecting a theological or metaphysical ground to religion, but on describing anthropological and historical realities in order to generate theoretically fruitful comparisons across cultures. This new phenomenology is ethnographically grounded, theoretically aware and historically reflexive, and has more in common with social anthropology and similar social science approaches than with the philosophical and indeed theological concerns of earlier generations.

This takes us to James Cox's second major contribution to the Study of Religions: his careful fieldwork on Indigenous experiences and identities in three continents – North America, Africa and Australia. Exposure to this material came at an early stage in Jim's career through his doctoral studies in missionary historiography, which helped him to re-think and re-work the colonial category of 'primal' as 'indigenous'. This category shift marks a major contribution to the wider decolonizing turn in the academy and was given sustained expression in Jim's monograph *From Primitive to Indigenous: The Academic Study of Indigenous Religions* (2007). This groundbreaking volume was followed in 2014 by *The*

Invention of God in Indigenous Societies, in which he takes up the debate on the construction or invention of 'religion' (and related categories) and explores its ramifications for Indigenous societies that typically lacked the concept, or whose people only recognized it insofar as they encountered it in colonizers' discourses. Jim has thus emerged as a major advocate for the study of Indigenous Religions both as a central ingredient in the Study of Religions as an academic field and as a comparative field of study in its own right, both located firmly within the decolonizing turn.

Third, Professor Cox has given abundant and unswerving service to international institutions for the academic study of religions. He was a co-founder, in 1992, of the African Association for the Study of Religions and served on its Executive Committee for ten years. Between 1997 and 2006 he served as Bulletin Editor, Secretary and finally President of the British Association for the Study of Religions. Between 2011 and 2014 Professor Cox was Deputy General Secretary of the European Association for the Study of Religions, to which he was elected an Honorary Member in 2015.

Finally, the cross-fertilization of critical mission historiography, phenomenological renewal and indigenous ethnography in Jim's research has been further refined through energetic classroom teaching over the years. Religious Studies students at Edinburgh on both the MA and MSc Religious Studies programmes invariably appreciated the content and presentation of Jim's courses on Indigenous Religions, shamanism, and phenomenological method and history. And this dynamic interplay between method, theory and data in Jim's teaching and research is abundantly evident in the essays gathered together in this collection. With the exception of the specially written Introduction and Conclusion, which contextualize the main content, these essays were written over a twenty-year period from 1998 to 2018. Read in sequence, they demonstrate a compelling coherence in voice and method, ranging lucidly across meta-theoretical debate, critical re-assessment of earlier scholars and – most importantly – Indigenous case studies from Alaska, Zimbabwe and Australia.

This volume is a fitting summation to Professor James Cox's distinguished career in the Study of Religions and makes a rich and compelling argument for the continuing vitality of phenomenology as method, Indigenous Religions as subject. It is highly appropriate that it should appear in the series *Advances in Religious Studies* which James Cox established with Peggy Morgan and which published its first volume in early 2008. Welcome back, Jim!

Dr Steven J. Sutcliffe
Senior Lecturer in the Study of Religion
University of Edinburgh

ACKNOWLEDGEMENTS

The idea for producing a book containing a selection of my previously published works was first considered in conversations I had with Lalle Pursglove, Religion Editor for Bloomsbury Academic, while attending the 2017 Conference of the British Association for the Study of Religions in Chester. This discussion was continued the following year at the BASR Conference in Belfast with Steven Sutcliffe, who was then President of the BASR and a member of the editorial team of Bloomsbury's Advances in Religious Studies Series. As one of its Founding Editors, along with Peggy Morgan of Oxford, I was urged to submit my proposal for inclusion in the Series. In later consultations with Lalle Pursglove and Steven Sutcliffe, I considered which articles and chapters from my previous publications to include and how to organize them under various themes. I am grateful for the encouragement provided by the Bloomsbury publishing team to pursue this project and for the guidance provided initially by Steven Sutcliffe, who so generously agreed to write the Foreword to this book, and to the other academic editors, Will Sweetman and Bettina Schmidt.

I was pleased to propose a collection of my writings for inclusion in the Advances in Religious Studies Series, partly because, as Peggy Morgan and I developed the Series in its early years, many of the contributors included my own PhD students or candidates for whom I served either as External or Internal Examiner. I am particularly indebted to my former students for their engagement with me on their topics, for their determination to complete their research projects and for their attention to detail when revising their PhDs for publication. It is often forgotten that much innovative, at times radical, research is produced by postgraduate students. I am proud to join this line of burgeoning academics who have contributed to advancing the study of religions through this Series.

At the outset, I wish to thank those who have helped me expand my opportunities for research on Indigenous Religions beyond my earlier projects developed in Alaska and Zimbabwe In particular, I am grateful to my colleagues in Australia and Aotearoa-New Zealand, who have facilitated my research on Indigenous populations in the southern Pacific region. I am indebted especially to Adam Possamai, Professor of Sociology in Western Sydney University, who supported my appointment as Adjunct Professor in the Religion and Society Research Cluster at Western Sydney University and has made it possible for me to travel to Australia to conduct research for the past ten years. I am also grateful to Will Sweetman, who promoted me for the De Carle Distinguished Lectureship at the University of Otago during the academic term 2011–12. In addition, I want to express my thanks to Carole Cusack, Professor in the Department for Studies in Religion at the University of Sydney, who agreed to an academic exchange with me in 2009. It was during the six months I was at the University of Sydney that I began exploring research opportunities in Central Australia. In this regard, I convey my deep gratitude to my colleagues in Alice Springs, particularly members of the Friends of the Strehlow Research Centre, who have welcomed me to Central Australia on numerous occasions since 2009 and have made my research projects there possible. I want to mention specifically the long-standing support I have received in Alice Springs from David and Susan Moore, David and Margaret Hewitt and Olga Radke.

Over the twenty years represented by the contents of this book, of course, I could mention many more colleagues, friends and supporters. I hope they will know who they are and will accept this as a collective thank you. I would be remiss, however, if I did not mention the numerous Indigenous people from Alaska through Zimbabwe to Australia, who have shared their knowledge with me so freely and generously. Without them, the rich experiences of my life, which are reflected in the chapters of this book, would not have been possible. Finally, for her technical advice in assisting me to produce the script for this book, but more importantly, for her unfailing encouragement, I express my deep gratitude to my wife, Valerie.

PERMISSIONS

Chapter 1: James L. Cox, 'Methodological Views on African Religions', in Elias Kifon Bongmba (ed.), *The Wiley-Blackwell Companion to African Religions*, 25–40. Chichester, England: Wiley-Blackwell. © 2012 Blackwell Publishing Limited. Granted a personal, non-exclusive, non-sublicensable (on a stand-alone basis), non-transferable, worldwide, limited license to reproduce the Wiley Materials for the purpose specified in the licensing process, License Date 29 January 2021.

Chapter 2: James L. Cox, 'The Contribution of TGH Strehlow to the Contemporary Global Study of Indigenous Religions', in Friends of the Strehlow Research Centre, Lynn Day (ed.). *Proceedings of the 2018 Symposium. Reflecting on the Past, Making Tracks for the Future*, 24–35, Friends of the Strehlow Research Centre: Alice Springs, NT, Australia. © 2019 James L. Cox. Permission to re-publish in a book granted by Friends of the Strehlow Research Centre, 25 February 2021.

Chapter 3: James L. Cox, 'Missionaries, the Phenomenology of Religion and "Re-presenting" Nineteenth-Century African Religion: A Case Study of Peter McKenzie's *Hail Orisha!*', *Journal of Religion in Africa*, 31(3): 336–53. © 2001 Koninklijke Brill NV, Leiden. Free permission on condition of acknowledgement of journal and Brill, granted 30 January 2021.

Chapter 4: James L. Cox, 'Religious Typologies and the Postmodern Critique', *Method and Theory in the Study of Religion* 10: 244–62. © 1998 Koninklijke Brill NV, Leiden. Free permission on the condition of acknowledgement of journal and Brill, granted 30 January 2021.

Chapter 5: James L. Cox, 'African Identities as the Projection of Western Alterity', in James L. Cox and Gerrie ter Haar (eds), *Uniquely African? African Christian Identity from Cultural and Historical Perspectives*, 25–37, Trenton, NJ: Africa World Press, Inc. © 2003 James L. Cox and Gerrie ter Haar. Free permission on the condition of acknowledgement, granted 29 January 2021.

Chapter 6: James L. Cox, 'Phenomenological Perspectives on the Social Responsibility of the Scholar of Religion', in Abraham Kovacs and James L. Cox (eds), *New Trends and Recurring Issues in the Study of Religion*, 133–51, Budapest: L'Harmattan. © 2014 Abraham Kovacs, James L. Cox and Contributors. Printed with permission of L'Harmattan Publishing House, Hungary, granted 1 February 2021.

Chapter 7: James L. Cox, 'The Transmission of an Authoritative Tradition: That without Which Religion Is Not Religion', in Afe Adogame, Magnus Echtler and Oliver Freiberger (eds), *Alternate Voices. A Plurality Approach for Religious Studies. Essays in Honor of Ulrich Berner*, 308–23, Göttingen: Vandenhoeck and Ruprecht. © 2013 Vandenhoeck and Ruprecht GmbH and Co. KG, Göttingen/Vandenhoeck and Ruprecht LLC, Bristol, CT, U.S.A. Permission granted for non-exclusive use only and is restricted to the types of use selected in the request, 5 February 2021.

Chapter 8: James L. Cox, 'Reflecting Critically on Indigenous Religions', in James L. Cox (ed.), *Critical Reflections on Indigenous Religions*, 3–18, Farnham, England and Burlington, VT: Ashgate. © 2013 from *Critical Reflections on Indigenous Religions* James L. Cox and contributors. Reproduced by permission of Taylor and Francis Group, LLC, a division of Informa plc., granted 28 January 2021.

Chapter 9: James L. Cox, 'Kinship and Location: In Defence of a Narrow Definition of Indigenous Religions', in Christopher Hartney and Daniel J Tower (eds), *Religious Categories and the Construction of the Indigenous*, 38–57, Leiden and Boston, MA: Brill. © 2017 Koninklijke Brill NV, Leiden, The Netherlands. Permission granted on condition of standard academic acknowledgement of the Brill title and Brill, 12 April 2021.

Chapter 10: James L. Cox, 'Secularizing the Land: The Impact of the Alaska Native Claims Settlement Act on Indigenous Understandings of Land', in Timothy Fitzgerald (ed.), *Religion and the Secular: Historical and Colonial Formations*, 71–92, Sheffield, UK and Bristol, CT: Equinox Publishing Ltd. © 2007 Timothy Fitzgerald and contributors. Permission granted on condition of acknowledgement of title and Equinox, 29 January 2021.

Chapter 11: James L. Cox, 'The Study of Religion and Non-Religion in the Emerging Field of "Non-Religion Studies": Its Significance for Interpreting Australian Aboriginal Religions', in James L. Cox and Adam Possamai (eds), *Religion and Non-Religion among Australian Aboriginal Peoples*, 25–43, London and New York: Routledge, an imprint of the Taylor and Francis Group, an Informa Business. © 2016 selection and editorial matter, James L. Cox and Adam Possamai; individual chapters, the contributors. Reproduced by permission of Taylor and Francis Group, LLC, a division of Informa plc, granted 27 January 2021.

Chapter 12: James L. Cox, 'Global Intentions and Local Conflicts: The Rise and Fall of Ambuya Juliana in Zimbabwe', in Greg Johnson and Siv Ellen Kraft (eds), *Handbook of Indigenous Religion(s)*, 366–77, Leiden and Boston: Brill. © 2017 Koninklijke Brill NV: Leiden, The Netherlands. Permission granted on condition of standard academic acknowledgement of the Brill title and Brill, 12 April 2021.

Chapter 13: James L. Cox, 'The Debate between E.B. Tylor and Andrew Lang over the Theory of Primitive Monotheism: Implications for Contemporary Studies of Indigenous Religions', in Paul-François Tremlett, Liam T. Sutherland and Graham

Introduction

BACKGROUND, CONTEXT AND CLARIFICATIONS

The main body of this volume contains fourteen previously published chapters and articles from books and journals that I have written during the most creative period of my career spanning twenty years from 1998 until 2018. This Introduction and the Conclusion are entirely new, the aims of which are to set the context for the book and to suggest ways forward in the academic study of religions and Indigenous Religions. I have chosen to include in the collection of previously published papers those that most clearly illustrate the development of my thought in theoretical and practical directions. The theoretical approach I have advocated is my version of the phenomenology of religion as I have adapted and modified it in its practical application to the study of Indigenous Religions. I have entitled this book *a* phenomenology of Indigenous Religions to indicate that I do not claim to have interpreted and implemented this method in a prescriptive manner. Rather, I have employed phenomenology as a dynamic tool suitable for describing specific Indigenous Religions and testing my conclusions about their place in the contemporary world.

I have chosen to organize the contents of this book thematically rather than chronologically. Had my aim been to produce an intellectual autobiography, obviously a chronological approach would have been preferable. One of my principal reasons for creating this collection, however, is to present Indigenous Religions in an empathetic manner that fosters widespread tolerance and understanding of practices that have been depicted widely in earlier literature as bizarre, strange, primitive or even alien to developed civilizations. Of course, such an aim is not limited to those who articulate phenomenological approaches, but I argue in this volume that the phenomenology of religion advocates an attitude towards others that fosters *intense* empathy. Another important goal in adopting a thematic approach is to counter increasing criticisms and widespread rejection of the phenomenology of religion. I have argued consistently that many of those who dismiss the phenomenological method do so on the basis of outdated and stereotypical characterizations that underestimate the continuing relevance of the method for the study of religions generally. I have chosen in the final three chapters of this book, including the new conclusion, to make a case for the potentially revolutionary contribution the phenomenology of religion can make to the study of Indigenous Religions by arguing that deeply rooted in phenomenological methodology lies an implicit commitment to privileging local agency in constructing research projects. The implications of this approach are just now beginning to be felt widely in interdisciplinary contexts, but not primarily by scholars in religious studies.

The subtitle of this book, *Theory and Practice*, suggests that theoretical constructs achieve their greatest value when they are applied pragmatically within concrete research projects. Theory devoid of application remains totally abstract and largely incomprehensible to the subjects of research and even for many academics. This volume challenges those who develop theories without actually testing them in practical settings to explain the relevance of their ideas for expanding our base of knowledge and for constructing future research projects. Admittedly, the essential link I assert between theory and practice as applied to the phenomenology of religion can cause confusion. This is because the phenomenology of religion often is discussed in terms of its method or approach, but frequently the theory beneath the method is left unexplored. I have tried to demonstrate throughout my writings on the subject that the phenomenology of religion represents a method that is grounded in a theoretical approach, one that was influenced in varying degrees by the late-nineteenth and early-twentieth-century German philosopher, Edmund Husserl. Phenomenology, in its Husserlian form, is best described as a theory of knowledge that seeks to clarify how we know what we know. In this sense, phenomenology, as a branch of epistemology, qualifies as a theoretical discipline that translates into a method that informs other areas within philosophy, including metaphysics, ethics, aesthetics and logic.

As I was nearing completion of this volume, a book that is relevant to my interpretation of the phenomenology of religion was published. Edited by Satoko Fujiwara, David Thurfjell and Steven Engler, it is entitled *Global Phenomenologies of Religion: An Oral History in Interviews* (2021). Some of those interviewed in the book, particularly Ulf Drobin (Thurfjell 2021: 34–9) and Jan Platvoet (Davidsen 2021: 254–61), challenge my interpretation of the phenomenology of religion as I presented it in my book, *A Guide to the Phenomenology of Religion* (2006). Drobin and Platvoet are critical especially of the significance I awarded to Edmund Husserl as a formative influence over later phenomenologists of religion.

I divided the contents of *A Guide to the Phenomenology of Religion* into three parts, as stated in the subtitle, *Key Figures, Formative Influences and Subsequent Debates*. The part on formative influences identifies three main themes: philosophical phenomenology, primarily as articulated by Edmund Husserl; theology, particularly the school of the nineteenth-century theologian Albrecht Ritschl; and the social sciences, principally as applied to 'ideal types' by scholars from different disciplines, including Ernst Troeltsch, Max Weber and C. G. Jung. In the section on philosophical phenomenology, I devoted considerable attention to Husserl's phenomenology, chiefly because he developed themes focusing on relationships between the subject and the object, the role of perception in determining reality and, quite importantly, because he formulated a theory of intersubjectivity that I found relevant to research on religious communities

(Husserl 1977: 92; Cox 2006: 28–30). Husserl introduced terms like the *epoché* and *eidos*, both of which were taken up in various forms by phenomenologists of religion, specifically by Gerardus van der Leeuw in his landmark book, *Religion in Essence and Manifestation* (1938). I contended that philosophical phenomenology was one 'formative influence', among others.

To provide a balanced perspective, I drew the reader's attention to the fact that the influential Dutch phenomenologist, C. J. Bleeker, downplayed the importance of Husserl's impact on the study of religions and criticized Van der Leeuw's phenomenology of religion for incorporating into it 'too many elements of the philosophical phenomenology' (Bleeker 1972: 41). I pointed out further that Bleeker contended that phenomenologists of religion used Husserl's terms *epoché* and *eidos* only in a 'figurative' way (Bleeker 1972: 40). Nonetheless, I have contended consistently in my discussions of this topic in numerous publications that Husserl's epistemological framework provides a solid foundation for constructing a phenomenology of religion. I maintain this position because, as I argue from different angles in Chapters 4, 5 and 6 of the current volume, it fosters a reflexive attitude that forces researchers to consider their own place in formulating and executing research projects in ways that I now contend are particularly relevant to the study of Indigenous societies.

Phenomenologists of religion have contended consistently that it is possible to gain an understanding of cultures that are largely alien to a researcher on the assumption that anything human ultimately is comprehensible to other humans. It is possible to cultivate a feeling for others that enables a scholar, using phenomenological principles, to share common experiences with religious communities without erasing the division between the self and the other, the subject and the object. The interpretations that follow can be communicated to other outsiders in ways that promote understanding and expand knowledge, both objectively and subjectively. To my mind, this represents a theoretical starting point that finds its practical application in concrete methods, or stages, that can be put into practice by researchers. These include employing the *epoché*, or suspending prior judgements, developing empathy for others and testing interpretations by recourse to the sources of knowledge themselves, the believing communities. Throughout this book, I have attempted to demonstrate how phenomenology, as both a theory of knowledge and a method for obtaining knowledge, can be combined to inform and guide research into particular, local expressions of Indigenous Religions.

The thematic divisions

Set between the new Introduction and Conclusion, Chapters 1 through 14 are divided into five parts, each reflecting a major theme in phenomenological approaches to the study of Indigenous Religions. Part I contains three chapters that explore how I have explained and interpreted the phenomenology of religion in specific contexts. In Chapter 1, I summarize how I have presented the phenomenology of religion in numerous earlier publications, including my *Guide to the Phenomenology of Religion* (2006) and *An Introduction to the Phenomenology of Religion* (2010). I review the thinking of key phenomenologists, such as Gerardus van der Leeuw, Wilfred Cantwell Smith, Ninian Smart and Mircea Eliade. In *A Guide to the Phenomenology of Religion* (Cox 2006: 4–6), I employed a modified case study approach under the category 'schools' of phenomenology, similar to the pattern used by George James (1995: 3) in his important volume, *Interpreting Religion*. Unlike James, who limited his choice of phenomenologists thematically, I organized my selection geographically, showing how those from distinct regions mutually influenced one another and how they shared many themes in common in their interpretations of the phenomenology of religion. Of course, this approach inevitably contains flaws since important omissions are required by the selection process. Although I concede this point, I would suggest that every academic must make decisions about which scholars and themes are most important to a specific research project, and how these should be organized. I made my choices on the basis of scholars within the phenomenological tradition that I thought were most influential, particularly among English-speaking audiences, and which as a consequence were most accessible to my students.

After presenting the main theories of the phenomenologists of religion I have chosen as representative of the method, in Chapter 1, I outline the objections of some chief critics of phenomenology, including Gavin Flood, Robert Segal and Paul François Tremlett. I follow this by offering a defence of phenomenology in response to their penetrating analyses. I conclude the chapter by applying the phenomenological method to a case study focusing on the postulated universal African belief in God. Chapter 2 explains the phenomenology of religion as a step-by-step method and demonstrates how it was used by the Australian linguist and researcher, T. G. H. Strehlow, in his life's work among the Arrernte peoples of Central Australia. In Chapter 3, I show how phenomenology should *not* be applied in practice, by critically examining the attempt of the late Peter McKenzie to use the phenomenological model developed by the German theologian Friedrich Heiler to interpret missionary records as a source for understanding how Yoruba religion in Nigeria was expressed at the time of first contact with English missionaries in the mid-nineteenth century.

Part II of the book focuses on specific issues that arise from a critical analysis of the role of the researcher in relation to the so-called objects of research. Chapter 4 looks at the development of religious typologies in the phenomenological tradition. After summarizing the use of ideal types as explained by Van der Leeuw, C. J. Bleeker and Ninian Smart, I review the postmodern critique of metanarratives, which can be applied to the way phenomenologists of religion traditionally have interpreted the creation of universal classifications of religious beliefs and behaviours. I conclude the chapter by using an early work of the philosopher Jean-François Lyotard to defend the creation of typologies for comparative purposes and suggest that the validity of constructing ideal types as paradigms must be tested by recourse exclusively to the humans, operating as both subject and object, who have engaged in the process of research. I follow this in Chapter 5 by exploring, more deeply than I had done previously, the relationship between the researcher and those being researched, the so-called objects of investigation. I argue that how a research question is framed tells us much more about the researcher than it does about those who are being studied. This insight encourages a reflexive application of the phenomenological *epoché* in which the 'other' is represented in the self, or as I put it, alterity is reflected in the ego. Chapter 6 follows my analysis of the subject–object problem by asking what responsibility a scholar holds with respect to the beliefs and practices of a community that might be detrimental to the health and well-being of its members. I discuss this by describing an African Initiated Church (AIC) in Zimbabwe that restricted its followers to healing by faith alone by prohibiting consultation with Western medical practitioners. I explore the dilemma created when researchers employ the phenomenological commitment to privileging believers' perspectives while at the same time refusing to comment on the truth or falsehood of a religious community's beliefs.

Part III of the book reflects a transition in my thinking in which I move towards a reductive, socio-cultural, definition of religion and Indigenous Religions. In some ways, this seems highly 'unphenomenological', since phenomenologists traditionally have been opposed to reducing religion to non-religious categories as proposed within other disciplines, such as sociology, psychology, economics, politics, cognitive science and so on. I was motivated to seek a socio-cultural definition of religion in part by the link that had been alleged between the phenomenology of religion and theology in which religion was related in Eliadean terms to a 'sacred', to Wilfred Cantwell Smith's 'transcendent' or to C. J. Bleeker's 'Divine'. Following the critique of the category 'religion' as veiling a theological agenda, as voiced by Timothy Fitzgerald in his important book *The Ideology of Religious Studies* (2000), I sought to define religion in terms that did not require beliefs about a 'sacred', a focus on a transcendent or reference to supernatural entities. I began refining my definition of religion following my interpretation of the work of the French sociologist Danièle Hervieu-Léger, who made the essential element in religion the transmission of an authoritative tradition. Chapter 7 represents one of my earliest attempts to limit religion following Hervieu-Léger by identifying the sine qua non of religion, that without which religion is not religion. I demonstrate my restricted interpretation of religion by describing two rituals I observed and documented from entirely different contexts: a rain ritual in Zimbabwe and a New Age trance dance conducted in Vermont in the United States. In Chapter 8, I outline the same method with respect to Indigenous Religions, which I restrict to two primary characteristics: kinship and location. In Chapter 9, I respond to criticisms of my reductive approach and argue that it is fully consistent with a phenomenological interpretation of religion and Indigenous Religions if the notion of the 'sacred' as an ontological category is bracketed out as a potentially distorting prior assumption.

Parts IV and V build on one another. The chapters that comprise Part IV explore the possible conflict between my restricted definition of Indigenous Religions as bound by kinship within limited local contexts and the fact that in today's world Indigenous societies simultaneously have been influenced by and have exercised influence over global movements. I exemplify the local–global conflict in Chapter 10 by describing how the US government 'secularized' the land of the Indigenous peoples of Alaska by transforming their traditional relationship to the land into stocks and shares in Native Corporations. This was written into law in 1971 when the Alaska Native Claims Settlement Act was signed by President Nixon. After outlining ancient Indigenous 'religious' understandings of the land that had been disturbed by the concerted effort to assimilate Indigenous peoples in Alaska through a capitalist solution to Indigenous claims to land ownership, I describe the resurgence of Indigenous challenges to the most discriminatory elements of the Act, which have in part resulted in achieving changes to the law that protect local ownership of the land and ensure the continuation of a subsistence economy. In Chapter 11, I examine the burgeoning academic field of 'non-religion studies' and analyse how, by clarifying the difference between religion and non-religion, we can identify criteria that determine if and, if so how, Indigenous Religions, as extensions of age-old customary practices, persist in an age of globalization. In Chapter 12, I argue that local traditions exercise immense power over movements with global intentions by describing the short-lived Ambuya Juliana phenomenon in Zimbabwe that came to prominence in the early 1990s. So influential was Juliana's organization that some leading scholars, such as the historian Terence Ranger, suggested it might develop into one of the most significant new religious movements to affect southern Africa during the late twentieth century. That this did not occur, I argue, resulted from the failure of the leader of the movement to respect local protocols and traditional authority by attempting to subvert them through her own global ambitions.

The final two chapters of the book, which comprise Part V, emphasize the central importance of local agency in directing and controlling the content and dissemination of traditional knowledge. In Chapter 13, which is partly historical, I contrast the opposing positions on the theory of primitive monotheism as advanced towards the end of the nineteenth century and into the early part of the twentieth century by the anthropologist E. B. Tylor and the Scottish poet, literary critic and self-styled anthropologist, Andrew Lang. I argue that this debate, which sought to identify the original beliefs of 'primitive' peoples, was dominated by the prior assumptions advanced by Tylor and Lang and had almost nothing to do with the Indigenous religious beliefs of the people they were discussing. I illustrate the power dimensions within the Tylor–Lang debate by referring to the contemporary case of the Rainbow Spirit Theology in Northern Queensland, Australia, where local agency was exercised when Aboriginal Elders transformed the Indigenous symbol of the rainbow-serpent into the incarnation of God, a move that represented a radically subversive act resulting in making the Rainbow Serpent Theology a genuinely Indigenous form of Christianity. This leads in Chapter 14 to my description of the repatriation of knowledge project now taking place at the Strehlow Research Centre in Alice Springs, Australia, which demonstrates the central place of local agency in reclaiming knowledge that had been lost or stolen by invading missionary and colonial forces. By acknowledging local ownership over knowledge, I conclude that future research projects among Indigenous societies must be conceived and executed in full cooperation among and dialogue between academic researchers and the communities they propose to investigate. This brings me back to the phenomenology of religion in my original conclusion to this volume, where I draw close connections between the phenomenological dictum, as expressed by W. Brede Kristensen (1960: 14), that 'the believers were always right', and the contemporary assertion by Indigenous people that their knowledge, which is sought by outside researchers, is accessible only by local consent.

Some clarifications

As with any book that contains contributions stretching over a twenty-year period, inconsistencies will appear in the chapters and certain overlaps will occur. This results from developments in thinking that inevitably transpire as a scholar engages over time with new ideas, responds to challenges levelled against earlier arguments, and engages in original research in a variety of cultural settings. For this reason, some chapters contain a re-statement of my definitions of religion and Indigenous Religions and some conclusions are reached based on the same descriptive material. Despite these commonalities, the aim of each chapter is different: to supply fresh applications of the data and to offer new interpretations of the topics considered.

Despite the necessary progression in my thinking about religion and Indigenous Religions, I believe that a careful reading of the core contents of this volume will display a generally consistent treatment of the themes under which I have organized the chapters. One term, however, may cause some confusion for the reader. I am referring to my use of the category 'sacred'. In exemplifying the stages in the phenomenological method, I discuss leading phenomenologists who identified what they regarded as the key to understanding religion in general, the stage referred to as 'the eidetic intuition', sometimes called 'the eidetic vision'. In particular, Mircea Eliade, as a leading figure in the history and phenomenology of religion in the mid-to-late twentieth century, identified the meaning of religion in terms of manifestations of 'the sacred' in space and time. He called these 'hierophanies' (Eliade 1987 [1959]: 11–2). Parallels to Christian theology in this scheme are obvious. I argue in my defence of the phenomenology of religion that the notion of an 'eidetic intuition', or the essence of religion, can best be understood in empirical terms as the sine qua non of religion, that without which religion is not religion. This results in a very different interpretation of the essence of religion than posited by Eliade. My minimal definition of religion, as I describe it in several chapters of this book, is rooted in social–cultural contexts and is entirely empirically falsifiable. My attempt to draw a clear line demarcating the academic study of religion from theology is closely related to my effort to separate 'the sacred' from 'religion' and in this way construct a non-theological definition of religion.

A potential confusion occurs at just this point. When I describe Indigenous Religions, particularly the religions of Australian Aboriginal peoples in Chapters

2 and 14, I refer frequently to 'secret-sacred' objects that were and are maintained as the property of particular clans whose lineage can be traced to the stories about their totemic ancestors. I also refer to 'sacred' rituals, myths and songs. The use of the term 'sacred' in these contexts refers not to a postulated ontological reality, as employed by Eliade, but in Durkheimian terms, as something set apart, which possesses power and conceivably is dangerous if used in ways that contravene rigidly enforced customary practices (Lynch 2020: 715). I have shown how objects, called *tjurunga* in Central Australia, are permitted to be viewed only by initiated men and how the inscriptions engraved on them are maintained with absolute secrecy. I also describe how, in past times, rituals relating to a particular totem were allowed to be witnessed exclusively by those who could trace their lineage through the totemic clan, violations of which were punishable by death. It is in this sense that I used 'sacred' with reference to the beliefs and ceremonies of the peoples of Central Australia, whose stories of the original totemic ancestors traditionally were enacted over and over in rituals and were transmitted from generation to generation with an overwhelming authority. I avoided applying an Eliadean interpretation that would have insisted that the symbols, rituals, songs, stories and objects, which were set apart from ordinary matters of life, represented intrusions of a 'sacred', conceived ontologically, into otherwise undifferentiated space and time.

It is true that in many places throughout this volume I have described Eliade as providing a clear example of a scholar who identified the phenomenological *eidos* or essence of religion as 'the sacred'. Nonetheless, I contend that there is an important difference between illustrating the ways that key scholars writing in the phenomenological tradition explained religion using ontological categories and agreeing with them that religion does not exist without such categories. Over the period covering the contents of this volume, I have argued repeatedly that the academic study of religion is entirely distinct from theology. At the same time, I have contended that the phenomenology of religion provides methods to study religion that are equally distinct from those employed in various branches of the social sciences. I have maintained consistently that the phenomenology of religion qualifies as a science of religion only if the theories it postulates about religious communities can be tested and potentially falsified.

An important point to note in this regard is that testing the results of research, on a phenomenological analysis, does not translate into claims to have attained pure objectivity. On the contrary, the value of the contribution of the phenomenology of religion to the sciences of religion rests on putting its theory into practice, whereby it bridges the gap between the subject and the object of research, between the insider and the outsider, by making believers' perspectives part of the scientific data regulating the design and outcomes of any research project. I will return to this critical argument in the conclusion to this book, in which I suggest how the fourteen chapters I have chosen to exemplify my interpretation of a phenomenology of Indigenous Religions can contribute positively to critical contemporary debates about future directions in the academic study of religions.

Part I

PHENOMENOLOGY OF RELIGION: THEORY, METHOD AND APPLICATION

Chapter 1

METHODOLOGICAL VIEWS ON AFRICAN RELIGIONS

When I first began lecturing in the University of Zimbabwe in 1989, I noticed after a few classes that students had warmed to a method of studying African Traditional Religions that drew on concepts derived from the phenomenology of religion. In fact, my students became so enamoured with the phenomenological method in the study of religion that often they wrote in their essays that phenomenology is *the* way, some said the *only* way, to study religions, particularly African religions. I now explain this overwhelmingly positive response by Zimbabwean students to the phenomenological method by the fact that many had been pupils in mission schools, or at least were active Christians, who had been taught that the Indigenous religion of their ancestors was demonic and that they should have nothing to do with traditional rituals. When they began to see that for academic reasons they should suspend such judgements, even if they maintained them personally, and should employ empathetic techniques to gain an understanding of any religion they were studying, it was as if a veil had been removed from their eyes, and they could view their own religious and cultural practices in a new light.

I refer at the outset to my Zimbabwean students because their experience of studying their own cultures using a basic understanding of phenomenological principles underscores at a deeper level two inter-related methodological questions I wish to consider: (1) What, if anything, can the phenomenological method, which has been much maligned in scholarly writings over the past thirty years, offer to contemporary understandings of African religions? (2) In light of the phenomenological method in the study of religion, as 'insiders' to their own cultures, do African scholars have an inherent advantage over non-African researchers of African religions? The first question focuses on the phenomenology of religion in general and the second considers a phenomenological interpretation of the relative value of 'insider' discourse. These questions relate to the study of all African religions, but I have chosen to exemplify my responses in the latter part of this article largely in terms of Indigenous beliefs and practices. Before I turn to these considerations, I need to outline the key principles underlying the phenomenology of religion and respond to some of the most persistent criticisms levelled at it by scholars of religion (see Cox 2010: 48–72; 151–64).

The phenomenology of religion

The three most important concepts found within the phenomenology of religion are *epoché*, empathetic interpolation and the eidetic intuition. Derived from the philosophy of the late-nineteenth and early-twentieth-century German philosopher Edmund Husserl, the term *epoché* was used by Husserl to suspend all judgements associated with what he called the natural attitude (which naively assumes that what is observed tells us all there is to know about the world) such as material objects, science, other humans, and the sequence and order of events. All the things we take for granted about what we perceive as real, to use a term Husserl borrowed from mathematics, must be 'put into brackets'. In solving algebraic equations, for example, the mathematician places the various components of the formula into brackets and works on solving each problem placed in brackets one at a time so that, at the conclusion, each limited solution can be applied to resolving the problem of the entire equation. In a similar way, although Husserl did not use the *epoché* to doubt the existence of the external world, he suspended judgements about it so that, like a mathematician, attention could be focused on another part of the equation, in this case, on an analysis of the phenomena of perception as they appear in the individual's consciousness. The effect of this method, according to Husserl, was to establish a new mode of consciousness in which the natural standpoint is put out of play or, as Husserl (1931: 111) put it, performing *epoché* 'bars me from using any judgment that concerns spatio-temporal existence'. By placing in brackets previously held beliefs or assumptions derived from the natural standpoint, the observer allows pure phenomena to speak for themselves.

Following Husserl, phenomenologists of religion advocated a method of bracketing out or suspending a researcher's previous ideas, thoughts or beliefs about the truth, value or meaning of any religion under study. Phenomenologists wanted to observe the phenomena of religion as they appear, rather than as they are understood through opinions formed prior to their being observed. This means suspending *personal beliefs* and withholding judgements on *academic theories* about religion. A leading advocate of the method was the Dutch phenomenologist Gerardus van der Leeuw, who followed closely Husserl's philosophical rejection of the natural attitude. Van der Leeuw (1938: 646) described *epoché* as a tool to ensure 'that no judgment is expressed concerning the objective world, which is thus placed "between brackets"'. He explained that this requires the scholar to observe 'restraint' by allowing only the phenomena that appear to manifest themselves, rather than the observer relying on presuppositions about what lies 'behind' appearances (Van der Leeuw 1938: 675). In Van der Leeuw's understanding, performing *epoché* should not be regarded as an effort to remove the observer from interacting creatively with the phenomena. The mind in its bracketed consciousness is not a blank tablet but, based on Husserl's rendering of the term intentionality, is employed precisely to enable the observer to interpret the phenomena as they appear, liberated from naïve or unchallenged assumptions. Because it eliminated potentially distorting biases, for Van der Leeuw, *epoché* enabled the observer to attain understanding of the subjective nature of religion (its internal structure) and its objective meaning (its broader connections).

Another important phenomenologist of religion was W. Brede Kristensen, under whom Van der Leeuw studied in Leiden University. Although his major work in English on theory and method in the study of religion, *The Meaning of Religion*, was not published until 1960, seven years after his death, his influence within the study of religions during the first half of the twentieth century was considerable. Despite the fact that he did not employ the term *epoché* in *The Meaning of Religion*, Kristensen began by insisting that the scholar must call into question any interpretation of religion that is potentially offensive to believers. He argued that a genuinely scientific understanding occurs only when the scholar is able to see through the viewpoint or perspective of adherents, since believers understand their own religion better than anyone from the outside ever could. In order to gain an insider's perspective, the scholar needs to suspend widely accepted presuppositions about the origin and meaning of religion. Kristensen believed that evolutionary theories in particular predisposed the scholar to evaluate religions from the outside and thus, in the words of Eric Sharpe (1986: 228), 'to have been responsible for inducing scholars to pass premature judgement on material they had learned to understand only in part'. By applying evolutionary assumptions to religion, the outside researcher produces an entirely biased interpretation to which believers could never accede. Kristensen (1960: 13) concluded: 'All evolutionary views and theories … mislead us from the start.' Van der Leeuw later used Husserl's term *epoché* to reinforce Kristensen's emphasis on the authority of believers to interpret their own religion.

A second key concept in the phenomenological method is what Van der Leeuw (1938: 675) called 'sympathetic interpolation', which he defined as the 'primitively human art of the actor which is indispensable to all arts, but to the sciences of the mind also', adding that 'only the persistent and strenuous application of intense sympathy … qualifies the phenomenologist to interpret appearances'. The British phenomenologist of religion, Ninian Smart (1973a: 54), preferred the term "empathy" to sympathy, which he explained, following Husserl's notion of intentionality, enabled the observer to recognize 'a framework of intentions' among the believers. Intentionality, for Smart, not only required the active involvement of the researcher but also included the acts of a believing community (what it intends by its myths, rituals and symbols), which must be apprehended by the observer if genuine understanding is to be achieved. The twin processes of using empathy and interpolating what is experienced into terms the researcher can comprehend defined for Smart how intentionality operates in a dual manner: first, by enabling the scholar to access the meaning of the religious life and practices for adherents and then by making sense of them intentionally in terms of the researcher's own culture.

The Canadian scholar of comparative religions, Wilfred Cantwell Smith, argued forcefully for this approach. In his popular book, *The Faith of Other Men* (1972), subsequently reprinted under the title *Patterns of Faith around the World* (1998), Smith provided examples of empathetic interpolation by selecting key symbols which he used to help interpret to outsiders the meaning of faith for adherents within four different religious and cultural traditions: Hindus, Buddhists, the Chinese and Muslims. For Hindus, Smith (1998: 35–48) identified the central symbol as the Sanskrit expression '*tat tvam asi*', which he translated into English as 'that thou art'. This terse statement points towards a deep religious truth affirming the identity of the individual soul (*Atman*) with the universal world spirit (*Brahman*). Smith (1998: 37–8) explained that for Hindus 'the individual self is the world soul' and thus 'each one of you reading this book' is 'in some final, cosmic sense, the total and transcendent truth that underlies all being'. Smith interpolated this difficult and seemingly contradictory idea for the Western mind by suggesting that in the areas of art, morality and theology people in European cultures, steeped as they are in Greek thought, seek a correspondence between what they appreciate aesthetically, do morally or believe ultimately and what *really is* Beautiful, Good and True. The unity sought between what the individual experiences and what is universal is familiar to the Western mind and thus interpolates empathetically what has often appeared enigmatic for Westerners within the Hindu tradition. Smith (1998: 49–62) does the same in the Buddhist tradition by describing a boys' initiation rite practised in Burma called the *Shin Byu* ceremony, within the Chinese tradition by exploring the significance of the *Yin-Yang* symbols of opposition and complementarity (Smith 1998: 77–90), and for Muslims by explaining the *Shahadah* or testimony of faith, 'There is no God but Allah and Muhammad is his prophet' (Smith 1998: 63–76). In each case, Smith draws from the everyday experiences common in Western culture to help Westerners gain an appreciation for and an understanding of what otherwise might appear incomprehensible, strange or even wrong in other religious traditions.

Ninian Smart (1984b: 264) exemplified this process when he asked his reader to consider the life and behaviour of Adolf Hitler, who for most people represents a historical figure with whom it would appear impossible to empathize or to cultivate a feeling for. Smart (1984b: 264) asks, 'Does it mean that I need to be a Hitler-lover to understand him?' In one sense, Smart (1984b: 264) answers this question affirmatively: 'If we are indeed to get into his soul we have to drop our preconceptions, and treat Hitler as a human being who had his own thought world.' This involves following him 'through his Austrian childhood and relationship to his father and dear mother; through his scholastic failures and outcast status in Vienna; through his years in the trenches fighting in France'. In other words, Smart calls on us to treat Adolf Hitler as a human being, but, he adds, 'All this is strictly *empathy*, "getting the feel of"' (Smart 1984b: 264). Empathy, he argues, does not require a person to condone Hitler's actions or approve 'in any way the rightness of his creed' (Smart 1984b: 264). Smart (1984b: 264) concludes: 'So we can still deplore his deeds once we have understood them.' This example shows that for phenomenologists of religion it is always possible to cultivate a feeling for anything human in order to induce understanding. Under the procedure of *epoché*, it is irrelevant whether or not scholars of religion are able to endorse the beliefs and practices of the communities they are seeking to understand.

A third key component in the phenomenological method is at the same time probably the most controversial: the eidetic intuition. Again, this idea is obtained from Husserl, who used the phrase, which he derived from the Greek *eidos* meaning form, idea or essence, to see into the meaning of the phenomena encountered while in the state of bracketed consciousness or *epoché*. By the eidetic intuition Husserl meant that the observer is able to apprehend not just particular entities or even universal classes of entities but their essential meanings as entities and classes of entities. This can occur only when one's preconceived notions are suspended, thereby enabling the observer to intuit the meaning of what actually manifests itself in the world. Husserl (1969 [1929]: 246) explains:

> The multiplicity of possible perceptions, memories, and, indeed, intentional processes of whatever sort, that relate, or can relate, 'harmoniously' to one and the same physical thing has (in all its tremendous complication) a quite definite essential style.

For Husserl, the combination of *epoché* and the eidetic intuition was required for the building up of an objective picture of the phenomena of existence. *Epoché* allows the observer to suspend theories of the world built on naturalistic assumptions, what Husserl calls the 'fact world', in order that consciousness, which forms the basis for all knowledge, can be analysed rigorously. In this way, the observer perceives the world as it comes fresh from the phenomena and is able thereby to intuit new realities or at least achieve a more complete understanding of reality than had been attained previously.

An important and influential figure in the academic study of religions throughout the latter third of the twentieth century was Mircea Eliade, who occupied the Chair of the History of Religions in the University of Chicago from 1958 until his death in 1986. Eliade's writings cover a wide range of topics from Shamanism to Australian Aboriginal Religions, but his chief contribution to theory and method resulted from his hermeneutical approach to the study of religions, an approach I have argued elsewhere is fully consistent with the phenomenology of religion (Cox 2006: 183–7). I am calling Eliade's interpretation of the meaning of religion a prime example of the eidetic intuition, although Eliade did not explicitly use the term, nor did he directly rely on Husserl in his writings, although clearly he was aware of Husserl's understanding of the *eidos* (Eliade 1969: 36). Nonetheless, Eliade constructed a general theory of religion which he believed applied in all cultural and social contexts, and thus can be regarded as providing a statement about the universal essence of religion.

For Eliade, the keyword that helps the scholar unlock the meaning of religion is the 'hierophany', the manifestation of the sacred, which locates for the religious person (*homo religiosus*) points of orientation around sacred centres. Eliade (1987: 9–13) contended that the sacred is unknown and unknowable in itself, but is revealed through manifestations in profane space and time. Hence, hierophanies are mundane, worldly objects which become the avenues for making known to humans what otherwise would remain utterly incomprehensible. As such, these manifestations, the hierophanies, constitute the subject matter of the history of religions. In his important book, *Patterns in Comparative Religion*, Eliade (1996: 29) explained that hierophanies reveal a 'paradoxical coming together of sacred and profane, being and non-being, absolute and relative, the eternal and the becoming'.

In what is arguably his most influential book outlining his theory of religion, *The Sacred and the Profane* (which significantly carries the sub-title, 'The Nature of Religion'), Eliade (1987: 20–4) asks his reader to imagine a time when there were no hierophanies, no sacred intrusions in space and time. He called this the chaos created by a profane homogeneity, where everything is the same, where no points of orientation can be located (Eliade 1987: 29–32). This is equivalent to being lost, where a person cannot identify any familiar landmarks and experiences utter despair and hopelessness as a result. In like manner, for the religious person, homogeneity, the inability to detect sacred points of orientation, results in a sense of absolute meaninglessness and total chaos. In the mythic beginnings of history, when space and time were undifferentiated, for religious people, the sacred manifested itself creating meaningful points of orientation. Stories about these primordial hierophanies are told within different religious traditions in their cosmogonic myths, which in turn are re-enacted in rituals.

Because religion primarily is about orientation, certain symbols recur in various forms throughout the world and across history. These primarily have to do with cosmic centres, which connect the layers of the world, the upper levels reaching to the heavens and hence to the gods and the lower levels extending to the foundations of the earth. As such, stories about the sacred are often associated with the sky and are symbolized by mountains, trees, birds, the sun and the moon. Ritual attention frequently is focused on the symbols, which are transmitted in the myths, and thus rituals transport the religious community repeatedly into a time of beginning when the world was 'founded'. This explains why for Eliade hierophanies, as told in myths and re-enacted in rituals, provide the key concept for interpreting religion universally (Eliade 1987: 63–4; see also Eliade 1975: 5–12).

It should now be evident from my description of the key elements in the phenomenology of religion that, as a method, it aims to promote understanding of religions in particular and of religion in general. Its techniques also attempt to bridge the gap between the subject and the object of religion, the observer and those that are observed, by drawing on common human ways of thinking which can be translated into multiple cultural contexts and individual inter-subjective experiences. The phenomenology of religion also seeks to alert the scholar to potentially distorting biases and unexamined assumptions (both personal and academic) in order that these do not predetermine the outcomes of research.

Criticisms of the phenomenological method and a rebuttal

During the period from around 1950 to 1980, the phenomenology of religion, including its application to historical studies in Eliadean terms, was probably the dominant method employed by scholars of religion. Since 1980 a mounting critique of the method has occurred, which has undermined its influence and, in the view of many contemporary writers, has made it irrelevant to contemporary studies of religion. If this consensus holds, of course, the questions with which I began this chapter investigating the application of the method within African religions are anachronistic. I want to counter this position by arguing that the declaration of the death of phenomenology is premature and that it provides still a cutting-edge approach to the study of religions with implications for new understandings of African religions. Before discussing the African context, I must rehearse some of the principal objections to the phenomenology of religion and respond to them briefly.

One of the main criticisms of phenomenology centres on its claim that by using empathy it can enter into specific religious contexts in order to gain a universal understanding of religious typologies and more generally, on the basis of typological comparisons, to ascertain the meaning of religion. According to the scholar of Hinduism, Gavin Flood (1999), this is a problem that the phenomenology of religion inherited from Edmund Husserl, who maintained that the individual consciousness is at the same time both particular and universal. The individual consciousness operates under the limitations imposed by being an individual consciousness, but at the same time it assumes a universal form of rationality. In other words, in Husserl's view, the observer, although particular and individual, asserts a common understanding of the world with others, or obtains intersubjectivity, through empathy. In the phenomenology of religion, this same process operates when the subjective observer, in this case the scholar of religion, is able to penetrate into the inner meaning of religious facts. This, according to Flood, has resulted in the overriding emphasis among phenomenologists on subjective states, conveyed in terms of numinous experience, faith or inner enlightenment. Flood argues that this can be seen clearly in the case of Eliade, where religion is construed in terms of the observer's ability to feel 'as if' one becomes religious by entering into the mind of the religious person. For Flood (1999: 108), this turns the study of religion into a study of the structure of the religious 'consciousness' because it is wedded to the idea it imported from Husserl that 'assumes the universality of the rational subject . . who can, through objectification, have access to a truth external to any particular historical and cultural standpoint'.

In response to Flood, I would emphasize the word 'interpolate', the second part of Van der Leeuw's phrase, 'sympathetic interpolation'. Sympathy (or empathy), considered by itself, can been regarded as an entirely subjective tool that depends on the ability of the individual observer to 'enter into' or 'cultivate a feeling' for that which otherwise would appear unusual, bizarre or alien to one's own understanding. For example, in his discussion of Australian Aboriginal cultures, Tony Swain (1985: 8) has argued that 'it is easy to be deluded into believing we have gained an empathic understanding of other people's religious life, when in fact we have merely seen ourselves reflected in their culture'. Nonetheless, as Smart demonstrated in his example of Hitler, to interpolate suggests that we insert consciously our own experience into the experience of the other on the assumption that nothing human ultimately is alien to other humans, since everywhere humans think alike, although the way thoughts are expressed culturally and socially differs dramatically. For this reason, it is possible to use one's own experience as an interpretative tool to gain an understanding of the experience of another. That is, one can interpolate out of one's own cultural setting meanings that help the student of religion, as an outsider, understand what occurs in another, seemingly alien, cultural context.

In one sense, Flood's objection cannot be answered since consciousness is accessible only to the one performing acts of consciousness. This means that the conclusions one reaches through the method of interpolation, which assumes that other minds operate in roughly the same fashion as one's own, cannot be tested empirically. It is based on a 'feeling for' the other, the technique Husserl used to overcome solipsism (the view that the individual consciousness is all that can be known to exist) through an alleged intersubjectivity between independent minds. In a like manner, phenomenologists of religion secure understanding of religious practices with which they are unfamiliar by appealing to a common humanity. In other words, even though the eyes of faith are denied to the scholar of religion, it is possible to imagine what it would be like to possess a vision based on faith.

Although solipsism can never be disproved, it remains an untenable philosophical position, since a theory of knowledge can never proceed without the assumption that other minds experience the world in similar ways (Popkin and Stroll 1986: 146). For this reason, Husserl can hardly be faulted for asserting common patterns of human thought that can be ascertained through assumed intersubjective experiences. In a like manner, the phenomenologist of religion takes for granted that religious people have common ways of expressing their beliefs and practices, understanding of which can be penetrated through a combination of empathy and interpolation. This means that the phenomenologist often refers to numinous experiences or, following Eliade (1987: 43), describes the longing of the religious person to be as near the sacred as possible in time and space, through myths and rituals. These represent scholarly interpretations generated by a careful analysis of data, but at the same time ones that are provoked by a subjective empathy. Such interpretations give insight into how the religious mind operates, or better, how the mind operates when it perceives the world religiously. So, on the one hand, Flood is correct when he argues that the phenomenologist of religion conceives the world by projecting the numinous experience of the believer onto the data. On the other hand, Flood overlooks the fact that this is done in the interests of objectivity, that is, to disclose the way the religious mind functions as part of a shared human way of thinking, which, at the same time, is expressed in multiple ways in specific social and cultural contexts.

This leads to a second major criticism levelled at the phenomenology of religion. Phenomenologists of religion repeatedly insisted that religion exists as an entity in itself, or as a classification sui generis, which requires specific methodological tools unique to its subject matter that are quite separate from any operating within the social sciences. For example, in his book on Australian religions, Eliade (1973: 196) commends the work of the anthropologist W. E. H. Stanner precisely because Stanner protested 'against the general notion that a study of totemism, magic, and ritual exhausts the understanding of primitive religion'. He then cites with approval the anti-reductionist position of Stanner, whom he commends for criticising 'the fallacious presupposition "that the social order is in some sense causal, and the religious order secondary and in some sense consequential"' (Eliade 1973: 197; see also, Stanner 2009). It is the fervent anti-reductionist stance of most phenomenologists that has brought charges from many scholars that the phenomenology of religion is ideologically based and therefore more akin to theology than to genuine scientific disciplines.

Following this line of thinking, Robert Segal (1999: 139–63) of the University of Aberdeen has launched a stinging criticism of the phenomenology of religion. In particular, Segal has attacked Eliade for confusing the study of religion in its own right with religious faith and thus of moving out of science into theology. Segal accuses Eliade of adopting a faith stance through his contention that the central component in religion is the sacred that believing communities apprehend through hierophanies. As we have seen, Eliade, and others writing in the phenomenological tradition, such as Kristensen and Van der Leeuw, insisted that all interpretations of religious beliefs and practices must be expressed in terms believers themselves can affirm, or at the very least in language that does not offend religious communities. Segal counters that, by subjecting academic interpretations to the believers' own authority, the scholar of religion not only describes the perspectives of adherents but actually endorses them. In Segal's words (1999: 143), this position forces phenomenologists of religion to abandon *epoché* by affirming that 'the conscious, irreducibly religious meaning for believers is its true one, which means at once its true one for them and its true one in itself'.

A similar appraisal of phenomenology has been proposed by Paul-François Tremlett, an anthropologist and lecturer in the Open University in the UK. Like Segal, Tremlett's chief offender is Mircea Eliade, whose primary aim in all his academic writings, according to Tremlett, is to restore authentic meaning to a world, which in modernity has deviated from its original, primordial spiritual orientation, defined by Eliade as seeking to be as near the sacred as possible. Tremlett (2008: 30) suggested that Eliade's mission is consistent with the phenomenological aim as a whole, which abandons its claim to 'value-neutrality by allowing certain assumptions about the reality or truth of the sacred to structure [its] mode of enquiry. This is consistent with Segal's charge that the emphasis within the phenomenology of religion on preserving a religious standpoint requires phenomenologists actually to endorse that standpoint. This view is confirmed, according to Tremlett, by Eliade's analysis of sacred space which 'founds, establishes and fixes the world, giving it meaning and moral content' (Tremlett 2008: 47). He added: 'Modernity is for Eliade a kind of pathological condition marked by alienation, loss, relativism, amnesia and ultimately nihilism' (Tremlett 2008: 47). This leads to Tremlett's conclusion that the phenomenology of religion is not only value-laden but based on an ideology, the purpose of which 'is to make a contribution towards the re-awakening of humanity's essential spirituality in order to re-enchant the world' (Tremlett 2008: 47).

These negative assessments of the anti-reductive stance of phenomenologists, although in many ways compelling, in my view are rendered less persuasive by their oppositional or dichotomous way of thinking. Both Segal and Tremlett insist that either the scholar of religion adopts the perspective of the non-believing social scientist and interprets religion necessarily as an outsider by giving no priority to a believer's own point of view, or the scholar, in the phenomenological tradition, acts like a believer and endorses the religious perspective as an insider. I have argued against this dichotomous view in previous publications by suggesting that the philosopher Ludwig Wittgenstein's analysis of language demonstrated that oppositional thinking does not provide the only, or indeed the best way, for understanding relationships in the world (Cox 1993: 103–23; Cox 1996a: 162–70; Cox 1998a: 94–7). Following Wittgenstein, as he was interpreted by the theologian David Krieger (1991: 110–8), I contend that, just like games we play in everyday life, we can move into and out of various methods in the study of religions without contradiction. In order to play a game, one must abide by the regulations of that game, but when one plays a different game, the operable rules vary. We cannot apply the rules of one game to another nor arbitrarily change the rules of a game, but we certainly can understand more than one game at once and know how to play many games well. When this analogy is applied to the study of religions, to argue that a non-believer cannot suspend personal judgements by using alternative methods to enter into the viewpoint of another is like saying we can never learn to play a different game from the one we know best and play regularly.

Certainly, Segal and Tremlett are correct in their assertion that the interpretations of religious communities employed by phenomenologists of religion differ from those employed within specific social scientific disciplines, but this neither invalidates the phenomenological method nor disparages the tools used by the other social sciences. It is like playing more than one game and understanding that different rules apply to each. The aim of the phenomenology of religion is to promote understanding in ways that can be affirmed by believing communities, but certainly not in confessional terms, as would be employed by members of those communities who are genuine insiders. The interpretations promoted by phenomenologists must speak to the academic community and must be able to withstand rigorous scholarly scrutiny. Where they do not, they require modification or, in some cases, rejection. In this sense, phenomenologists are playing by the same rules as other social scientists. Yet, by limiting their interpretations to theories that encourage understanding of a religious community in terms acceptable within the community, phenomenologists adhere to a self-imposed rule within a discipline devoted exclusively to the study of religion. This method does not dictate to other disciplines in the social sciences what interpretations are permitted or feasible. This is like playing a game that, although related to other games, operates according to its own rules. Only dichotomous thinking prohibits the scholarly community from playing by many rules. It is Segal and Tremlett, rather than phenomenologists of religion, who unduly restrict the freedom of interpretation in a scientific sense by their unwavering commitment to dualistic thinking.

Implications of phenomenology for the study of African Religions

If I am correct, the phenomenology of religion remains an important method for studying religions and by extension for studying African Religions. Yet, some points can be made specifically about applying the method in Africa, and thus I return to the two central questions with which I began this chapter: What, if anything, can the phenomenology of religion contribute to contemporary understandings of African religions? In light of the phenomenological method, as 'insiders', do African scholars possess an inherent advantage over non-African scholars of African Religions? I address the first question by exemplifying the value of *epoché* as a technique to limit what I regard as one of the most distorting assumptions made by scholars of African religions, the claim that African Indigenous peoples have always and everywhere believed in a Supreme Being. I respond to the second question by subjecting 'insider' discourse to a brief analysis in light of 'empathetic interpolation'. In the end, I argue that interpretations of the meanings of African religions, the phenomenological eidetic intuition, must be accountable to the data while at the same time avoiding the naïve assumption that the facts present themselves to the observer in a 'pure' form.

One of the first critiques levelled by an African at Western interpretations of African Indigenous Religions was introduced into scholarly debates by the Ugandan poet, philosopher and anthropologist, Okot p'Bitek, in his now-classic book entitled *African Religions in Western Scholarship*, first published in 1970. P'Bitek (1990: 80) opens the tenth chapter of his book, which he called 'Hellenization of African Deities', with the following words: 'When students of African religions describe African deities as eternal, omnipresent, omnipotent, omniscient, etc. they intimate that African deities have identical attributes with those of the Christian God.' He closes the same chapter with an indictment of such conclusions, which he labels 'absurd and misleading' (p'Bitek 1990: 80), by referring back to the same attributes: 'African peoples', he writes, 'may describe their deities as "strong" but not "omnipotent"; "old" but not "eternal"; "great" not "omnipresent"' (p'Bitek 1990: 88). P'Bitek was critical of Western missionaries, like Edwin W. Smith, who edited the highly influential book, *African Ideas of God* (1950) and E. G. Parrinder, whose book *African Traditional Religion* at the time did perhaps more than any other to interpret African belief systems in simple terms to Western audiences (1954). P'Bitek, however, was most scathing in his appraisal of African Christian apologists, like Parrinder's student, E. B. Idowu, and the Kenyan theologian, J. S. Mbiti. P'Bitek believed that Idowu's and Mbiti's books, which were published in the 1960s and early 1970s, undermined the pride Africans had in their own religions and cultures by making them acceptable only insofar as they conformed to Christian values (Idowu 1962; Mbiti 1969; Mbiti 1970).

To be fair, the writers who were most subject to p'Bitek's stinging critique must be seen, in part at least, as trying to correct prior degrading descriptions of African religions as 'fetishistic', 'tribalistic' and 'primitive'. For example, Edwin W. Smith, as a missionary, postulated a universal African belief in a Supreme Being as evidence that God had been active in Africa before missionaries brought the message of

Christ to them. Smith (1950: 34) wrote: 'When the Christian missionary comes with the Good News of God revealed in Jesus Christ as loving Father – whatever else in his teaching they find it hard to accept, this [belief in God] at least they readily take to their hearts.' Smith's contention that Africans universally believe in God, although expressed in Christian theological language and arguably, as p'Bitek implied, was patronizing towards traditional African cultural expressions, must be understood in its historical context as aiming to counter earlier prejudicial attitudes towards African religious beliefs.

Recent developments suggest that the assumption that Africans have always believed in some form of a Supreme Deity, rather than simply reflecting the historical background that produced it, has become even more widespread than when p'Bitek so damagingly exposed the faults with this idea. Part of this can be explained by the continued popularity of Mbiti's writings, especially in Africa, but other more recent publications have spread the same idea. For example, the African scholar of religions, Jacob Olupona (2000: xvi), refers in the introduction to his edited volume, *African Spirituality*, to the wide variations within African myths and the deities they portray, but concludes nevertheless that they all 'yield images' of the Supreme Being. Or, in his article on 'Christianity' in John Hinnells's widely read *A New Handbook of Living Religions*, in line with the widespread notion that the Supreme Being throughout Africa was a withdrawn High God, the historian Andrew Walls (1998: 147) maintains that 'the coming of Christianity was less bringing God to the people than bringing God near'. And, in a book prepared to introduce the study of African Traditional Religions into the secondary school curriculum in Zimbabwe, the editors, Gerrie ter Haar, Ambrose Moyo and S. J. Nondo (1992: 7) assert: 'The Indigenous religions of Zimbabwe share a common faith in the existence of a Supreme Being who is believed to be the Creator and Sustainer of the universe.' More recent evidence that academics today are perpetuating the notion that Africans believe universally in a High God is found in two highly acclaimed books written by respected scholars of African history and religions, one co-authored by Jean Allman of the Centre for African Studies in the University of Illinois and John Parker of the School of Oriental and African Studies in London, and the other by David Westerlund of Södertörn University, near Stockholm. I will deal with the Allman and Parker book first.

In their volume entitled *Tongnaab: The History of a West African God*, published in 2005, Allman and Parker describe the primary aim of their study as challenging the widespread notion that African Indigenous Religions only entered history when they encountered Christianity and Islam or when they were affected by the slave trade, colonialism and eventually African nationalism. They observe: 'Too often scholars have privileged the processes of conversion to Islam and Christianity as the central historical dynamic of African religion, thereby consigning Indigenous belief to the realm of unchanging tradition' (Allman and Parker 2005: 6). In order to counter this idea, the authors trace the history of Tongnaab, a deity found in northern Ghana in the Tong Hills among the Tallensi ethnic group. This emphasis on historical change, of course, makes the question, 'Who is Tongnaab?', extremely difficult to answer, but Allman and Parker (2005: 44) contend that local people still believe that Tongnaab 'was embedded in the rocky heights of the Tong Hills before the emergence of mankind' and that 'Tongnaab – like the ancestors – is generally perceived as a readily accessible refraction of the withdrawn High God, Naawun'. I find this conclusion remarkable in light of the overall analysis of the book. The authors appear, perhaps unwittingly, to confirm the widespread notion that the African Supreme Being, after having created the world, withdrew from it. The present deities, including autochthonous beings, are refractions of the Supreme Being. This fits nicely into a Christian interpretation of African Indigenous Religions, whereby God is seen as the source of all things, and is superior to any lesser gods. In the end, the deities that receive the bulk of ritual attention are reduced to acting as mediators between the people and God. That the authors rather uncritically re-enforce this view suggests that, although they have attempted to rescue African Indigenous Religions from a time warp, in the case of the Supreme Being at least, they have fallen into the very trap they have so assiduously sought to avoid.

David Westerlund, even more explicitly than Allman and Parker, presents God as an integral part of African cosmology in his book *African Indigenous Religions and Disease Causation*, published in 2006. Westerlund, who is a highly respected international expert in the history of religions, examines the understanding of disease causation among five ethnic groups: the San of southwestern Africa, the Maasai of southern Kenya and northern Tanzania, the Sukuma of north-western Tanzania, the Kongo, the majority of whom today live in the province of Lower Congo in Democratic Republic of Congo, and the Yoruba of Nigeria. In his study, Westerlund discusses what he calls beliefs in 'supra-human' beings in each of these groups and seems unconcerned about employing the word God as part of his descriptions about such beings (Westerlund 2006: 6). Amongst the San, he discusses 'heavenly beings' and describes God as creator, suggesting that various names used to designate the Supreme Being normally are associated with the sky (Westerlund 2006: 43–4). He follows this with a chapter on 'God in Maasai thought', and, although he qualifies belief in the Supreme Being by admitting that not all Maasai believe in God, he argues nonetheless that 'God is associated particularly with the heavenly realm, yet he is not identified with it. He may also be said to be omnipresent' (Westerlund 2006: 67–8). The Sukumu, who are a Bantu speaking people, place a heavy emphasis on ancestors, but Westerlund (2006: 89) adds, 'When people invoke ancestors, they often invoke God as well.' Among the Kongo people, Westerlund notes that the name of the Supreme Being or God the creator is Nzambi. 'It signifies someone who is higher, stronger, more powerful than other beings; it also denotes something incomprehensible and mysterious, or, in short, divine' (Westerlund 2006: 118). And, of course, following the many studies on the Yoruba, Westerlund observes that the most important names for God are Olodumare and Olorun, which point to the Yoruba belief that God is Creator, 'the Supreme Being who is immortal and unchanging'

(Westerlund 2006: 124). It is important to note that Westerlund is fully aware that Christian and Islamic influences have elevated the notion of God above that which may have existed several hundred years ago. Yet, the fact that he draws attention to the local word for God or the Supreme Being in each of his examples seems to imply that every African people has some idea of a Supreme Being or God, which generally can be translated into terms commensurate with Christian (or Islamic) notions of a Creator.

In each of these cases, I am arguing that what began as a theological idea in the writings of Smith, Parrinder, Idowu and Mbiti has now become uncritically accepted and incorporated into works that are not written for theological purposes. It is at this point that the use of the phenomenological *epoché* becomes most relevant. By employing the technique of *epoché*, a scholar is able to suspend such judgements or at least develop a healthy suspicion towards them. Part of the analysis which follows, of course, will necessarily need to frame the question concerning the African belief in God historically, since to study African Indigenous Religions today cannot avoid taking into account the long contact such religions have had with Christianity and Islam and at the same time take cognizance of the impact of Western educational, political and economic influences. Since African societies were oral, tracing a universal belief in a Supreme Being historically is problematic, but insight from linguistics, archaeology and early accounts of contact with African societies written by explorers, ethnographers and missionaries can provide some tools for drawing conclusions. The important point is that the phenomenology of religion calls on the researcher to challenge uncritical assumptions, just as Husserl challenged the 'natural attitude'. In this way, on many topics related to the study of African Indigenous Religions, but particularly on the largely unexamined notion of the ubiquitous belief in God, the scholar seeks to limit potentially distorting biases and base conclusions on the data, which then can confirm the original theory, modify it or lead to entirely new interpretations (e.g. see Cox 1995: 339–55).

The second important contribution the phenomenology of religion can make applies much more generally to the 'insider/outsider' discourse in the study of African religions. The African scholar, as an 'insider', according to a phenomenological analysis, has no inherent advantage over non-African 'outside' researchers. This is because the method of empathetic interpolation emphasizes that humans all think alike and that it is possible to gain an understanding of cultures other than one's own, if a proper attitude based on *epoché* is employed and if the time and skills for attaining understanding are cultivated. From a phenomenological perspective, the interpretation that scholars, African or not, give to the data never simply replicates the language of believers nor even necessarily uses concepts derived from their cultural settings. This is evident in the terminology employed by phenomenologists, such as Eliade's concept hierophany. Believers would not use such technical language to describe the way the sacred is known in their traditions, but if the meaning of the term were understood by them, it certainly would not be offensive. This suggests that the scholar of religion, by using empathy, while interpolating what is unfamiliar in terms of one's own cultural and social background, can enter into any cultural setting and provide a sound academic interpretation of what might at first sight appear incomprehensible, strange or bizarre. This process is intended, as Van der Leeuw argued, to overcome the division between the subject and the object in the study of any religion. It does not, however, guarantee that the interpretation provided by the scholar is accurate; it simply affirms that accurate interpretations are open to all researchers regardless of their social or cultural backgrounds.

On this point, it is important to emphasize that the eidetic intuition proposed by any scholar must remain accountable to the phenomena themselves. If the interpretative structure of meaning is incapable of being tested in the data, it must be rejected. Eliade provides a case in point. As we have seen, some of Eliade's fiercest critics have accused him of basing his conclusions on a personal pre-commitment to the value of a religious view of life. Thus, even if Eliade's interpretations of religion proved inoffensive to believers and demonstrated an acute sympathy towards religious communities, that would not ensure that his interpretation of the essence of religion is correct. In fact, in his discussion of Eliade's interpretations of Australian Aboriginal Religions, Tony Swain (1985: 7–8) argues that Eliade's emphasis on the sky as a symbol of transcendence is not confirmed by the data. The point stressed by the phenomenology of religion on this question thus is two-pronged: following the method of empathetic interpolation, the meanings scholars assign to the data must in theory be capable of being affirmed by 'insiders' within the religious communities under study and such interpretations must be capable of being tested by recourse to the phenomena on which the eidetic intuition is based.

Conclusions

My review of the continued relevance of the phenomenology of religion for the study of African Indigenous Religions, and more broadly, for all religions in Africa, is critically important for two reasons. One has to do with academic integrity, and the other touches on ethics in academic research. I have made the first point repeatedly throughout this chapter when I have contended that a defining task of scholarly research is to question and, where appropriate, to challenge, widely accepted assumptions by showing the underlying presuppositions that inform them. On the second point, the phenomenology of religion insists that African Indigenous Religions in their many forms should be studied in their own right, and not as a preparation for Christianity or as a base on which all religious beliefs are constructed. If we accord other religious traditions the dignity of studying their histories, oral or written traditions, rituals and beliefs in their own right and not as a subset of another tradition, then it appears, on grounds of academic fairness alone, we ought to do the same with traditions whose records are largely oral and presentational, sometimes small scale and largely kinship orientated. This is precisely what Okot p'Bitek (1990: 111) intended, when near the end of his book he concluded: 'The aim of the study of African religions should be to understand the religious beliefs and practices of African peoples, rather than to discover the Christian God in Africa.' I regard this as thoroughly consistent with phenomenological principles and why I contend that the phenomenological method continues to make a constructive contribution to the academic study of religions in Africa.

Chapter 2

THE CONTRIBUTION OF T. G. H. STREHLOW TO THE CONTEMPORARY GLOBAL STUDY OF INDIGENOUS RELIGIONS

In my 2007 publication, *From Primitive to Indigenous: The Academic Study of Indigenous Religions*, I analysed the developing academic interest in the global study of Indigenous Religions (Cox 2007a: 8–31). Since the publication of that book, the study of Indigenous Religions has gained momentum and is rapidly becoming an important subject in religious studies, as well as in multi-disciplinary contexts. For example, a current project is being organized by Professor Geoffrey Davis, Former International Chair of the Association for Commonwealth Literature and Language Studies and G. N. Devy, Founder of the People's Linguistic Survey of India, who are editing a ten-volume series to be published by Routledge. The series is entitled, 'Key Concepts in Indigenous Studies'. In an email addressed to me dated 7 April 2015, Davis and Devy wrote that 'the field of Indigenous Studies has been one of the more important emerging fields of scholarship in the Humanities during the last two decades'. They note that 'leading universities in many countries have established specialized Departments of Indigenous Studies' (Personal correspondence: Davis and Devy to Cox, 7 April 2015). An example of this is located at the University of Tromsø, the Arctic University of Norway, which on its website claims to be 'one of the very few in the world to offer an international Master's degree programme in comparative Indigenous studies' (https://uit.no/utdanning/program/270446/Indigenous_studies_-_master). Key figures in the study of Indigenous Religions at Tromsø are Bjørn Ola Tafjord and Siv Ellen Kraft, who have collaborated with Greg Johnson of the University of Colorado in Boulder on the *Brill Handbook of Indigenous Religions*, published in 2017. Tafjord, Kraft and Johnson have developed a project on Indigenous Religions that has involved Arkotong Longkumer, Lecturer in Religious Studies at the University of Edinburgh, who in December 2016 organized a workshop on Indigenous Knowledge at Kohima, Nagaland, that also included the participation of the Africanist scholar, Rosalind Hackett of the University of Tennessee, who is the former President of the International Association for the History of Religions. In the United Kingdom, Graham Harvey of the Open University, continues to promote the study of Indigenous Religions, something he has been developing through a series of publications since the appearance of his groundbreaking edited volume, *Indigenous Religions: A Companion* (2000).

In Australia, initiatives have been launched at Western Sydney University by the School of Social Sciences and Psychology and at the University of Sydney in the Department of Studies in Religion. On 12 September 2016, Western Sydney University held its Inaugural Aboriginal and Torres Strait Islander Research Symposium on topics focusing on 'lived experience' and 'perspectives on research'. This was timed to follow the 2016 National Aborigines and Islander Day Observance Committee (NAIDOC) theme of 'Songlines: The Living Narrative of Our Nation', which was observed from 3 to 10 July 2016. The School of Social Sciences and Psychology at Western Sydney University followed this with a second one-day symposium on 11 April 2018 that considered 'Aboriginal and Torres Strait Islander Peoples' Knowledges, Religions and Cultural Diversity'. The intention at Western Sydney University is to make symposia on research themes related to Indigenous Peoples in Australia annual events.

The Department of Studies in Religion at the University of Sydney sponsored a one-day symposium on 18 October 2013 that reflected on issues surrounding the category Indigenous Religions, which in 2016 resulted in the publication of the book, *Religious Categories and the Construction of the Indigenous*, edited by Christopher Hartney and Daniel J. Tower. In addition to leading Australian academics, such as Garry Trompf, Emeritus Professor of Religious Studies in the University of Sydney, an expert on Indigenous Religions in Melanesia (Trompf 2016: 8–37), the book contains articles by international scholars including Bjørn Ola Tafjord (2016: 138–77) and Graham Harvey (2013a: 74–91), and my own submission in which I defend my restricted definition of Indigenous Religions against critics, such as Tafjord and Harvey (Cox 2016: 38–57).

In the context of these new developments in the global study of Indigenous Religions, the importance of introducing the work of T. G. H. Strehlow to scholars working in this field around the world becomes critical. Strehlow (1908–78) was the son of the Lutheran missionary-linguist, Carl Strehlow. He grew up on the Hermannsburg Mission around 130 kilometres west of Alice Springs in the Northern Territory of Australia, where he learned the local Arrernte language as one of his mother tongues. At the age of fourteen, when his father died, he went to Adelaide with his mother to complete school and later enrolled in the University of Adelaide to study Classics and Linguistics. In 1932, as a part of his MA degree at the University of Adelaide, he returned to Central Australia to begin work on an Arrernte grammar, but soon learned that language and culture were intricately connected. This began a lifetime of research on the Indigenous peoples of Central Australia during which he compiled a massive collection of data based on interviews and observations that resulted in detailed research notes, sound recordings, films, genealogical records, maps of totemic clan wanderings, accounts of myths and detailed descriptions of secret ceremonies. He was also entrusted with a number of secret-sacred objects (*tjurunga*) by Indigenous Elders because he had gained their trust, partly due to the lasting influence of his father and because many of them remembered him as a child on the Hermannsburg Mission. In 1936, he became the Native Patrol Officer responsible for the southern half of the Northern Territory, a post he held for six years. His research was interrupted during the Second World War, but he was able to resume his work in 1946 when he was appointed Research Fellow in Australian linguistics and Lecturer in English literature at the University of Adelaide. After spending two years from 1950 to 1952 studying under the noted anthropologist Raymond Firth at the London School of Economics, Strehlow was appointed Reader in Australian Linguistics in the University of Adelaide, which provided a solid base for his continued research and writing on the Indigenous cultures of Central Australia. He was awarded a Personal Chair in Linguistics by the University Adelaide in 1970 and was conferred an Honorary Doctor of Letters from Adelaide in 1973.

Strehlow was widely known within Australia, particularly among anthropologists, but his potential contribution to the international study of Indigenous Religions has never been realized. He made limited contributions to publications in the study of religion, the most relevant of which for religious studies was an article that appeared in a volume edited by the European scholars of religion, C. J. Bleeker and Geo Widengren (Strehlow 1971b: 609–28). Strehlow's paper provided an overview and introduction to Aboriginal Religions in Australia for scholars for whom the subject was new or outside their fields of expertise. Strehlow also achieved global recognition within the international study of Aboriginal societies when in 1978 he was awarded an honorary doctorate by the University of Uppsala in Sweden. Despite these notable achievements, Strehlow's works remain largely unknown among current researchers in the burgeoning field of Indigenous Religions within religious studies departments outside Australia.

Strehlow's Theoretical and Empirical Methods in the Study of Indigenous Religions

I begin my analysis of Strehlow's contribution to the global study of Indigenous Religions by considering him as a phenomenologist of religion. In my book, *Restoring the Chain of Memory: T. G. H. Strehlow and the Repatriation of Australian Indigenous Knowledge* (Cox 2018: 129–47), I argue that, although Strehlow never claimed to use the phenomenological method in his research among the Indigenous peoples of Central Australia, he utilized aspects of this approach, particularly in his three major publications: *Aranda Traditions* (1947), *Songs of Central Australia* (1971a), and *Central Australian Religion* (1978a).

In order to justify this claim, I need first to outline the main elements within the phenomenological method. For the sake of simplicity, the phenomenological method can be organized into a step-by-step system following three main phases: (1) the attitudinal phase, (2) the descriptive phase and (3) the interpretative phase. The first step in the attitudinal phase involves performing the technique of *epoché* (from the Greek 'to hold back') through which scholars bring to their awareness and attempt to limit the impact of their most powerful and potentially distorting pre-judgements, both academic and personal, which may determine the outcome of their research before any empirical investigation has taken place. The second stage in the attitudinal phase encourages scholars to see as believers see by fostering an empathetic attitude that interpolates from one's own experience into the experience of the religious believer in order to make comprehensible to outsiders what otherwise might seem bizarre or even offensive in the religion the phenomenologist is seeking to understand. The process of getting inside a believer's mind requires a deep empathy through which researchers cultivate a feeling for the religious communities they are describing and interpreting (Cox 2010: 52). This is followed by the third stage in the attitudinal phase, which I have called 'maintaining *epoché*' (Cox 2010: 55–7). By this I mean that, in the process of cultivating empathy, scholars must take particular care to separate academic conclusions from confessional statements concerning the beliefs of the communities they are studying. In other words, students of religion do not actually become believers in the religion they are studying, even though they seek to include the believers' perspectives in their eventual interpretations. To avoid what has been called 'going native' (see, for example, O'Reilly 2009: 89–92), researchers must suspend judgements, not only about their own potentially distorting academic or personal opinions (performing the *epoché*), but they must continue to hold in abeyance any judgements about the truth or value of the beliefs and practices of the religion they are studying (maintaining *epoché*).

After the steps in the attitudinal phase of the phenomenological method have been employed, scholars then are ready to enter the descriptive phase in which they present the data observed as accurately as possible. This means that 'words, actions, gestures, songs, symbols, explanations by adherents and stories must be recorded in detail' (Cox 2010: 57). This is followed by the next step in the descriptive phase, 'naming the phenomena', or put in other terms, the creation of classifications or typologies into which the observed and recorded data can be sorted and organized. Phenomenological categories include, among others, myths, rituals, beliefs, religious practitioners, art, ethics and morality. These classifications can be sub-divided into further types, such as cosmogonic, socio-moral and quasi-legendary myths; lifecycle, calendrical and crisis rituals; shamanistic, priestly or holy person types of religious practitioners. Such classifications and sub-categories are created by the scholar not only for organizational purposes, but also for comparative reasons. This makes it possible to compare and contrast diverse societies in varying time periods with different types of source material. Of course, it is important not to make naïve or superficial comparisons, but by creating typologies and sub-categories, the salient factors that comprise the classifications can be compared according to the criterion on which the classification has been constructed.

This leads to the stages in the third phase where scholars interpret the data that have been inserted into typological categories and compared. It is important to underscore that comparisons are done primarily for empirical reasons and thus they must be rooted in specific and local contexts. The aim of comparisons, however, is interpretative, to elucidate the meaning of particular religious practices, which, in turn helps academics make generalizations about the classifications themselves. This was done, for example, by the anthropologist Victor Turner, who analysed life-cycle rituals, such as male initiation ceremonies, among the Ndembu of Zambia. Turner, following the outline of the classical anthropologist, Arnold van Gennep (1960), divided male initiation rituals into three main stages beginning with the first stage, separation from the community, followed by a liminal stage, betwixt and between, where the males are neither children nor yet adults, and then finally the incorporation stage, when they return to the community as adults (Turner 1985: 205–10). The stages, which mark significant changes in the social status of young males, are punctuated throughout with rituals that mark different phases in their passage from children to men. Turner's model operated as a paradigm or structure for initiation ceremonies everywhere, but the specific content, context, rituals, and symbols varied according to local situations. It is possible using Turner's formal structure of initiation rituals to make comparisons that help to promote understanding of the religious significance of life-cycle rituals in general while at the same time insisting that the model must be filled with specific content. In this sense, the interpretative stage in the phenomenological method is shown to be based largely on the ability to generalize beyond specific contexts and thus to create informed comparisons that help elucidate the larger meaning of the categories of religious phenomena according to formal structures or what I have called paradigmatic models (Cox 1998a: 8–9; Cox 1998b: x–xiv).

Traditionally, phenomenologists of religion have sought to offer interpretations not only of the meaning of specific classifications and sub-categories of the phenomena of religion; they have also identified general patterns that can be applied to religious life everywhere. This final step in the interpretative phase is called 'the eidetic intuition', whereby the scholar constructs a paradigm for religion in general. Examples of influential academics who have formed models for religion include Mircea Eliade (1996 [1958], 1987 [1959]), who found 'patterns in comparative religion' by constructing themes around the sacred and the profane, Gerardus van der Leeuw (1938: 23–8), who described the key concept in religion as 'power' and W. Cantwell Smith, whose prototype for religion focused on 'personal faith' in a 'transcendent power' that was embodied in a 'cumulative tradition' (1964: 141). These formal structures of religion provided a framework on which religious phenomena could be placed for the purposes of interpreting their meaning and as a system for promoting an overall understanding of the place of religion in human history.

In brief, as a method for the study of religious communities, the aim of the phenomenology of religion is to promote understanding of religions in particular and of religion in general. Its techniques attempt to bridge the gap between the subject and the object of religion the observer and those that are observed, by drawing on common human ways of thinking that can be translated into multiple cultural contexts and individual inter-subjective experiences. Because all phenomenological interpretations follow from the attitudinal and descriptive phases in the research process, testing the interpretations is two-fold: they must be supported by the most careful attention to empirical descriptions and they must be capable of being affirmed by believing communities themselves. This final point means that phenomenologists of religion acknowledge and respect the agency of the so-called objects of study by involving them in the research process and by making their voices heard in the final interpretations presented by scholars to the wider academic community and more broadly to the general public.

Strehlow as Phenomenologist of Religion

I now turn to examine how T. G. H. Strehlow fits into the stages in the phenomenological method in the study of religion. Strehlow's use of the technique, 'performing *epoché*', is demonstrated in his highly critical assessment of the presuppositions that dominated so-called scientific theories about Aboriginal Australian communities in the late nineteenth and early twentieth century. In the 'Introduction' to his book *Aranda Traditions*, Strehlow refers to the Report of the Horn Expedition, which, funded by the wealthy businessman William Horn, constituted the first scientific investigation into the remote regions of Central Australia. The Expedition was conducted over a three-month period in 1894 and comprised a multi-disciplinary research team under the auspices of the Universities of Sydney, Melbourne and Adelaide. The participants on the Expedition included experts in the fields of botany, geology, anthropology, ethnology and zoology. Baldwin Spencer, who in 1887 had been appointed Professor of Biology at the University of Melbourne, was the Expedition's zoologist and photographer, as well as the author of the Expedition's official report (Spencer 1896). Strehlow cites a lengthy quotation from the Report, which refers to the 'Central Australian aborigine' as 'a living representative of a stone age' and graphically describes the Aboriginal person as 'a naked, hirsute savage'. As to the religion of the Aboriginal of Central Australia, the Report states: 'he has none', nor does he have any 'traditions'. Rather, the Aboriginal 'continues to practise with scrupulous exactness a number of hideous customs and ceremonies which have been handed from his fathers, and of the origin or reason of which he knows nothing' (cited by Strehlow 1947: xvi–xvii). Strehlow argues that this section from the Horn Report clearly exposed the assumptions that prejudiced its conclusions:

> Such an observation suggests that the Australian aboriginal was then regarded merely as a highly specialized offshoot of the human species – primitive and incapable of further development, and therefore inevitably and naturally doomed to total extinction from the day when the superior white man entered upon his domains. (Strehlow 1947: xvii)

The Horn Expedition stimulated Spencer's interest in studying further the Aboriginal peoples of the central desert region. He returned to Central Australia in 1896, and in close cooperation with the Alice Springs postmaster, F. J. Gillen, whom Spencer had met during the Horn Expedition, began a study of Indigenous societies in the region. Despite not being a trained ethnologist and whose knowledge of Indigenous languages was poor, Gillen was useful to Spencer because he had forged good relationships with Aboriginal people. As a result, Gillen was able to organize a series of initiation ceremonies and other rituals for Spencer's benefit that formed a major part of Spencer and Gillen's book published in 1899 under the title *The Native Tribes of Central Australia*. In 1927, fifteen years after Gillen's death, Spencer published a new and enlarged edition of the original book in two volumes under the title *The Arunta: A Study of a Stone Age People,* to which he attributed Gillen as co-author.

Strehlow repeatedly condemned the assumptions that informed the writings of Spencer and Gillen claiming they had influenced a generation of scholarly opinion about the Indigenous Religions of Central Australia. Spencer and Gillen persistently referred to Arrernte peoples as living representatives of a 'Stone Age' culture that was quickly being superseded by an advanced European civilization. This fundamental presupposition prompted Spencer and Gillen, following an evolutionary model, to conclude that Arrernte culture would inevitably be replaced by the beliefs and values of the higher, more scientific and rational world-view, just as other Stone Age peoples around the world had succumbed to the superior forces of Western civilization. This pre-judgement was voiced by Spencer in the opening words of the Preface to *The Arunta* (1927: vii) in a well-known statement that reveals in quite bold language the assumptions that underpinned his research:

Australia is the present home and refuge of creatures, often crude and quaint, that have elsewhere passed away and given place to higher forms. This applies equally to the aboriginal as to the platypus and kangaroo. Just as the platypus, laying its eggs, and feebly suckling its young, reveals a mammal in the making, so does the Aboriginal show us, at least in broad outline, what early man must have been like before he learned to read and write, domesticate animals, cultivate crops and use a metal tool. It has been possible to study in Australia human beings that still remain on the culture level of men of the Stone Age.

Strehlow regarded the attitude Spencer voiced in the Preface to *The Arunta* as just one example of many 'nauseating insults' that Spencer 'heaped upon his aboriginal informants' (Strehlow 1978b: 3). That the presuppositions of Spencer and Gillen influenced the reliability of subsequent anthropological findings was confirmed, according to Strehlow, by the 'silence' of later anthropologists, who uncritically accepted Spencer and Gillen's evaluation of the 'primitive' state of Aboriginal peoples. In *Central Australian Religion*, Strehlow argued that work on the religion of Central Australian people had suffered from the failure of scholars to recognize and acknowledge the prejudicial impact of the distorting preconceptions voiced in the works of Spencer and Gillen. He singled out in particular Spencer's biases, which caused his studies of the Arrernte to be dotted with errors and misinformation. Strehlow's criticism of Spencer on just this point is severe, as expressed in *Songs of Central Australia*:

It is hard to believe that Spencer, a highly trained man about whose accuracy Sir James Frazer wrote such a glowing eulogy, could ever have stooped to set down his own personal views about the Western Aranda beliefs when he had never bothered to ascertain the relevant information from the Western Aranda natives themselves. (Strehlow 1971a: xxxi)

Strehlow provides an example of how Spencer had influenced the work of J. G. Frazer by citing a section extracted from Frazer's seminal multi-volume work *The Golden Bough*. Strehlow criticizes Frazer for describing the Indigenous peoples of Australia as 'the rudest savages as to whom we possess accurate information' and for ascribing to them the universal practice of magic, whereas 'religion in the sense of propitiation or conciliation of the higher powers seems to be nearly unknown' (cited by Strehlow 1978a: 8–9). Strehlow credits Spencer and Gillen as the primary source for Frazer's negative judgement of Australian Aboriginal peoples claiming that based on their writings Frazer ranked them lowest on the evolutionary scale (1978a: 8). Strehlow also criticized Lucien Lévy Bruhl, the French anthropologist well known for his theory of 'primitive mentality', whom Strehlow claimed had been influenced significantly by Spencer and Gillen. Strehlow asserted that Lévy Bruhl was guilty of making 'attacks upon the "pre-logical mentality" found in "primitive societies"' and 'sneered at the crude nature of "primitive languages"' (Strehlow 1978a: 9).

The phenomenological stage, performing *epoché*, was developed in part as a reaction against preconceived theories that ranked cultures according to their stage of evolutionary development. This clearly applies to Strehlow's criticisms of academic theories that were rooted in the writings of Spencer and Gillen. Strehlow also criticized the practice of finding explanations for the meaning of Arrernte myths and rituals by reference to a single causative factor. Strehlow voiced strong objections to singular interpretations of religion in his book *Songs of Central Australia* when he observed: 'I do not for a moment believe that all our present-day psychological or sociological explanations about the aboriginal Australians and their institutions are sufficiently well-attested or statistically validated to survive the criticism of later generations' (1971a: xvi). In particular, he criticized the theories of Géza Róheim, the Hungarian-American Freudian psychoanalytical ethnologist, who in 1928 studied the peoples of West Central Australia, which resulted in his book *The Riddle of the Sphinx*, published in 1934. Strehlow (1971a: xvii) claims that Róheim 'nowhere gives us full and unabridged versions either of the sacred myths or of the songs of this area'. Rather, 'he has selected from them only those portions which he could use as illustrations from his preconceived theories' (1971a: xvii). So predetermined were Róheim's methods of collecting data, Strehlow suggests, that 'before placing these carefully selected and cooked chunks before his readers, Róheim has masticated the tougher lumps for the benefit of his readers and saturated them with the saliva of Freudian suggestions so as to make his characteristically Freudian stew easier to swallow' (1971a: xvii).

The *epoché* was used by phenomenologists of religion to filter out biases, such as those based on theories of cultural evolution as expressed by Spencer in the Horn Report and in his later books, the predetermined notion of 'pre-logical mentality' as articulated by Lévy-Bruhl or psychoanalytical reductionism as exemplified by Géza Róheim's selection of research data to prove his own Freudian theories. According to Strehlow, the failure to bracket out such distorting preconceptions made producing accurate descriptions and fair interpretations of religious communities impossible. So severe were prior errors in judgement, description and analysis that 'a complete restatement of the aboriginal religious concepts which underlie Australian mythology and ritual' was required (Strehlow 1978a: 10). To do this Strehlow called for close attention to detail in collecting data which would enable the scholar to note the 'connection between religion, ritual, social organization, and certain purely geographic aspects of the environment' (1978a: 10). Although he did not use the term *epoché*, Strehlow clearly conducted his research in a way that attempted to limit the impact of scholars' prejudgements on their research conclusions.

A hallmark of the phenomenological approach relates to step two in the attitudinal phase whereby researchers attempt to get 'inside' the communities they are studying through empathetic interpolation and in the process reflect the perspectives of believers in their detailed descriptions at phase two and in their scholarly interpretations at phase three. Strehlow explained that one of his principal aims in *Songs of Central Australia* was 'to draw attention to the mental attitudes, common human emotions, and uninhibited subconscious drives which seem to find a safe and convenient outlet for their expression through the medium of these songs' (Strehlow 1971a: xvi). To describe fairly the attitude, emotions and drives of his research subjects required Strehlow to develop an appreciation of what he called 'the language of ordinary conversation' (Strehlow 1971a: xvi). This involved fostering a sympathetic feeling for the groups about whom he was writing, part of which was deepened by his knowledge of the Arrernte language, but was also enhanced because he had earned the trust of those who shared knowledge of their traditions with him. He explains: 'I have been able to speak Western Aranda since my childhood, and … I have known intimately many Northern, Southern, and Eastern Aranda informants' (1971a: xvi).

Communicating to outsiders a sense of what it is to think like an Arrernte person required Strehlow to interpolate symbols and meanings gained from studying an Arrernte cultural context into terms familiar to a European audience. Strehlow applied this method repeatedly throughout *Songs of Central Australia* by drawing parallels between Arrernte beliefs and practices, which to the Western reader may appear bizarre or even offensive, and themes commonly found in European, and particularly Old Norse, literature and poetry. On the surface, this might seem to reflect an entirely unempirical method by constructing comparisons between cultures which have no historical, linguistic or geographical relations. But Strehlow's aim was to cultivate a feeling for Arrernte traditions among his European readers by encouraging them to interpolate from their own traditions, beliefs and practices what might equally appear bizarre or offensive if placed into an Arrernte context. In this way, the seemingly 'strange' aspects of the foreign religion became more familiar to the European mind and hence comprehensible. Strehlow makes this method clear in the Introduction to *Songs of Central Australia*:

> The European parallels are designed to achieve a more sympathetic attitude in the mind of the white reader towards aboriginal verse and towards the aboriginal

world of ideas. For once it can be shown that some of these apparently crude, cruel, strange, or disgusting ideas were once to be found also in ancient pagan Europe, then more thoughtful readers may hesitate to reject them as utterly valueless. (Strehlow 1971a: xl)

Strehlow and Phases Two and Three in the Phenomenological Method: Description and Interpretation

Having established that Strehlow called for prior assumptions to be questioned and the resulting judgements from them suspended and that he encouraged an empathetic attitude through the process of interpolation, we are now ready to consider how he approached the descriptive stages in the phenomenological method. Strehlow indicates that the 'main material' contained in *Songs of Central Australia* was obtained on numerous research trips he made to Central Australia between 1932 and 1960 (Strehlow 1971a: xiv). He recorded many of the songs that are presented in the book in the Arrernte language, since, as he clarifies, 'I often found it easier to set down the explanation of a new word just as it was given to me in Aranda rather than translate it into English' (1971a: xiv). He adds that during his research trips he 'gathered four thousand two hundred and seventy aboriginal song verses', most of which were from various Arrernte groups living across the region (1971a: xiv). Strehlow notes that in *Songs of Central Australia* he had described in detail 'the traditional sacred texts used at the various religious rites, initiation ceremonies, and festive occasions' (Strehlow 1971a: xv). In the process, he claims to have provided 'a cross-section of every type of native song once found in the Central Australia area' (1971a: xv).

The term 'songs' is Strehlow's attempt to create a general overarching category according to which the verses he collected could be named or classified. He explains that by 'songs' he means 'the traditional native poems of Central Australia which are intoned according to traditional rhythmic measures' (1971a: xiii). Each song, he adds, 'is associated with a definite ceremonial centre and with a mythical supernatural being or mythical group of totemic ancestors' (1971a: xiii). He admits that he had considered terms other than 'songs' as a general category under which he could organize his data, principally 'poems' or 'chants'. Both words would have been appropriate, but he preferred 'songs' as the most comprehensive term and one that best fitted what he was trying to convey to the reader. In line with a second step in descriptive phase of the phenomenological method, Strehlow then sub-divided the general classification 'songs' into more specific categories for purposes of distinguishing their content and use. He explained that the 'songs' he collected and documented could be classified as 'musical compositions, as literary productions, and as traditional, religious, ceremonial, and social documents' (Strehlow 1971a: xv).

In the final phase of the phenomenological method, the scholar offers interpretations that clarify the meaning of the material that has been described, and because the attitudinal phase has been followed, lead to in-depth understanding of the religious communities being studied. In this sense, Strehlow has followed a phenomenological method by summarizing the essential elements within the classifications and sub-categories he has identified and then suggesting a composite term that encapsulates the overall structure through which Arrernte religion can be portrayed and through which understanding the traditional Arrernte way of life can be enhanced. The essential social structure within Arrernte traditional religion, according to Strehlow, is found in his pregnant phrase, 'personal monototemism in a polytotemic community' (Cox 2018: 60–80). Studying this concept in detail, based on Strehlow's intensive empirical research, provides the reader with a key to understanding Arrernte Indigenous Religion. This concept builds on the principal classifications or typologies Strehlow identified: Arrernte myths of creation, Arrernte songs and ceremonies, and Arrernte customary morality. It is important to underscore that Strehlow's phrase, 'personal monototemism in a polytotemic community', was derived entirely from empirical studies, and hence was testable and open to modification as circumstances changed and as new research was conducted. This strategic social descriptor indicating the structure of Arrernte Indigenous Religion is meant as an interpretative tool useful for promoting understanding of how the authority of the inherited Arrernte tradition translates into specific local contexts.

Towards the conclusion of *Central Australian Religion* Strehlow made generalizations about the essential nature of religion, and in this sense, contributed to the broad understanding of religion in the wider phenomenological tradition. He summarized the core of religion as showing 'a way of linking ... Time-limited existence with the riches and truths of Eternity by means of a faith formulated in terms that harmonized with a scientifically-validated view of the universe' (Strehlow 1978a: 52). Strehlow did not intend his comments on religion in human life to be prescriptive; he offered them at the conclusion of his detailed discussion of Arrernte myths, ceremonies, songs and social organization primarily to demonstrate to his readers that Arrernte Traditional Religion was consistent with the religious longings of humans everywhere. He argued that 'civilized man could improve his prospects of a more secure future by adopting some of the concepts of toleration and cooperation on which the aboriginal Australians based their social and political systems' (Strehlow 1978a: 52). This comment formed part of his resistance against ranking religions from higher to lower and also was consistent with his attempt to foster empathetic attitudes towards Arrernte religious beliefs and practices.

In the end, we see that by conducting research on Arrernte culture, Strehlow's primary aim was not to produce a general theory of the structure of religion. His principal focus was on the Arrernte peoples themselves, which made his generalizations very close to testable data and one in which he stressed the local character of the Indigenous Religions he wrote about. He could be said to have been ahead of his time in this regard, since contemporary studies of religion are notoriously hesitant to make broad statements about religion, precisely because they are difficult to test and because they foster the tendency to find in the data material that confirms the predetermined theory of religion the scholar has formulated (see, for example, Segal 1999: 139–63; Tremlett 2008; Flood 1999). Hence, we come back to the beginning: In Strehlow we find a scholar who, following principles consistent with the phenomenology of religion, was wary of theories that predetermined the results of research and as an interpreter of Arrernte Religion made his conclusions amenable to empirical testing and verification.

Strehlow's Significance beyond the Phenomenology of Religion

Although I have demonstrated that Strehlow can be interpreted as a phenomenologist of religion, his research methods and findings carry significance beyond phenomenological applications to the study of Indigenous Religions generally. In the first instance, his empirical methods included the scrupulous collection of data, which was documented with precision and clarity. His field notes were detailed so that any reader could trace how and where his research was conducted and what his aims were in conducting the research. He travelled vast distances, making in the process detailed maps showing the most important ceremonial sites, the tracks followed by the totemic ancestors and drawing attention to the central geographical features that were regarded as sacred embodiments of the founding ancestors. His photographs, films, recordings and transcripts of songs and chants were done with absolute precision. The testimony to his exacting empirical method of collecting data is now found in the Strehlow Collection housed in the Strehlow Research Centre in Alice Springs, which is so valuable that it can be regarded as occupying the place of the Elders themselves, who transferred their knowledge to Strehlow, and which now is providing the link between the current and the past generations. Strehlow also demonstrates how critically important it is for successful researchers to gain access to communities and in the process to win their trust. Without this, a researcher is unlikely to obtain accurate information or develop trustworthy interpretations of the data collected. Strehlow's criticism of shallow research underscores this point: promoting understanding of other cultures takes time and commitment, which Strehlow has shown requires not only sound theoretical and empirical skills, but also demands competence in local languages.

Strehlow's findings confirm that for the Arrernte groups he studied in Central Australia, local stories about totemic ancestors, which were tied to places on the landscape, define who they are and inform their complex kinship relations, including how marriage partners are selected. For the study of Indigenous Religions, Strehlow's intensive research demonstrates that Indigenous Religions in Central Australia were restricted to the two key factors, kinship and location, which I have made central to my definition of Indigenous Religions generally. His findings also indicate that the Indigenous Religions of Central Australia, although containing beliefs in the power of the original ancestors, did not magnify these to occupy the place of a sky god, a high god or contain elements of belief in one God. The ancestors emerged from the earth at the beginning of time and they returned to the earth in the form of significant geographical features on the landscape.

That these ancestors were so fundamentally intertwined with locality and kinship provides another example of how Indigenous Religions are best understood in terms of social categories rather than being confined to beliefs about supernatural beings or determined by alleged supernormal experiences.

Strehlow's descriptions of Arrernte Indigenous Religions also have implications for a sociological interpretation of religion in general. It is clear from the way in which traditions were maintained and ceremonial protocols enforced that the authority of the Arrernte way of life was rooted in age-old customary law, the knowledge of which was passed on to each new generation beginning with initiation ceremonies. Authority was vested in the Elders, who painstakingly safeguarded their secret knowledge, keeping it hidden from women, the uninitiated and outsiders. The Indigenous Religions of Central Australia, following Strehlow's analysis, precisely fit into a definition of religion as the transmission of a tradition that is endowed with an overwhelming authority over members of each kinship group and totemic clan.

Strehlow's frank discussion of the decline of Indigenous Religions in Central Australia and his noting of changes that he observed over the period he conducted his research confirms that his aim was not to depict a people in the present as if they were exact replicas of the past, the so-called error of the ethnographic present. He recognized and documented change, even if at times he lamented the loss of the traditions he was witnessing. By studying Strehlow's writings, as outsiders, we see him wrestling with the significance of disputes between Elders and younger men over the proper use of ceremonies; we see him describing the attitudes of young men who had come under the influence of white bosses and how that detracted from their respect for traditional ways of life; we see him struggling with the changes he experienced when Elders first entrusted him with their secret knowledge and how twenty years later that knowledge was largely unknown among the next generation of Elders in the line of succession. We also witness Strehlow's own changes from the time he was a young researcher to his period as Native Patrol Officer through his time as a more senior academic when ultimately he felt estranged from many of his academic colleagues, whom he believed encouraged methods based on superficial field research that were both inadequate and self-interested. In these ways, we see that Strehlow represents a scholar who was fundamentally aware of the dynamics of historical, social and cultural change as it impinged on the traditional way of life in Central Australia and that he responded personally to these changing situations.

Finally, we find in Strehlow an academic who firmly believed in social engagement. Whether one agrees with the policies he endorsed or not, from the time he accepted the appointment as Native Patrol Officer in 1936, he became committed to providing a more humane approach to the government's interaction with Indigenous people, and he set up a way to provide them with food supplies when they were in need. Admittedly, he used corporal punishment, but this was not just to establish his authority but served as a way of using culturally accepted methods without falling into the excessive abuse of Indigenous people that was practised earlier by colonial officers and representatives of the police. Later, he became an advocate of Indigenous rights against assimilationist policies; he intervened in the case of Rupert Max Stuart, the Indigenous man accused of raping and killing a young girl in South Australia; he was consulted as the legal status of customary law in Australia was being debated. In these ways, Strehlow demonstrated that he was a socially involved scholar, not one that remained aloof or indifferent to his research subjects. His frequent public lectures and talks, as well as his pamphlets and articles written for consumption by the general public, in terms of contemporary academic jargon, demonstrated that his research had 'impact' on public perceptions of Indigenous peoples in Australia. That he regarded his Collection as a depository that served to preserve knowledge of traditions that had disappeared also supports my contention that Strehlow exemplified a scholar who balanced his commitment to serious and detailed academic research with a recognition that his research had social implications.

Strehlow's Contribution to the Global Study of Indigenous Religions: A Summary

A summary of Strehlow's extensive research draws together and confirms his important contributions to the international study of Indigenous Religious. These fall under the following seven points:

1. His theoretical methodology was consistent with the basic tenets of phenomenology of religion.
2. He gave scrupulous attention to detail in conducting his empirical research.
3. He demonstrated the importance of gaining the trust of informants.
4. He underscored the central place of totemic ancestors among the Indigenous peoples of Central Australia, which in turn confirmed the fundamental themes of kinship and locality among Indigenous religious practitioners everywhere.
5. He exposed the errors in previous conclusions about Central Australian Religion, particularly assumptions about 'Dreaming', High Gods and One God.
6. He avoided the error of 'ethnographic present' by tracing and substantiating the important changes that had been imposed on the Indigenous people of Central Australia through colonial structures and missionary efforts.
7. As an active participant in contemporary policies that affected Indigenous Australians, he exemplified and modelled the social engagement of the scholar of religion.

If I apply the characteristics I have just listed that belonged to Strehlow the scholar, researcher and academic to his potential impact on the current international study of Indigenous Religions, we find that Strehlow combined a sound theoretical approach with in-depth empirical methods, which in turn help us delimit what we mean by the term Indigenous Religions and, more generally, by religion itself.

Reading T. G. H. Strehlow's works in-depth provides for contemporary scholars of Indigenous Religions an exemplary model for how research should be done while contributing significantly to our knowledge of a specific Indigenous people in Central Australia. Strehlow demonstrates to students of religion that our aim is to enlighten a wide range of audiences about Indigenous Religions, while accepting that the use of this knowledge thrusts us immediately into arenas of power and involves us in questions of possession. Through this tangled web of complicated issues, introducing the work of T. G. H. Strehlow into contemporary global academic studies in Indigenous Religions offers methodological clarity and serves as a paradigm for anyone who wishes to research and write about the religious life and traditions of specific Indigenous peoples in local contexts.

Chapter 3

MISSIONARIES, THE PHENOMENOLOGY OF RELIGION AND 'RE-PRESENTING' NINETEENTH-CENTURY AFRICAN RELIGION: A CASE STUDY OF PETER MCKENZIE'S *HAIL ORISHA!*

In this chapter, I am exploring one central question: By applying methods derived from the phenomenology of religion, can a scholar determine from missionary accounts what African Indigenous Religions were like at the time of first extensive contact with Christian missionaries? From this question, a series of sub-questions follows:

1. Are the accounts so distorted by missionaries' own evangelistic interests that they miss the actual focus of African Indigenous Religions and thereby minimize the usefulness of their records for scholarly research?
2. Does the phenomenology of religion provide a method for filtering out the potential distortions in missionary records?
3. Are phenomenological typologies themselves so influenced by Christian theological categories that they obscure for the scholar the actual focus of African Indigenous Religions?

An underlying assumption in this chapter is that African societies have radically expanded their world-views since the mid-nineteenth century, primarily under the influence of Western educational, economic, political, medical and religious systems. This is based in part on Robin Horton's thesis that colonialism caused traditional societies to undergo a shift from a 'micro' to a 'macro' world-view (Horton 1975: 219–20). Horton postulated that in religion this would result in a lessening of emphasis on local deities and ancestor veneration while increasing cultic attention towards the High God or Supreme Being. Horton's position is summarized helpfully by Jan Platvoet (1996: 56):

> In the relatively bounded and closed 'microworlds' of precolonial times, ritual attention would be greatest towards the ancestors and/or (lower orders of) gods and spirits of nature … but … the incorporation into the much wider and much more open 'macro-worlds' of colonial society – into which several traditional societies were simultaneously incorporated, and which was itself part of a global

colonial empire with a centre far away – would cause an important shift …,
and … the cult of the creator god would expand.

Although, as Platvoet notes, Horton's thesis was 'hotly contested', I agree with
Platvoet's conclusion that 'the shift from more limited to wider horizons through
incorporation into wider contexts of communication caused major changes in the
religious scene of Africa' (Platvoet 1996: 57).

Elsewhere, Andrew Walls (1996: 191) calls this 'the magnification of the
God component', which has resulted from extensive contact between traditional
societies and Christianity and Islam. For Walls, the fact that African religions
almost everywhere today maintain a belief in a Supreme Being makes the question
as to whether or not African societies in pre-colonial times actually conceived
of a Creator God largely irrelevant for discussions of contemporary African
world-views (Walls 1996: 187). Walls's position implies that even when traditional
rituals are practised today, with the apparent focus remaining on local deities or
ancestors, the Supreme God lurks in the background influencing the stories and
ritual dramas of traditional African religions.

The 'God question' is just one issue in an overall understanding of African
Indigenous Religions, but it underscores how interpretations of 'original' religion
in Africa have become important for scholars from many disciplines, but chiefly
for Christian apologists of African religions, such as E. B. Idowu (1962, 1973),
Kwesi Dickson (1984), J. B. Danquah (1944), and J. S. Mbiti (1969). For theological
and missiological reasons, these writers have asserted that Africans always had an
inherent belief in God, which is comparable to a Christian understanding of the
deity.

Today, many, if not most, books on African religions, written by Western and
African scholars alike, assume that Africans universally believe in a Supreme Being
(see, for example, Shorter 1997; Mitchell 1977; Magesa 1997; Banana 1991). This
relatively unchallenged assertion may disguise the sources and motivations behind
it. For the purposes of understanding the nature of African Indigenous Religions
in their own right and how they have come to be depicted in scholarly accounts, it
would be extremely useful to develop phenomenological descriptions of Indigenous
religious beliefs and practices at the time of first missionary contact. To test if
phenomenological methods can be used to reconstruct African Indigenous Religions
based on letters and reports from missionaries, in this chapter, I examine a specific
case where this has been attempted. In his volume of nearly 600 pages, entitled *Hail
Orisha! A Phenomenology of a West African Religion in the Mid-Nineteenth Century*,
Peter McKenzie (1997) 're-presents' phenomenologically Church Missionary
Society (CMS) accounts of Yoruba religion between 1840 and 1880.

Since McKenzie's work is so central to this analysis, a brief biographical note
about him should be included at this point. McKenzie, who is from New Zealand,
earned his PhD from the University of Edinburgh in 1953, in the Department
of Church History at New College. He taught religious studies at the University
of Ibadan, Nigeria, between 1965 and 1970 and then moved to the University of
Leicester, where until his retirement in 1989 he lectured in the history and

phenomenology of religion and served as Head of the Department of Religious Studies. While he was in Leicester, he made several field visits to Nigeria, one of which resulted in his 1976 book, *Inter-Religious Encounters in West Africa: Samuel Ajayi Crowther's Attitude to African Traditional Religion and Islam*.[1]

McKenzie's understanding of phenomenology

McKenzie introduces his study of mid-nineteenth-century Yoruba religion by placing himself firmly within the phenomenological approach to the study of religions. He announces at the outset that his work proposes 'to go behind the works of the last hundred years to material on Yoruba religion provided by the missionaries in the mid-nineteenth century' and to 'arrange that material in a phenomenology' (McKenzie 1997: viii). McKenzie aligns himself with the late-nineteenth/early-twentieth-century German philosopher Edmund Husserl, to whom contemporary movements in philosophical phenomenology can be traced (Cox 1996b: 18–9). Specifically, McKenzie (1997: viii) affirms Husserl's concept of intentionality, which he defines as being 'against ideology' and 'indirect reporting' in favour of presenting the world as it is through the method of 'bracketing out value-judgements' (otherwise known as the *epoché*). McKenzie (1997: viii) admits that the missionary records he has consulted are marked by 'unreflected subjectivity', but he hopes to use phenomenological methods 'to reveal the way the world of the *orisa* worshippers actually presented itself'. In other words, McKenzie wants to do for the nineteenth-century missionary what the missionary could not do, namely to present value-free, scholarly descriptions of Yoruba religious beliefs and practices.

Phenomenological methods do more than promote empathetic attitudes that encourage objective descriptions of religious activities. The phenomenologist also creates classifications or typologies to make sense of the descriptions through a rational ordering of religious practices. In this way, descriptions are assimilated under predetermined categories so that comparisons can be made among different religious communities in a variety of contexts. McKenzie (1997: viii) affirms this comparativist objective for his own research: 'The phenomenological approach provides ... a kind of yard stick by which to measure the status of Yoruba religion in terms of other religious traditions'. He adds later, 'The religious profile [of the Orisa cults] enables comparisons to be drawn with *other religious traditions*, not *in globo* but broken down into ... individual categories' (emphasis in original) (McKenzie 1997: 1).

McKenzie's typologies are derived from the phenomenological approach of the German scholar of religions, Friedrich Heiler, particularly from his book *Erscheinungsformen und Wesen der Religion* (1979 [1949]), a lengthy, systematic ordering of religious phenomena derived from secondary sources, which describe religious practices from around the world, both historically and contemporaneously. Heiler's work represents the classical phenomenological attempt, in Eric Sharpe's (1986: 245) words, to establish 'types, patterns, morphologies – all with a view to penetrating the "essence" of religion. McKenzie replicates Heiler's categories in his descriptions of mid-nineteenth-century Yoruba religion, but he claims to depart from Heiler's search for an 'essence' of religion. 'No attempt is made to penetrate behind the phenomena to some kind of religious "essence". *The nature of religion is, we believe, seen in the phenomena themselves*' (McKenzie 1997: 3) (emphasis in original).

Heiler organized his typological scheme into three concentric circles, each of which was intended to elucidate an aspect of a religion's understanding of and relationship to what McKenzie calls the 'sacred', but Heiler referred to as the 'holy' or 'numinous'. The outer circle (using McKenzie's terminology) comprises the following categories: sacred objects, sacred space, sacred time, sacred action, sacred person, sacred community and sacred word (including oral traditions). Within this circle is found a middle circle comprising the concept of the deity, creation stories, revelation, ideas of salvation and beliefs about the last things. The innermost circle refers to religious experience, which is divided into two categories: basic and supernormal. Basic forms denote awe, fear and anxiety, faith, trust, hope, joy, confidence, devotion, love, peace and zealous defence of the faith. Supernormal experiences include visions, trances, out of the body experiences, dreams and possessions and other experiences that transport the individual outside normal space and time.

Heiler believed that all religions can be understood within these various categories. He portrayed them as concentric circles because he believed that at the core of religion is the experience of the numinous, which is articulated in beliefs (the middle circle) and expressed in various symbolic forms (the outer circle). As one penetrates deeper towards the core of religion, the personal, experiential form becomes central. The scholar of religion can describe and classify the various ways a religion symbolizes the core inner experience and how it conceives the experience through beliefs, but religion fundamentally must be understood in some sense as an ineffable experience of the numinous or sacred reality.

McKenzie (1997: 3) accepts Heiler's structure of religion as applicable to 'the study and interpretation of Yoruba religion as disclosed in the archival materials from the mid-nineteenth century'. He finds the correlation between Heiler's categories and his own description of nineteenth-century Yoruba religion 'remarkable since there was no way of knowing in advance how the material would shape up' (McKenzie 1997: 3). In Yoruba religion, for example, numerous sacred objects can be identified, including rocks, hills and mountains, earth and water, lightning and storm, groves and trees, animals and birds. Sacred space can be divided between open and enclosed areas, which are comprised of various shrines with cult objects surrounding them. Sacred time can be observed in the new year and new yam festivals based on annual agricultural cycles. Sacred action consists of various rituals of sacrifice and purification, which in turn lead to a unification with the deity. Sacred persons can be found in numerous ritual settings and in the roles assigned to them within the community. These include family members assuming particular responsibilities in rituals, and religious specialists, such as healers, diviners and mediums. Each of these categories reveals to the scholar how the Yoruba think about the deities, the creation of the world, salvation, the last things and revelation.

In his analysis of religious experience among the Yoruba, McKenzie omitted Heiler's basic categories, hope and joy, he explains, 'not because hope and joy might be lacking, but because material on these has not been noted at the time' (McKenzie 1997: 541). He cites Yoruba examples of Heiler's 'supernormal forms of religious experience', including inspiration, dreams, visions, auditions, conversion, healing and incubation, although he admits these 'cover only in part Heiler's list' (McKenzie 1997: 546–55).

For McKenzie, such a study ultimately discloses the type of religious experience known to the Yoruba in beliefs that are expressed symbolically through rituals, stories and numerous observable practices. The similarity between the variety of religious expressions among the Yoruba and Heiler's morphology of religion convinces McKenzie (1997: 3) that 'the categories were not being imposed upon the archival materials, rather they are simply there, as a well-tried series of headings, under which the diverse materials may find their natural grouping'.

McKenzie's use of archival materials

McKenzie claims that by the 1890s Yoruba religion was being forced on the defensive because of the activities of Christian missions, particularly the work of the CMS, and the Wesleyan Missionary Society. During the period of his study, from 1840 to 1880, however, he claims that traditional Yoruba religion was still in a strong position. McKenzie chose 1840 as his starting point because this date roughly marks the beginning of the work of the CMS and the Methodists in Yorubaland and thus corresponds to the time when missionary records of Yoruba religion first began. It was also a period when independent Yoruba kingdoms still existed. He concluded his study at 1880 because the way the CMS arranged its incoming papers changed after that and because during the last twenty years of the nineteenth century the British and French colonial powers exercised increasing influence in the region (McKenzie 1997: 15).

McKenzie obtained most of his material from the CMS archives in Birmingham, but he also consulted the archives of the Methodist Missionary Society, now held at the School of Oriental and African Studies in London. He was particularly interested in the reports of missionary pastors and catechists, many of the latter being Yoruba converts to Christianity. Among the reports sent to Britain in this period, McKenzie discovered numerous references to the Yoruba *orisa* cults. He notes that 'almost on a daily basis there occurred encounters between missionary agents and *orisa* worshippers' (McKenzie 1997: 15). The most important of the letters, reports and journals were from those working for the CMS, 'not only because this mission was the largest one in the area, but also because the Society required its servants to send their journal extracts to London at regular intervals' (McKenzie 1997: 15).

In the appendix to his book, McKenzie explains that gathering the material was a lengthy process extending over many years. He began with the journals and letters of Africans, 'so as to hear the African voice first of all' (McKenzie 1997: 560). The letters and journals of the African catechists and pastors were faithfully sent to the CMS offices in London, where they were edited and frequently published in periodicals such as the *Church Missionary Intelligencer*. He describes in detail how he obtained the material from the archives.

> A typical day was spent by the present author in the CMS archives in Birmingham, earlier in London, where most of the relevant materials were ordered under authors' names from the O[riginal] papers of CA 2 (Yoruba Mission) with help obtained from William Ajayi's (1965) checklist of CMS missionaries in the Yoruba country. On the train back to Leicester, looking over the day's 'haul', one noted the various *orisa* and religious phenomena. (McKenzie 1997: 560)

McKenzie explains that he engaged in a lengthy process of sifting out material that was not directly related to the *orisa* cults. He then arranged the material chronologically and charted missionary encounters with worshippers of particular *orisa* according to 'city, town and village' across what, by studying maps of CMS mission stations, he divided into seven geographical regions (McKenzie 1997: 562). The most difficult and vital step in all of this followed, that of arranging the material according to what McKenzie (1997: 564) calls 'Heilerian phenomenology', which he adapted in categories and sub-categories as the material presented itself. In this way, he claims to have avoided the danger of 'offering a prefabricated set of categories' because 'there was no way of knowing in advance how the material would shape itself under which headings' (Mackenzie 1997: 564).

A sampling of McKenzie's material

It is clear from just a cursory review of McKenzie's material that he was attempting to describe Yoruba religion objectively, in a non-judgemental fashion, and, in so far as possible, empathetically and in terms of the believers themselves. An excellent example is found in his discussion of images and cult objects, which he notes are written about frequently in the reports of the pastors and catechists, primarily because such objects testify 'to the importance of the visual image for the *olorisha*' [*orisa* devotees] (Mackenzie 1997: 52). McKenzie (1997: 52) wants to know why amulets and images (referred to by the catechists as 'fetishes') 'shaped by human hand' seem so important for Yoruba religious practitioners. Citing the report of one African pastor, McKenzie (1997: 52) notes that for the Yoruba 'God is so far, far, far away'. McKenzie (1997: 15) concludes from this that images form vital parts of Yoruba religious life because they 'need a visible medium for the worship of the invisible God'. He adds: 'The in-dwelling of the divine in the image has to be remembered when considering the forms of devotion paid to it' (McKenzie 1997: 15).

Another, related, account falls under McKenzie's discussion of 'apotropaic' sacrifices, ritual activities undertaken to ward off evil. McKenzie notes that many pastors make references to *orisa* who guard and protect the people and hence are capable of helping them avoid calamities. The evils to be avoided, in McKenzie's (1997: 225) words, 'consisted of warlike enemies (and their dangerous charms), death as an enemy, serious illness leading to death (sent, it may be from an *orisa*), smallpox, fire and the anger of the Orisa, death by drowning, and evil in general'.

McKenzie (1997: 226) cites in detail a report by Samuel Pearse, an Egba catechist, who describes a mass gathering of people to drive death away. Pearse witnessed the event in 1859 at Porto Novo, where he estimates as many as 50,000 people gathered. While women 'invoked and praised the deities', the men were divided into groups of about twenty-five under the leadership of a 'priest' who was possessed by a deity. The priests used sticks and brooms to drive death away from every 'corner or tree'. They then ritually employed mud images, called '*sugudu*', made in the forms of humans and animals, to kill death. In Pearse's words, 'These *Sugudus* are made to sit on mats surrounded with various kinds of atoning sacrifice and after exposure from morning to evening as emblems of death, are wrapped, bound and packed up in two or more canoes, pulled into the middle of the river and then drowned' (McKenzie 1997: 226). McKenzie then proceeds to describe without comment various other rituals that are intended to avert various calamities, thus limiting his interpretative role largely to classifying the data, such as noting that blood is a 'sacred substance' (McKenzie 1997: 239) and that rituals of purification can be 'linked with the thought of asceticism' (McKenzie 1997: 241).

In his chapter entitled 'Sacred Action: Unification', McKenzie provides numerous descriptions of rituals of possession. A typical example is based on two reports written in 1850 describing the possession of a girl initiate dedicated to the deity Dada at Aradagun. McKenzie (1997: 291) summarizes the accounts of Van Cooten, a Dutch mission surgeon, and William Marsh, an Egba catechist, as follows:

1. A *procession of female olorisha* pass by, at their head a priestess ('an old one').
2. There follows 'immediately after … a *little girl dedicated to the god Dadda*'.
3. She has reached 'a certain age, when [the parents] are able to make *sacrifices* to this [*orisa*], … and the child is released from the [initial] *vow* made by its parents'.
4. The little girl has a *calabash* half full of cowries upon her head.
5. *Possession-State:* The initiate 'threw herself into various postures as if moved by a Spirit'.
6. She is under 'supernatural power and may well be capable of 'prophesying' (emphases in original).

McKenzie (1997: 291) draws the reader's attention in this account to the 'active rather than passive trance' of the girl under possession and to the fact that the 'initiate is regarded as being in a position of great spiritual power'. One further example, drawn from his section on religious experience, will show how inner states and feelings elucidate Yoruba symbols of the sacred. McKenzie analyses Yoruba religious experience according to Heiler's list of basic and supernormal forms. On the basic religious experience of trust, McKenzie (1997: 543) cites the report of the Egba pastor Thomas King, who, writing in 1850 about the cult of *Orisa-Oko,* noted: 'In perilous times of difficulty or imminent dangers by war, *Orishako* affords great protection, much respect and undue reverence to its professors.' The experience of fear is also widely reported by the catechists, often in response to the threat of illness. For example, T. B. Wright, an Egba catechist at Faji Lagos, reported speaking with a priest who confessed that he 'feared the wrath of the *orisa* if he were to forsake them' (McKenzie 1997: 542).

McKenzie (1997: 548–49) notes that many dreams and visions (supernormal experiences) reflect the religious conflict created by the missionaries, and that they often are associated with conversion. One example is that of Tifa, a skilled traditional drummer and a Christian convert. He was refused baptism by the missionary James White on the grounds that he had two wives. Subsequently, he became ill. Many of his relatives believed he was ill because he had offended the *orisa* by becoming a Christian, but, to White, Tifa confessed to seeing 'strange things', not in a dream but in reality, 'though no one sees them'. His vision consisted of a heavenly being who had bound him and was ready to take him away. However, he was not ready to be taken away and thus in the vision is set free. Despite having been given his freedom by the heavenly being, he says he still must go, 'for the Messenger is standing by me and is waiting for me'. Later, he is reported as having become quite delirious, but eventually after much prayer, recovered his health. Subsequently, according to the account, he 'gave up his *Ifa* – and also his drumming'. McKenzie (1997: 549) concludes that these clearly represent 'a series of conversion visions, partly traditional (in form) and partly Islamic-Christian (in content)'.

McKenzie's conclusions

After nearly 550 pages of descriptive material similar to the sampling shown above, McKenzie devotes just three pages to a conclusion. This is primarily because he was intent on using a phenomenological method through which, as he notes in the conclusion, 'the materials themselves have been allowed to shape and steer the various sections of the work' (McKenzie 1997: 556). The resulting product is a kind of phenomenological profile of Yoruba religion in the mid-nineteenth century, which, he claims, 'broadly fits a composite picture of the religions of mankind' (McKenzie 1997: 556).

His conclusions (McKenzie 1997: 556–9) thus are quite modest. They consist of the following points:

1. Symbols of nature (mountains, stones, rivers, animals) are much less important during the period under study than images and cult objects.

2. Yoruba religion 'holds its own in relation to other religious traditions' with regard to the importance given to sacred space and sacred time as demonstrated by the central feature of festivals and life cycle rituals.
3. Sacred action, including sacrifices, forms a central part of Yoruba religion.
4. Sacred word, in the form of oral traditions, also plays a pivotal role in the accounts of the pastors and catechists.
5. Sacred persons likewise have been shown to be critical for the religious life of the Yoruba. The category includes women, which, McKenzie notes, is rather surprising given the altitudes of male dominance in the society at the time of writing.
6. Material on the sacred community was less satisfactory, partly because the reports tended to emphasize individual as opposed to group responses.
7. Information on the conceptual world of the Yoruba appears to reveal more about the efforts of the pastors and catechists to provide alternatives to traditional beliefs than it does about Yoruba concepts of creation, salvation and eschatology. The exception to this relates to ideas of the deities, about which the material provides extensive reports.
8. The basic and supernormal forms of religious experience proved to be 'questionable' categories, because they seem foreign to the *orisa* cults and because it might have been better to have regarded dreams, visions and healing as 'basic' rather than 'supernormal'.
9. *Orisa* worship is shown to be profoundly tolerant of other traditions despite the rapid social changes affecting it during the mid-nineteenth century.
10. The Yoruba are shown during the period from 1840 to 1880 as being involved increasingly in a 'trialogue' between traditional religion, Christianity and Islam. The present work 'reinforces the claims of Orisa Worship to equal partnership both in Yorubaland and also more widely among the World Religions' (McKenzie 1997: 559).

An evaluation of McKenzie's project

As I noted at the outset of this chapter, McKenzie's ambitious undertaking provides an exemplary model for analysing the usefulness of classical phenomenological categories for filtering out prejudices in missionary journals, letters and reports and thereby revealing symbols, practices, beliefs and inner states as they existed at the time of Yoruba Religion's first encounters with missionaries. He also offers ample material against which we can assess the reliability and usefulness of the missionary records themselves. I want to examine this latter point regarding the reliability of McKenzie's sources briefly before evaluating in more detail his underlying methodological assumptions.

From the limited examples cited above, it will be clear that a good deal is left to the imagination of the reader in the accounts provided by missionary pastors and catechists. In Pearse's description of the mass gathering in which rituals were performed to ward off evil, for example, we have to guess what occurs in the 'atoning sacrifices' and picture what is meant by 'emblems of death'. In McKenzie's summary of two accounts of a possession ritual, we have the barest descriptive material and can merely conjure up what might have occurred. These accounts are typical of the material used by McKenzie and result, so it would seem, not from his unfamiliarity with the need for adequate descriptions, but from the limitations of the missionary reports themselves.

We must remember that the missionaries and catechists cited by McKenzie were writing primarily to missionary boards in England with the clear understanding that their accounts would be used in conveying to the church at large what missionaries were doing and how they were encountering religions in the field. This may explain why the sections on supernormal religious experiences seem more complete than the ritual descriptions. As McKenzie notes, dreams and visions frequently were connected to conversion, and thus would have been reported enthusiastically by those writing to the mission boards in Britain.

McKenzie readily admits that the missionary pastors and catechists were slanting their versions of Yoruba religion for consumption in England. He also acknowledges that missionary records and letters are highly unreliable for descriptive purposes without a method for minimizing the distorting effect of the authors' biases. This is precisely why he chose to sort the data he collected so painstakingly into Heilerian phenomenological categories. It is not possible, therefore, to discredit McKenzie's work on the basis alone of the incomplete, inaccurate and biased sources he consulted. Rather, his study must be regarded as having a wider application beyond CMS archival accounts of Yoruba religion in the mid-nineteenth century and be judged primarily as a project characteristic of scholars in the phenomenological tradition.

Heiler's morphology of religion, it should be emphasized, is not idiosyncratic, but corresponds quite closely to other classificatory schemes developed by phenomenologists during the first half of the twentieth century, such as those proposed by Gerardus van der Leeuw and C. J. Bleeker (Cox 1998c: 245–50). Heiler's emphasis on religious experience, moreover, reflects the thinking of Rudolf Otto, who clearly can be cited as influencing somewhat later scholars of religion in the phenomenological tradition, such as Mircea Eliade and Wilfred Cantwell Smith. Any flaws we discover in McKenzie's project thus are shared by other scholars in the phenomenological tradition, who claimed to have identified universal categories of religion based on neutral observations. It is this claim to universality, accompanied by the phenomenological 'bracketing out' of prior assumptions, that suggests the most fundamental conceptual error beneath McKenzie's work.

The analytical constructs McKenzie adapted from Heiler, like those conceived by other phenomenologists of the period, are neither universal nor neutral, but are derived almost entirely from a Western, Christian theological framework. The concept of 'the sacred', Heiler's 'numinous', ascribes to a transcendental referent in religion the status of ontological reality. The 'sacred' manifests itself, or appears, in revelatory acts, in a way fully consistent with Christian theological constructs of God's interventions in history. The symbols employed in Heiler's morphology, such as place, time, nature, people and community, fit neatly into Christian notions of sacred boundaries symbolized in church buildings, sacraments and congregations. Moreover, the beliefs into which Heiler organized his conceptual categories read like a Christian systematic theology: God, creation, revelation, salvation and the end times. By endorsing Heiler's structure of religion, despite his claims to phenomenological neutrality, McKenzie imposes on Yoruba religion a Christian configuration. This is why, in the end, he can quite easily compare Yoruba religion with monotheistic religious traditions.

As one reads more deeply into McKenzie's text, it becomes clear that his 're-presentation' of Yoruba religion on a Christian model was no accident or a simple oversight. At least one of McKenzie's underlying purposes in writing the book was to depict Yoruba religion sympathetically, as being on a par with Christianity and Islam. This is seen at the outset of his discussion of charms and amulets, which he assumes manifest 'the sacred' for believers (McKenzie 1997: 52). Moreover, the place of God in Yoruba religion seems a persistent concern throughout for McKenzie, resulting in his interpretation of images as concrete representations of deities, which themselves mediate between the people and an otiose God. In this way, McKenzie legitimates Yoruba religion as an equal partner in what he calls the trialogue with Christianity and Islam. His assertion that CMS missionary accounts show that mid-nineteenth-century Yoruba religious practices quite naturally and without premeditation fit into universal categories thus is contradicted by his own predetermined Christian interpretation of Yoruba religion. By assigning Heiler's phenomenological typologies a universal and timeless status, McKenzie ensures that religions in the Jewish-Christian-Islamic traditions will define the categories through which, not only Yoruba religion, but all religions are analysed.

Despite holding to what can be identified clearly as prior ideological convictions, McKenzie maintains throughout that he has allowed the phenomena to speak for themselves. He does so while at the same time affirming the value to contemporary thinking of postmodern and feminist critiques of overarching explanations of reality (McKenzie 1997: 7–11). Nevertheless, he seems not to have grasped the significance of such critiques for his own methodology. After discussing postmodern 'deconstructionism' and feminist readings of religious data, he then affirms, 'the phenomena are their own meaning' (McKenzie 1997: 10), seemingly missing or dismissing the central role of the interpreter in the construction of meaning, and most importantly, failing to acknowledge the Christian intentions hidden beneath Heiler's phenomenological categories.

One last, but critical, point regarding McKenzie's assumptions about religion must be made. In a single paragraph, he addresses and then jettisons the debates that have dominated religious studies over the past twenty to thirty years. This debate centres on the critical issue as to whether a scholar is able to isolate strictly religious from other types of data, such as those which emerge from political, economic, social, psychological and geographic contexts, among others. McKenzie affirms Heiler's phenomenology partly because it maintains that the 'religious' falls within a classification of its own (sui generis), and that this is further justified because such a view 'accords with the view of many Africans' (McKenzie 1997: 2) (emphasis in original).

In a recent review of McKenzie's book, J. D. Y. Peel (2000: 401–3) argues that, quite apart from debates among scholars about the essence of religion, it is certainly clear that McKenzie's assertion that religion held a unique place within Yoruba society at the time of missionary contact does not accord with the view of many Africans. This is because the Yoruba had no concept of religion before they acquired it from the world religions. Where their 'religion' ended, and their politics or economics began, is an unintelligible question from a pre-modern Yoruba point of view (Peel 2000: 402). McKenzie's argument is shown by Peel to rest on the tenuous assumption that religion as a conceptual category among the Yoruba pre-dated the CMS accounts and thus can be studied by later scholars using phenomenological methods. If, however, the Yoruba had no concept of religion (in the Western academic understanding of the term), all such systematic analyses are disclosed as having been imposed from without and, therefore, as contradicting McKenzie's principle that the phenomena must be allowed to speak for themselves.

Conclusions

Peter McKenzie's *Hail Orisha!* sheds light on the central question and its sub-questions with which I began this chapter. The phenomenology of religion, as a method, clearly does not provide the scholar with the interpretative tools required to 're-present' any religion as it once appeared in history. This is because the phenomenologist starts with ideological constructs which are themselves interpretations of the data. Moreover, the sources used by the phenomenologist are also interpretations. The idea that the scholar can suspend judgements and objectively represent religions by directly observing religious behaviour has largely been challenged today as lacking academic credibility (see, for example, Flood 1999; Smith 1999; Chidester 1996). That a scholar could do so using incomplete records written in an entirely different context, in a time period and culture far removed from the present, and quite clearly for ideological purposes makes the proposal quite unfeasible. The answers to the sub-questions I posed further underscore this conclusion, Missionary accounts, of course, are distorted and biased, but, in some ways, all accounts suffer from the same problem. In the case of the missionary records, what they do not do is to provide descriptions of religious behaviour in the way a social scientist would require. For this reason, although they may help to clarify certain historical developments or offer insight on the missionary encounter with other religions, they do not provide something other than what they were intended to supply: reports to missionary headquarters about the progress of the Christian work in a region. To transform them into documents of social scientific research is untenable.

With regard to the second sub-question, it is clear that the phenomenology of religion cannot provide a method for filtering out biases in the missionary records. The phenomenologist may try to examine the documentation neutrally and eliminate distorting language, but the process of interpretation goes much deeper than that. The phenomenologist cannot 'invent' the descriptive detail that is missing, re-word the questions relevant for understanding the practices of the people at the time or re-order the criteria defining what is important and what is not in the source material. The central hermeneutical role of the original source and the context for its writing can be understood and analysed by the scholar, but the scholar cannot infer what the original sources did not investigate.

Finally, phenomenological typologies, understood as essential characteristics of religion, fail to acknowledge the historical, social and cultural contexts out of which they developed. Typologies only make sense as pragmatic, limited terms to help facilitate communication and promote understanding. If they are regarded as universal categories, the scholar who uses them will inevitably fit the data to suit the categories. For this reason, it is important for scholars to adopt self-reflexive approaches whereby they position themselves historically and ideologically as they engage in their investigations. If this is done, the categories selected are understood as reflecting the scholar's context and are regarded as bound by particular and declared academic interests. In the case of Heiler, and many of the classical phenomenologists working during the first two-thirds of the twentieth century, the categories through which they analysed data seemed self-evident and were promoted as universal without acknowledging their roots in Western academic and theological traditions.

As noted at the beginning of this chapter, it would be extremely useful if missionary records, accompanied by phenomenological methods, would allow us to reconstruct African Indigenous Religions as they existed at the time of first extensive contact with missionaries. A series of important answers to numerous questions of interest to scholars from many disciplines would thereby be provided. Unfortunately, for the reasons I have just cited, *Hail Orisha!* reveals not only the futility of seeking to represent Yoruba religion phenomenologically as it existed in the mid-nineteenth century, but it confirms the fruitlessness of any similar enterprise. The positive results of this disappointing conclusion force us towards self-reflexive research with due attention maintained always to contextual study.

Part II

THE PHENOMENOLOGICAL SUBJECT AND
OBJECT OF STUDY

Chapter 4

RELIGIOUS TYPOLOGIES AND
THE POSTMODERN CRITIQUE

The Penguin Dictionary of Religions, edited by John Hinnells, defines typology in the academic study of religions as 'the method of analysis and classification according to type' (1984: 338). A religious typology refers to observable phenomena which a researcher contends share enough common characteristics to be classified within one category, despite the fact that data which are placed together originate from diverse cultures, communities and geographical regions. Examples include sacrifice, purification, prayer, myth, ritual and their various sub-classifications or more general typologies, such as the distinction between universal and local religions or between prophetic and mystical religious experiences.

Late in his academic career, F. Max Müller, whom Van Baal (1971: 26) calls 'one of the most outstanding promoters of religious and ethnographical studies of the nineteenth century', argued that abstract theories should always be rooted firmly in history: 'All that I maintain is that it is better to test the truth of … general principles by history, and not by theory only' (Müller 1898: 4). Although through his extensive translations and comparisons of religious texts Müller assumed that religions can be classified according to the stage of their moral and theological development, he maintained throughout that historical facts determine the value of any theory. 'The true science of religion', he explained, 'is the history of religion' (Müller 1898: 4).

The problem of creating religious typologies, which this chapter addresses and to which Müller indirectly referred, has plagued the academic study of religion since its entry into the modern era during the nineteenth century. The problem centres on the capacity of scholars to create broad generalizations for the purpose of making informed comparisons while still maintaining an accurate account of specific data on which the generalizations are based. In the postmodern debate, serious doubt has been cast on the ability of researchers to do just that. The creation of religious and moral universals can be regarded as the invention of what Zygmunt Bauman (1993: 42) calls 'make believe' points of agreement (1993: 42). Nevertheless, the history of the discipline called the 'science of religion' has maintained persistently that universal forms, structures and essences can be identified which aid in the scholarly understanding of human religious experience.

In this chapter, I ask if religious typologies form part of a grand interpretative scheme constructed by academics rather artificially for the purpose of fashioning cross-cultural comparisons. If so, it raises the further question: 'Can we sustain an empirical approach within religious studies while still speaking in meaningful categories about the religious data scholars uncover?' I will approach these questions first by describing briefly how three scholars of religion, operating at different times during the twentieth century, have insisted on creating ideal types for the purposes of understanding religious phenomena. I then will turn to the critique which comes from postmodernist circles before offering my own observations as to how this critical issue for the comparative study of religions can be addressed.

The need for religious typologies: Van der Leeuw, Bleeker and Smart

Among those who were instrumental in developing an academic approach to the study of religion during the first half of the twentieth century was the Dutch phenomenologist Gerardus van der Leeuw, who, in his classic book *Religion in Essence and Manifestation,* called the creation of typologies 'absolutely imperative' for a science of religion (1938: 593). By a typology, he meant an 'ideal type', 'form' or 'structure' (Van der Leeuw 1938: 672–3) resulting from the scholarly application of two interrelated methods. The first approach involves the researcher moving from specific observations to general conclusions by apprehending 'the specifically historical, to the highest attainable degree, under quite general points of view' (Van der Leeuw 1938: 593). The other method stresses the need for all generalizations to be tested in the light of what is 'historically given' (Van der Leeuw 1938: 593). For example, scholars of religion may identify a broad typology called religions of compassion, but they must be careful at the same time to relate the ideal type to Buddhism 'as the historically living form of this religion' (Van der Leeuw 1938: 593).

Despite his emphasis on the 'historically given', it is important to note from the outset that Van der Leeuw did not begin *Religion in Essence and Manifestation* with a methodological discussion of either how generalizations can be derived from specific observations or how they must be confirmed within concrete situations. Rather, he left such a discussion to the concluding sections of his book. The first part focuses on the 'object' of religion with which the subject or adherent of religion interacts. Van der Leeuw (1938: 23) simply asserts from the first page of his text that the 'object' is firmly associated with concepts of power: 'Man remains quite content with the purely practical recognition that this Object is a departure from all that is usual and familiar; and this again is the consequence of the *Power* it generates' (emphasis in original).

This assertion is not substantiated initially by any detailed empirical studies, but it is intuited in advance based on the scholar's own sense of the religious. This represents Van der Leeuw's movement from the general to the specific, a movement which culminates for him at the end of the study once more in the general. The preliminary intuition emphasizes, to use phenomenological terminology, the intentionality of the subject in the apprehension of the object of research. The interplay between subjective consciousness and the objective world produces the interpretations researchers offer about the meaning of their observations. For Van der Leeuw, there is a clear process at work; it involves a movement from initial conceptions through specific observations to the concluding interpretations of meaning. The eidetic vision, in the fullest sense of the term as a seeing into the meaning of religion, occurs only at the end of the process, but this can never be achieved without some preliminary, intuitive sense of what constitutes the nature of religion.

Van der Leeuw defined the operation of creating ideal types as beginning with the appearances or manifestations of religious phenomena. To these appearances, the phenomenologist assigns names such as 'sacrifice, prayer, savior, myth' (Van der Leeuw 1938: 688). The next stage is to interpolate these into the phenomenologist's own experience to encourage sympathetic understanding. This allows the researcher at the third stage to step aside from any personal biases to observe the phenomena just as they appear. The next step leads to comprehension of what has appeared through a process of clarification. Finally, the phenomenologist interprets meanings within what has been observed and ultimately testifies to what has been understood. This process is fully scientific because in the end 'science is hermeneutics' (Van der Leeuw 1938: 676).

These stages do not necessarily follow on one from another sequentially; frequently, they transpire simultaneously. Moreover, the appearance of a religious phenomenon always occurs in relation to other appearances, but it is a relation which is perceived by the observer who forms, from empirical research, what Van der Leeuw (1938: 673) calls 'structural connections'. Such connections do not exist in themselves factually or causally. They are perceived connections and thus are formed by the phenomenologist into an ideal type. Van der Leeuw (1938: 673) explains:

> 'Type' in itself ... has no reality; nor is it a photograph of reality. Like structure, it is timeless and need not actually occur in history. But it possesses life, its own significance, its own law.

Maintaining the close connection between the general and the specific defined, for Van der Leeuw, the central challenge for creating religious typologies. He endeavoured to secure this connection by linking phenomenology to the history of religions. History cannot proceed without interpreting data, a task Van der Leeuw assigned to the phenomenologist of religion. The phenomenologist, however, cannot interpret apart from collecting and organizing historical data. Because interpretation and data collection are so intimately intertwined, they are undertaken frequently by the same researcher. Their differing functions, nonetheless, must be noted. Van der Leeuw (1938: 672) described the resulting process as 'the sketching of an outline within the chaotic maze of so-called "reality"'.

Another Dutch phenomenologist, C. J. Bleeker, who during the 1960s was Professor of the History of Religions in the University of Amsterdam, and for twenty years served as Secretary-General of the International Association for the History of Religions, sought to clarify the meaning and application of ideal types. In his book, *The Sacred Bridge,* which largely considers methodological issues in the study of religion, Bleeker (1963: 40) argued that detecting the structure of religion would be aided by identifying 'a key word of religion, by which the heart of religion would be touched, so to say in one shot'. Bleeker's keyword is intuited: 'The student of the history of religions and the phenomenology of religion starts his study with an intuitive, hardly formulated, axiomatic notion of what religion is' (Bleeker 1963: 36). Empirical studies follow the intuition by producing 'an inclusive formulation of the essence of religion', which, when constructed, comprises 'the crowning of the whole work' (Bleeker 1963: 36). The keyword provides the connection between the initial intuition and the completion of empirical studies through the identification of the fundamental structure of religion.

After rejecting a number of possibilities for the keyword, such as power (Van der Leeuw) because it is too vague, 'personal god' (Geo Widengren) because it is too limited, and 'the holy' because it is too individualistic, Bleeker (1963: 46) offered his own suggestion for the keyword of religion: 'the divine'. The selection of 'the divine' as the keyword of religion assigns historians and phenomenologists of religion the task of enquiring 'into the original significance of the terms by which the deity is indicated in the different religions' (Bleeker 1963: 46). It should be noted that Bleeker's method is to agree on the defining characteristic of religion prior to undertaking the empirical study. After first intuiting 'the divine' as the keyword of religion, the scholar then can study how the concept has been understood and practised in various religions.

Bleeker admitted that to produce conclusive results his method would have to involve a vast empirical study, one that is beyond the range of any one scholar. It would be impossible for a researcher to catalogue all the ways the divine has been understood throughout the history of religions. An alternative would be to study a limited number of the notions of God in various religions which could then serve as a paradigm for all religions. The conclusions of such a limited study would be open to debate and modification, but this process 'would at any rate shed new light on the question of the key word of religion' (Bleeker 1963: 46).

Bleeker exemplified how this process occurs in Egyptian, Semitic, Indian, Iranian and Roman contexts, where the divine has been conceived variously as (1) a numinous force; (2) a cult-place deity; (3) a being invoked by offerings; (4) a sovereign being controlling the affairs of human history; (5) a sky god; (6) one who distributes or withholds the necessities of human survival and well-being; (7) a wise and active being who represents truth and order (Bleeker 1963: 50). Bleeker's keyword, which began as an investigation into the meaning of a single unifying concept for religion, thus disperses into a plurality of meanings. The implications of this exercise are not lost to Bleeker (1963: 50): 'There is not one single key word of religion, but ... there are many of this kind'. This might even lead to the more radical conclusion, one which Bleeker rejected, that 'it is an illusion to think that all phenomena, which are generally called religious, can be covered by the same term "religion"' (Bleeker 1963: 50–1). Bleeker did not arrive at this conclusion because he remained convinced to the end of his academic career that in a formal sense 'religion always has been and still is man's relation to a superhuman power' (Bleeker 1963: 51). In a 1975 publication, he reiterated this point: 'Religion is a universal human phenomenon. Everywhere in the world and at all times since the evolution of *homo sapiens*, people both collectively and individually have worshiped superhuman force' (Bleeker 1975: 7). For Bleeker, an analysis of keywords exposes the complexities and dynamic character of religious phenomena and for that reason remains a useful method for identifying structural connections within religions.

A third scholar of religion who has employed a form of the ideal types of religion is Ninian Smart. During his distinguished academic career, Smart wrote numerous books on the world's religions and on methodologies in the study of religions. One of his later books, *Dimensions of the Sacred: An Anatomy of the World's Beliefs* (1996), as the title implies, clearly outlines his understanding of how religious beliefs and experiences can be classified according to shared characteristics. Smart (1996: 7) argued for a 'dynamic phenomenology' distinct from the 'synchronic and static' forms of earlier phenomenology (presumably the philosophical essences sought by Van der Leeuw). A dynamic phenomenology is also a 'dialectic phenomenology' that exposes the relationship 'between different dimensions of religion and world-views' (1996: 7). By dimensions, Smart was referring to seven components of human religious behaviour. He preferred to give each a 'double name, which helps to elucidate them' (Smart 1996: 8). The dimensions are the ritual or practical, the doctrinal or philosophical, the mythic or narrative, the experiential or emotional, the ethical or legal, the organizational or social, the material or artistic (Smart 1996: 9–11). In effect, Smart's dimensions are typologies for understanding how common religious characteristics interrelate within a variety of settings.

Smart assigned two purposes for his schematic presentation of religions. The first intends to provide a balanced picture of religious experience, which overcomes the tendency in the West to emphasize the doctrinal or philosophical dimension of religion. A second purpose is to avoid defining religion as if it possessed a single content. For this reason, Smart did not define religion in terms of a divine–human interaction, as Bleeker did, but preferred to study how religion functions within the dimensions identified.

A brief look at his description of the ritual or practical dimension will demonstrate how he employed religious typologies. In *Dimensions of the Sacred*, Smart (1996: 73) defines ritual as 'an act involving performative uses of language (for example, in blessing praising, cursing, consecrating, purifying) and a formal pattern of behaviour either closely or more loosely followed'. He adds that religious ritual, as opposed to other ritual acts, focuses on such things as deities or ancestors or on meditation to achieve an elevated plane of consciousness. Religious rituals, moreover, are characterized by the operations of internalization and superimposition. Internalization refers to the interior meaning for the believer who participates in an outward ritual act. All communal rituals have external requirements in order that they can be performed accurately and practised uniformly by adherents. Nevertheless, a component of ritual involves transferring that which is exterior in practice into the interior spiritual life of the believer. Superimposition refers to the way rituals acquire significance by use and over time. Examples include the study of the Torah, which develops into a ritual fulfilling the Law, or practising yoga as a form of sacrifice (Smart 1996: 72–6).

Smart acknowledges that his dimensions of religion are untidy because the data which comprise them are all connected and interrelated. Moreover, each emerges from a specific context which may render the comparisons at times superfluous. Nonetheless, he contends that the dimensions provide a useful way of demonstrating the complexities of religious phenomena while still speaking of them in meaningful categories. To think otherwise is self-defeating because it leads to the conclusion that 'there is no vocabulary which can properly describe the offerings of different cultures' (Smart 1996: 6). He claims that his book demonstrates that this is not the case since 'the theoretical and descriptive similarities' he has identified 'stand up to the necessary contextualities' (Smart 1996: 7).

In Van der Leeuw, Bleeker and Smart, we find three scholars of religion who spanned most of the twentieth century and who, each in his own way, decisively influenced methodological approaches within religious studies. Each acknowledged the need for understanding the context in which religious phenomena occur, largely historically in the cases of Van der Leeuw and Bleeker, and broadly in cultural dimensions for Smart, and each insisted that the academic study of religion depends on the creation of typologies under which the vast diversity of human religious practices, beliefs and activities can be made intelligible.

The postmodern critique of universals

In his book on ethics in a postmodern age, to which I referred earlier, Zygmunt Bauman summarizes the general postmodern critique of modernity. He claims that modernity lived in a 'veil of illusions' and 'had the uncanny capacity for thwarting self-examination' (Bauman 1993: 3). One of the principal illusions of modernity was its search for universals to which a wide variety of complex human activities could be reduced and by which they could be explained. In contrast to the modernist effort to encapsulate human experience within all-encompassing principles, postmodernism, in the words of Huston Smith (1992: 232), is 'blurred and amorphous ... Not only does it lack an embracing outlook; it doubts that it is any longer possible (or desirable) to have one'. In Smith's view (1992: 232), it is the postmodern rejection of universals which 'signals the new chapter in intellectual history'.

According to Thomas Docherty (1993: 9), the modernist principles of unification, against which postmodernists have so strongly objected, are exemplified in structuralist schools which have sought to decode symbols by deciphering their inner, but hidden forms, 'such as myth in anthropology, desire in psychoanalysis, or grammar in literature'. Related to this is semiotics, a discipline which searches for equivalence between apparently different signs. The process of translation of one language to another could not proceed without such assumed equivalencies. Hence, structuralism and semiotics converged, in the words of Christopher Norris (1995: 85), under the principle 'that cultural forms, belief systems and discourses of every kind can best be understood by analogy with language, or with the properties manifest in language when treated from a strictly synchronic standpoint that seeks to analyse its immanent structures of sound and sense'.

Both structuralism and semiotics, according to Docherty, proceed on the basis of abstraction. By reducing particularities to abstracted generalizations, dissimilarities disappear. Docherty (1993: 9) explains: 'Abstraction must wilfully disregard the specificity of the material objects under its consideration.' This results in negating historical facts, as exemplified in the great metanarratives of Marx, Darwin and Freud. These grand schemes for explaining society, life or the psyche construct total systems aimed at fitting each piece of specific data into them. Docherty (1993: 11) asserts that 'in order to accommodate widely diverging local histories and traditions, they abstract the meaning of those traditions in a "translation" into the terms of a master code, a translation which leaves the specific traditions simply unrecognizable'.

The process of abstraction closely relates to what Docherty condemns as 'historicism', which ignores the historical causal relations emanating from the moment it wishes to investigate and brackets out or suspends judgements concerning the historical event itself. This implies an empathy for the event that excludes critical examination resulting in an interpretation of history which is highly favourable to the powerful elite. According to Docherty (1993: 11):

> Historicism benefits and is complicit with the ruling class at the moment of the historian's own writing. The victors in history thus proceed in triumphant procession, bearing with them the spoils of their victory, including those documents which record, legitimize and corroborate the necessity of their victory.

The postmodern view refuses to write history as if it were flowing in a single strand from one overriding world perspective or metanarrative. There are multiple histories depending on the perspective of the historian and on the historian's involvement with events. It is proper, Docherty (1993: 18) explains, to speak of history as 'a network of forces which all proceed in their own directions, heterogeneously'. For example, modernism created the historical and economic categories we still refer to as 'First World' and 'Third World', as if vast regions of the planet with its cultural diversities could be comprehensively understood and explained within a rubric familiar to the dominant perspective of one region and culture. Postmodernism would rather think, again according to Docherty (1993: 18), 'that the world is simply lived at different speeds, in different times, in different places ... at different rhythms, none of which need ever converge into harmony'.

Postmodern analyses have profound effects on epistemology. Knowledge does not proceed in a progression towards the gradual uncovering of a single reality. What we know is limited by our own restricted cultural communities. For postmodernism, this signals the end of metanarratives, defined as overarching explanations of meaning within any field of enquiry, including history, the social and physical sciences and religion. As Stanley Grenz (1996: 45–6) suggests, we are left only with local narratives: 'Each of us experiences a world within the context of the societies in which we live.' Scientific rationality, which is founded on the modernist method of discovering what is real by applying universal and consistent laws, gives way to multiple perspectives on and various horizons within experience.

The postmodern attack on universals outlined above can be summarized under the following three related points:

1. Unified knowledge about human societies and cultures is not achievable;
2. Grand interpretative theories of histories, cultures or societies are empirically unverifiable;
3. Any attempt to produce a comprehensive conceptual picture of cultures and societies is indefensible academically.

Such conclusions appear to discredit the search within religious studies, as demonstrated by Van der Leeuw, Bleeker and Smart, for ideal types, keywords or dimensions within human religious experience. If the postmodern critique applies to the creation of religious typologies, we would be forced to conclude that no essential characteristics or common categories of religion exist under which historically unrelated, culturally diverse and socially disparate religious practices can be classified, compared and understood.

A phenomenological response to the postmodern critique

One way to respond to the apparent postmodern critique of religious typologies is to attack the concept of postmodernism itself as an extension of modernist tendencies. This has been done, for example, in an article by Phillip Mellor and Chris Shilling (1994: 27), who suggest 'that what is mistaken for postmodernity is in reality a series of circumstances and experiences which are the direct product of certain features of modernity'. Mellor and Shilling (1994: 28) prefer the term 'reflexive modernity' which, as a product of the thought of the Enlightenment, 'eventually leads to the deconstruction of that thought' because 'modernity cannot limit the reflexivity it has unleashed'. They conclude:

> Postmodernism expresses contemporary disorientations about the nature of reality, identity and meaning, but cannot offer a satisfactory explanation for how those disorientations arose. These can be understood as the outcomes of the breadth and depth of reflexivity in contemporary societies. (Mellor and Shilling 1994: 29)

Although I think Mellor and Shilling offer a helpful analysis of the roots of the postmodern discussion and an alternative approach to interpreting it, I do not want to follow them by attempting to discredit the postmodern critique itself. What they are saying, at any rate, does not sound very different from that voiced by the French philosopher, Jean-François Lyotard, whom they clearly place within the postmodern camp, but who himself acknowledged the ambiguity of the term: 'A work can become modern only if it is first postmodern. Postmodernism thus understood is not modernism at its end but in the nascent state, and this state is constant' (Lyotard 1993: 44).

Rather than disputing the terminology used to define the contemporary distrust of universals, I propose rather to explore a methodology consistent with the postmodernist critique that can lead to new ways for understanding the way religion can be studied. In order to argue my case from within a broadly phenomenological position, I want to analyse an early contribution on phenomenology by Lyotard. His small book, entitled *Phenomenology*, was first published in 1954, although the English translation did not appear until 1991. This could lead to the conclusion that Lyotard's *Phenomenology* represents an early phase in his thinking and cannot be used as an example of a postmodern analysis. This seems to be the position adopted by Geoffrey Bennington who argues that Lyotard's *Phenomenology* 'is criticized and displaced' by his later work, *Discours, Figure* (1971) (cited by Ormiston 1991: 20).

There are two reasons to reject Bennington's dismissive attitude towards *Phenomenology*. The first is that Lyotard's early work went through ten revisions under the supervision of the author, with the latest revision occurring in 1986. (It is this edition from which the English translation is derived.) We can infer from this that Lyotard himself regarded his discussion of phenomenology as having continued relevance to his ongoing contribution to postmodern analyses.

A second, more substantial, reason for taking *Phenomenology* seriously relates to the content of the book itself. As I will try to demonstrate, Lyotard's attack against radical empiricism, what I would call a scientific metanarrative, is fully consistent with the postmodern rejection of all-encompassing explanations of reality. His treatment of Husserl's phenomenological reduction (*epoché*) and the preliminary intuition (the eidetic vision) are also consistent with postmodern holistic pluralism. I am not suggesting that *Phenomenology* represents Lyotard's mature thought, but as Gayle Ormiston (1991: 20) notes in his comments on the English edition, in it 'there are several elaborate discussions of certain phenomenological themes as they appear in some of Lyotard's later writings, especially with respect to Lyotard's examinations of Marxism, psychoanalysis, and semiotics'.

In *Phenomenology*, Lyotard (1991: 37) criticizes what he calls 'psychologism' for identifying 'the subject of knowledge with the psychological subject'. Psychologism insists that the entities that the subject observes are not independent from the one who does the observing. For example, as I write this, I am sitting in my office observing my green wall. I say, 'My wall is green.' Does this mean that the wall is green because I perceive it to be or does it possess characteristics independent of my perceiving it, such as extension in space and alteration over time? This restates the philosophical question regarding the real existence of objects in the world apart from a subject perceiving them. Lyotard argues that psychologism would answer my question by saying, 'The green wall I observe possesses no independent reality apart from my perceiving it.'

This version of Berkeley's radical empiricism ('to be is to be perceived') transforms knowledge into a pragmatic activity; the real world is determined by the success of the subject's observations. The empiricist tests theories endlessly, posing one hypothesis after another. Verification depends on the proper operation of the methods for testing. Such an approach excludes perceiving meaning within the data, because knowledge is reduced to a series of trial and error experiments. This does not give knowledge of the world as such, but it establishes constant relations among symbols, such as power and energy in physics. We are not permitted to ask questions that science cannot answer, leading Lyotard (1991: 38) to conclude, 'All these theses converge in scepticism.' Following Husserl, Lyotard argues that radical empiricism is based on a devastating contradiction. It assumes that experience provides the source for knowledge, an assumption, which to be accepted on empirical grounds, would need to be verified within experience. Experience, however, relies on what is relative and particular and thus can never verify a universal principle. Therefore, the fundamental assumption on which empiricism is based cannot be verified according to its own methods.

This leads Lyotard to postulate a science of essences, which forces us to consider the appearances of the 'things themselves'. He gives an example of the colour yellow. Can the colour be imagined apart from its being attached to something? Could we conceive of an unextended yellow? Lyotard regards this as impossible, since when we visualize the colour yellow, we always see it as it presents itself, such as a yellow automobile or a yellow flower. We never see 'yellow' in the abstract (Lyotard 1991: 39).

For Lyotard, the essence of objects is determined by 'the consciousness of impossibility'. When we conceive of anything, we conclude, 'I can or I cannot' (Lyotard 1991: 39). I cannot envisage unextended yellow. The essence or the *eidos* of the object is thereby resolved as 'that which is constituted by the invariant that remains identical throughout the variations' (Lyotard 1991: 39). In other words, the essence is always experienced in concrete, actual situations and is derived from the 'things themselves'. Essence should not be confused with a metaphysical concept, such as a Platonic Idea, but 'is revealed to me in an *ordinary givenness*' (Lyotard 1991: 39) (emphasis in original).

Empiricism, which appears on the surface to reject metaphysics, actually offers an all-encompassing explanation of reality. By limiting knowledge to that which can be apprehended within experience, empiricists unwittingly remain metaphysical, referred to by Lyotard (1991: 40) as 'a pragmatist-empiricist prejudice' on what we are able to know. Phenomenological analysis demonstrates that knowledge of perceptual data (the 'things themselves') cannot be limited to direct perception, but instead requires a 'seeing into' or a prior intuition, defined by Lyotard (1991: 40) as 'primordial dator consciousness'. Prior to any experimental study, the essence of any physical or human science must be intuited. This is the eidetic science of phenomenology, which stands as a prolegomenon to the empirical sciences. Lyotard (1991: 41–2) explains:

It is already clear, for example, that no serious empirical psychology can be undertaken if the essence of the psychological has not been grasped in a manner avoiding all confusion with the essence of the physical .... Likewise, all natural objects have spatial being as their essence and geometry is the eidetics of space.

This same process applies to all disciplines of scientific enquiry since 'to each empirical science there corresponds an eidetic science' (Lyotard 1991: 42). That this conclusion coincides with Husserl's interpretation of phenomenology is confirmed by Marian Hobson (1987: 110), who argued that the entire aim of Husserl's philosophy was 'to get beyond mere facts of experience and of worldly presence ... to "eidetic structures", that is, forms of experience which are prior to facticity'.

Lyotard applied phenomenological principles to three principal disciplines within the human sciences – psychology, sociology and history – each of which by extension can be related to religious studies. He contended that phenomenology acts as an introduction to the human sciences by defining 'the object eidetically prior to all experimentation' (Lyotard 1991: 76). It also aids analysis since it tries to draw out fundamental meaning from all forms of experimentation. The phenomenological contribution within the human sciences can be summarized as identifying 'the essence *in* the concrete itself' (Lyotard 1991: 76). A review of how Lyotard related this interpretation of phenomenology to sociology will be instructive for the problems I have raised concerning religious typologies.

Lyotard's phenomenology of sociology

Lyotard (1991: 95) begins his phenomenology of sociology by claiming that the aim of any form of experimental science is 'to establish constant relations between phenomena'. When the relations occur repeatedly under similar conditions, scientists conclude that the connection between the relations is verified. Simply to affirm such connections does not complete the scientific act; it must culminate in explanation. Science is not concerned just to know *how* certain operations occur but *why* they occur. From observation of facts, the scientist confirms relationships between phenomena and then suggests why such relationships occur. According to Lyotard (1991: 96), the resulting explanation is then 'universalized into an absolute constant'.

When the experimental method is applied to human behaviour, such as occurs in sociology, the result is to 'treat social facts *as* objects' (Lyotard 1991: 96). This enables the sociologist to treat social institutions as if they operate just like objects do in physics, which in turn enables the social scientist to determine universal laws applicable to all societies. Lyotard opposed this method by appealing to Husserl, who, according to Lyotard, exposed the flaws in the inductive approach of the empirical sciences by showing that 'the hypothesis of constancy the empiricist claims to *find* through his observations is *constructed* by the mind' (Lyotard 1991: 97). Sometimes the constant relationship is based on just one such occurrence, but it is the clarity of the occurrence which convinces the researcher that it is constant.

This, Lyotard (1991: 97) concludes, demonstrates that induction and statistics, so central to sociology, involve 'a creative act of the mind'.

Lyotard cites Durkheim as an example of this process in sociology. In his *Elementary Forms of Religious Life*, Durkheim argued that the sacred, defined as that which is set apart from the profane, has its origin in totemism, which, in Lyotard's words (1991: 74), 'is a sublimation of the social'. In his Introduction to the *Oxford Dictionary of World Religions*, John Bowker (1997: xvi) appears to agree with Lyotard when he suggests that Durkheim 'regarded religion as being the social in symbolic form'. Already, in Durkheim, we can see that prior notions are assumed: the nature of the social institution and the character of the sacred. These assumed essences, according to Lyotard (1991: 98), 'constantly correct observation, lest the observational results be blind' (1991: 98).

The scientist thus begins by seeing into the essences of things before beginning research. One must have an idea of what is being studied and how it is defined before commencing the enquiry. Only then can the observational work begin, not blindly as objectivists would have us believe, but by grasping through intuition what the essential character of our study entails. The researcher then moves to the 'things themselves', not simply to describe connections and correlations, but to discern within descriptions, in Lyotard's words (1991: 98), 'an interpretation of their *meaning*', which 'is the only true objectivity'.

In many statements of scientific methodologies, the assumption of meaning is omitted. To include meaning in one's methodology, so it is asserted, would imply from the outset that the researcher is seeking to discover something beyond what can be immediately investigated using empirical instruments. As we have seen, on the contrary, Lyotard argued convincingly for inserting meaning into a research methodology. Even if researchers fail to understand the basic structures of societies that may be culturally alien to them or historically distant from them, the assumption of meaning implies a purpose in the research. Lyotard contended that admitting that the researcher seeks meaning in the phenomena destroys the objectivist contention that only by detachment can the scientist gain an understanding of what is being observed. When meaning is inserted into the methodology, immediately the central role of the researcher becomes apparent. 'In other words', Lyotard claims, 'we must first do a sociology or psychology of the observer in order to understand his understanding' (Lyotard 1991: 99). This does not imply that we must rely on simplistic or spontaneous interpretations of data as if the investigator comprises the primary component in research. A middle ground must be identified between such naivete and what Lyotard (1991: 99) calls 'brutal objectivism', a mediating position that can only be found in the interpretation of meaning or, as Lyotard expresses it, in 'a *recovery* of explanatory data which seeks to express the unity of their latent meaning' (Lyotard 1991: 99) (emphasis in original).

Lyotard's phenomenology of sociology asserts the necessity of developing sociology into an eidetic science: 'Only an adequate eidetic definition of the social permits a fruitful experimental approach' (Lyotard 1991: 100). Although this sounds as if researchers must reach conclusions prior to conducting their investigations so that their findings will confirm their prior intuition of what constitutes the social, Lyotard (1991: 100) explains that 'in reality this indispensable eidetic must construct itself in the course of an exploration of the facts themselves, and even afterwards'.

In sociology, as in all the human sciences, the human defines the meaning inherent in the phenomena. This involves the researcher in an engagement with the Other, an engagement which affects and directs the meaning obtained. The comprehension of the phenomena, of the things themselves, is a human comprehension undertaken in dialogue between humans. Lyotard (1991: 100) concludes that sociology is not the study of social objects, but of human interaction, 'of the relation of person to person, of Me to You'. A phenomenology of sociology is predicated on an eidetic intuition which acknowledges the active role of the researcher in the formulation of the essence of what is being studied prior to the research being undertaken. It engages with the 'things themselves', which in sociology means an engagement between the researcher and the researched in a dialogue between Others, a dialogue which produces a meaning inherent in the human interaction itself. In the end, this is the only 'objective' knowledge of the social that is obtainable.

What Lyotard says about sociology can be applied with very little alteration to a phenomenology of religion. We must possess a concept of the religious prior to our engaging in religious research. The religious 'objects' of our investigations are human and hence not objects at all. The scientist of religion approaches the study as a social being, as an Other who enters into dialogue with Others, a Me and a You, an ego and an alter ego. Through the dialogue meaning emerges which is unique to that particular encounter.

It will be noted from this description that phenomenology does not produce static essences or objective knowledge in the sense of the externally detached observer studying things. Because the engagement is human, it is open to innumerable interpretations and a constant flow of meanings. Lyotard (1991: 109) confirmed just this conclusion when he asserted: 'These truths are inexhaustible since they are those of concrete human beings'. The essence is found in the concrete, but the essence has been demonstrated to be plural and as open to as many fresh results as the number of human interactions.

Application to the creation of religious typologies

From the above discussion of a phenomenological interpretation of the postmodernist critique of universals, and the detailed philosophical methodology expounded by Jean-François Lyotard, I would argue that religious typologies are best understood as part of an eidetic science. We need to intuit in advance what we mean by religion and its dimensions in order to study it. This is true of all natural and human sciences. This is not the same as creating grand systems or constructing metanarratives. All typologies, as Van der Leeuw, Bleeker and Smart each acknowledged, are provisional and are accountable to the data of religious life. Religious typologies are not the 'things themselves'; they do not constitute the phenomena of religion. They describe essential characteristics of the phenomena, not as abstract entities, but as concrete expressions of religious communities. As such, they enable the researcher to conduct research about and from within the dimensions of religious life. Moreover, religious typologies demonstrate that the researcher plays an active role in the development of the research project. To deny this is to portray a false objectivity. Acknowledging this should not be understood to imply that the scientist of religion approaches research with predetermined theories into which the data are then forced to fit. The typologies proposed always remain accountable to the facts uncovered and are subject to persistent revision.

Although conducting a scientific project begins in a framework and from a perspective determined by the one who guides the research, the researcher, as a human engaging with other humans, needs to acknowledge in advance what that perspective entails. This means revealing to the religious community under investigation the aims, prior assumptions and purposes of the research itself. This disclosure invites from the members of the community, not only assent in the project, but participation in its ultimate shape, a participation which will influence the results. The objectivity that follows has been formed in the concrete moment through a specific human interaction.

The meaning, which is rendered from the interaction, can be regarded in a limited sense as paradigmatic for other similar situations, but the paradigms suggested do not entail systematic explanations or grand theories of religion in general. From detailed comparative studies, certain religious types can be identified that seem to operate generally within other social situations. The validity of the types as paradigms, nevertheless, is tested by recourse exclusively to the humans who have engaged in the process of research. Religious typologies thus are posited at the beginning of research as an indication of the active role of the researcher in practising an eidetic science and at the end of research as a result of specific interactions within religious communities (understood as a dialogue with adherents). Religious typologies advance the process of scientific inquiry from its formulation through its field studies to its interpretation of the meaning of data.

I admit that religious typologies bear a resemblance to theological models and philosophical essences. They are easily confused with the assertion that abstracted entities are real and can be removed from their concrete expressions. Nonetheless, as I have tried to show through my references to Lyotard, in a phenomenological sense, typologies are neither theological nor metaphysical ideals. My defence of the value of maintaining typologies cannot be found in their potential value for creating academic abstractions for the purposes of understanding religion as a unified, unchanging entity, but because they demonstrate the uniquely human character of religious studies research in which knowledge transports itself through potentially endless horizons of interpretation.

Chapter 5

AFRICAN IDENTITIES AS THE PROJECTION OF WESTERN ALTERITY

The academic study of African cultures, religions and societies originated in the late nineteenth and early twentieth centuries from disciplines as diverse as linguistic and textual studies, anthropology, history, sociology, archaeology and what became known as the science of religion (*Religionswissenschaft*). The primary aim of such scholarship until the 1960s was to provide an objective description, largely for the Western academic community, of various aspects of African life. For example, historical studies sought to determine the development of African religions, often with a view to exposing the primitive nature of their rites and beliefs (Evans-Pritchard 1965; Thrower 1999). Anthropologists identified a wide range of subjects from clan structures and lineage systems to processes operating within rituals, particularly life cycle rituals (Cox 1998b). Scholars within the phenomenological approach emphasized 'understanding' African religions, but often from within Western categories such as belief in a Supreme Being, concepts of evil and how salvation is achieved (Cox 1995: 339–55).

Postmodern analyses, which have dominated methodological discussions during the latter part of the twentieth century, have introduced significant changes in the way African societies are being studied. These include acknowledging that no objective or reified knowledge of African communities is attainable. Understanding, in the phenomenological sense of understanding in depth (*Verstehen*), reflects not so much an African perspective as it does the perceptions of the researcher. This viewpoint destroys all-encompassing explanations of African cultures, limits knowledge to specific interchanges between particular researchers and researched communities, and challenges assumptions that descriptions from any of the major fields studying African societies can be regarded as 'true'.

Postmodern research methodologies can be classified as 'deconstructionist', but ones which result from Western self-reflection where the questions posed and problems identified are relevant exclusively to Western scholarship. For example, in his discussion of postmodernism and Buddhism, Stephen Batchelor (1998: 122–3) suggests that postmodern thinkers take for granted 'the plurality and ambiguity of perception, the fragmented and contingent nature of reality, the elusive, indeterminate nature of self'. Such a radical dispersion of knowledge has resulted from the deconstruction by Western philosophers of unitary explanations of reality, the metanarratives of what Batchelor calls the 'European Enlightenment Project' (1998: 123). This same point has been made by Phillip Mellor and Chris Shilling (1994: 27), who suggest that what is mistaken for postmodernity is in reality a series of circumstances and experiences which are the direct product of certain features of modernity. Mellor and Shilling prefer the term 'reflexive modernity' to postmodernism because it shows clearly that the contemporary deconstruction of thought remains fully consistent with the principles of the European Enlightenment. The domination of intellectual discourse by Westerners perpetually restricts Africans to the role of foreigners in the academic language game until they learn to play according to rules of scholarship dictated by disciplines operating in Western universities.

A similar analysis has been suggested by Terence Ranger (1996: 271) who, in his discussion of postcolonial methods, refers to 'hybridity' not only as 'the cultural condition of Third World intellectuals' but as 'the condition of all contemporary society'. Ranger (1996: 272) argues that the traditional methods of Western social anthropology, for example, in such an intellectual climate are inadequate for understanding contemporary African realities: 'The old colonial relations of dominance and authority need to be replaced by social science as dialogue, as participation.'

Colonial dominance and authority persist on a practical level today through African universities, which as mirror images of Western institutions, are facing increasing problems, some of which are financial and others political, but at their core may be ideological. Many African universities, such as those in Nigeria, Sierra Leone and Zimbabwe, have been closed periodically by governmental authorities. Despite such problems, African students continue to be trained in African universities in Western methods and African students still travel at great personal cost to Europe and America to obtain higher degrees. Methods for discovering African identities could clarify if part of the crisis in African higher education can be traced to the imposition of Western methodologies in preference to viable African alternatives.

Western educational models for studying African cultures and religions have spread throughout Africa carrying with them the methodological assumptions implicit in an all-encompassing explanatory scheme supported by scientific rationality, even when these have been posited in a Christian guise. Although, as I have noted, postmodern analyses have challenged these assumptions, they have operated more like an intra-familial squabble rather than offering radically new perspectives; postmodernism makes little sense outside of the modernist context. I propose in the remainder of this chapter to outline a method which suggests ways not only to surpass the modernist agenda, which prescribed how concepts such as culture, religion, education and nationhood were introduced from the West to Africa, but how to transcend the postmodern critique itself. In order to provide a context for this analysis, I begin by outlining the current debate, which I regard as highly divisive among scholars of religions, between those who stress either 'insider' or 'outsider' methodologies.

Polarities in methodologies in the study of religions

In their introduction to *Religion in Africa*, Walter van Beek and Thomas Blakely define religion in a way which demonstrates that Western academic approaches to the study of religions tend to fall into two rather polarized camps, one which may be called broadly empirical and the other theological. Van Beek and Blakely's definition of religion as 'human interaction with a culturally postulated nonfalsifiable reality' underscores the opposition between what sociologists (borrowing from a linguistic distinction) call the *etic* (outsider's) and the *emic* (insider's) approach (Van Beek and Blakely 1994: 2). The outsider is one who conducts research on religious communities of which he or she is not a member. The insider is one who portrays what it is to be a member of a religion as one who actually is (or at least knows what it feels like to be) an adherent and a participant in the religion under study.

In the Van Beek-Blakely definition, the outsider's view is shown by their emphasis on religion as a culturally specific human response to what must always remain from a scientific perspective a merely postulated, but entirely non-falsifiable, reality. Van Beek and Blakely suggest that this definition safeguards the study of religions from theology. Just like other disciplines in the human sciences, such as anthropology, psychology or sociology, scientific approaches within the study of religions seek to understand and interpret aspects of human religious behaviour, without passing judgements on their truth or value.

Van Beek and Blakely (1994: 2) call their approach an example of 'methodological agnosticism', a phrase used widely in religious studies by scholars as diverse as Ninian Smart (1973b) and J. G. Platvoet (1990). The term 'methodological agnosticism' indicates that the postulated beliefs of any community are non-falsifiable utilizing any scientifically accepted instruments for testing. The approach is methodological in the sense that it employs techniques of description and observation to arrive at an understanding of the phenomena under study. Since what is non-falsifiable cannot be observed, the academic study of religion limits itself to describing how believers relate to and understand what they postulate to be real. Van Beek and Blakely (1994: 1) explain:

> Most people do not claim that they can – at will – directly observe God, an ancestor, or a witch at work. However, this does in no way detract from the reality of widely held beliefs; in fact, the fundamental impossibility to falsify religious content is one major foothold of religion and a source of the bewildering variation and multiplicity of forms.

Those who maintain the Van Beek and Blakely position frequently refer to scholars, such as Mircea Eliade or W. C. Smith, who seem to affirm the reality of the believer's object of faith, as religionists, defined by Platvoet (1990: 21) as those who study 'religions not only for academic reasons, i.e., for the sake of the religions themselves ... but also for a religious reason, for the sake of their own religious view of life'. By contrast, religionists refer to those like Van Beek and Blakely, who deny the verifiability (and hence, falsifiablity) of the transcendental source of religion, as 'reductionists', defined again by Platvoet (1990: 21) as those who study 'not the religions themselves, but the ways in which religions function in societies and in the human psyche and the ways in which religions are determined by non-religious factors'.

That these opposing positions remain polarized today can be demonstrated by a quick review of some recent writers who have commented on methodological issues in the study of religions. One scholar who highlights the polarity is John Hick, who in his book entitled *An Interpretation of Religion* maintains a religionist position or what he calls 'a religious interpretation of religion' in opposition to 'reductionist accounts advocated by such thinkers as Feuerbach, Freud, Durkheim and their successors' (Hick 1989: 1). Although he acknowledges the value of reductionist critiques of religion, particularly in the light of religious diversity with its implications for cultural relativity, Hick (1989: 9) contends that 'this vast and multifarious field of human faith is nevertheless not wholly projection and illusion, ... but constitutes our variously transparent and opaque interface with a mysterious transcendent reality'.

Hick's position is strongly opposed by advocates of reductionism, such as Ivan Strenski, who in his book *Religion in Relation* argues that competing theories of explanation form part of any scientific methodology. Accepted explanatory theories are challenged and superseded using specific or reductionistic disciplinary tools, which are derived from varying fields such as sociology, psychology, economics or politics. Reductionism in this sense does not represent a closed system of analysis that explains everything in terms of its own presuppositions, but what Strenski (1993: 5) calls an empirical 'openness to theoretical change'. In Strenski's view, religionists actually limit the field of enquiry in the study of religion because they depend on a 'theological programme', which contends that if a transcendent reality does not exist, 'the history of religions would be impossible' (Strenski 1993: 2).

Opposition to methodological agnosticism emanates not only from theologians such as Hick and W. C. Smith, and from Eliade (whom Strenski calls a crypto-theologian), but also from social anthropologists such as Michael Bourdillon of the University of Zimbabwe. In an article discussing anthropological approaches to African religions, Bourdillon argues that academic neutrality on religious matters is based on the flawed premise that the scholar of religion can or should exclude personal judgements from academic discourse. Bourdillon contends (1996: 151) that 'our personal judgements are relevant to academic debate, and academic debate can affect our personal judgements'. By accepting this, scholars acknowledge that they view reality from limited perspectives. Bourdillon (1996: 151) explains: 'If we are aware of our limitations, we can enter into academic debate in an undogmatic way, ready to listen and to learn.' He concludes that the best way to do this, rather than denying that we hold personal judgements, is to 'make explicit the value judgements behind our academic work' (Bourdillon 1996: 151).

At this point, Bourdillon appears to be calling for honesty on the part of the researcher by disclosing personal perspectives both to the community being researched and within the academic arena. What he means by a personal judgement, however, seems to go beyond intellectual honesty. He notes that in today's world, each person has a number of religions to choose from and 'our choices arise from judgements about what different religions offer and how true are their perspectives' (Bourdillon 1996: 149). In this multi-cultural and pluralistic situation, it seems to Bourdillon that responsible academic work aims at assisting individuals within changing cultural settings to decide on positive values they wish to adopt. Bourdillon (1996: 150) admits that his position could be regarded as theological since it often is asserted in the study of religions that 'theology requires some kind of commitment while the study of religions is essentially neutral'. Against this view, he says, it is difficult, if not illegitimate, to distinguish between personal and academic judgements. Although the task is difficult, academics in the study of religions need to define 'cross-cultural criteria for judgements' (Bourdillon 1996: 150).

Methodological conversion as a starting point

In the debate over methodologies in the study of religions, the polarities I have just outlined, created by advocates of what may variously be called the insider-outsider, reductionist–non-reductionist, religionist–empiricist positions, suggest a need for innovative thinking in methodologies. In my book, *Rational Ancestors* (1998a: 99–115), I develop a theory based on Raimundo Panikkar's (1979: 9–10) 'diatopical hermeneutics' and David Krieger's (1991: 53) 'methodological conversion', in which I affirm my own faith in scientific rationality while seeking to understand and interpret Indigenous religious expressions in Zimbabwe. I have sought to apply the method in a concrete situation to demonstrate an innovation in religious methodologies going beyond the traditional phenomenological categories of *epoché* and empathy and also attempting to overcome the problems Bourdillon notes in academic neutrality or the position of methodological agnosticism. Although I am not going to repeat here what I have written elsewhere, I do want to press forward with the basic concept that to understand an 'other' requires me in some sense to adopt the identity of the other. This forms the basis for Panikkar's method, which he says comes naturally to him, since his identity is composed of two religious 'others', the Hindu and the Christian (cited in Krieger 1991: 21). Following Panikkar, Krieger (1991: 51–60) suggests that we must internalize the other into our own identities, so that we can, like Panikkar, be both-and, rather than either-or, in Panikkar's case both Hindu and Christian, or as I suggest in my book, both a scientific rationalist and an Indigenous African believer (Cox 1998a: 117–36). This process is strictly methodological and intended to promote understanding of both the subject and the object of research.

As this is outlined by Krieger in the context of interreligious dialogue and adapted by me for the purposes of scholarly research, seven stages emerge:

1. The researcher begins by employing what Krieger (1991: 75) calls 'all reliable methods', including the empirical, historical–critical, philosophical and phenomenological to critically analyse his or her own tradition.
2. The same critical tools are then applied to the tradition the researcher wishes to understand.
3. Understanding of the tradition changes to conviction, just as the scholar is committed to his or her own tradition.
4. This enables an internal intra-religious dialogue to occur within the researcher, which is characterized by the search for a 'common language capable of expressing the truth of both religions' (Krieger 1991: 75).
5. The internal dialogue becomes external when the scholar's interpretation is presented to representatives of the other tradition.
6. The same stages are presupposed for those the scholar is seeking to understand.
7. New interpretations are tested in the dialogue between the traditions. Where they are found inadequate, the researcher returns to the level of intra-religious dialogue and starts afresh (Krieger 1991: 75–6).

The Krieger-Panikkar approach, as I have adapted it, assumes that the researcher is committed to, and by using the proper critical tools, can speak for his or her own tradition. It also assumes that the scholar can learn to experience what it is like to adhere to the tradition under study and thus apply the same critical analysis to it as was done with the original tradition. In this way, the scholar interprets both one's own and the other's 'faith' through an intra-personal dialogue (just as Panikkar did as a Hindu-Christian) before actually testing the interpretations reached through the methodology in actual field studies. Although this approach eventually involves the researched community in the process of research, I believe recent studies of the 'other' can deepen the method by making it less dependent on a model of inter-religious dialogue and hence more valuable for empirical research.

The other within

In recent years, the study of Otherness, or what is called 'alterity', has become a central theme across many academic disciplines. This has been documented in a book that appeared in the Amsterdam Studies on Cultural Identity series, edited by R. Corbey and J. Th. Leerssen entitled *Alterity, Identity, Image* (1991). In their introduction to the book, Corbey and Leerssen note: 'The Other has been placed on the agenda by pursuits as diverse as women's studies, literary image studies, psychology, philosophy, and most importantly perhaps, in the social sciences' (1991: viii). Although Corby and Leerssen fail to include the academic study of religions in their list (unless they subsume it under the social sciences), the movement to study alterity and identity is precisely what Panikkar and Krieger have sought to do, and what I have tried to apply in an African context.

In the Corby and Leerssen volume, a particularly helpful paper for the discussions of African identities is presented by Ernst van Alphen, who at the time of writing was lecturer in literary theory in the University of Nijmegen. In his article, entitled 'The Other Within', Van Alphen does not address religion directly, but he is concerned with the same issues implied by the insider–outsider discussions I described above (Van Alphen 1991: 1–16). By examining the categories of hermeneutics, epistemology and psychoanalysis, Van Alphen sheds light on how 'outsiders' gain knowledge of and understand culture and societies of which they are not a part.

Van Alphen suggests that, from a hermeneutical perspective, we have tended either to idealize or to denigrate the 'other'. He calls the former tendency 'exoticism' and the latter 'nationalism'. From an exotic perspective the culture of the other is regarded as superior to one's own, thereby implying a negative regard for one's own identity. A hermeneutic of nationalism on the other hand regards one's own identity as superior to the identity of the other, thereby creating images of other cultures as dangerous, weird, inferior or evil (Van Alphen 1991: 2–3).

In either an exotic or nationalistic depiction of the other, the interpretation provided results entirely from the image which the subject holds of itself. The alleged superiority or inferiority of the other is not based in objective reality, but on an imputed value based on self-identity. Van Alphen (1991: 3) asserts 'that the concept of alterity does not have the same status as that of identity. While "alterity" is a screen for the imagination, "identity" is the content of that imagination'. This leads Van Alphen (1991: 3) to conclude that alterity '*is* nothing, has no meaning' (emphasis in original). It operates simply as a device for meaning-production induced by self-identities.

An epistemology delineating how we project identity and alterity as objects of knowledge thus becomes critical. Van Alphen, following the philosopher J. L. Austin's distinctions between locutionary, illocutionary and perlocutionary speech acts, argues that identity and alterity are defined not by what is said about them, but by the effects they produce in those who speak about them and in those who hear what is spoken about them. Austin (1963: 25) defined locutionary speech as the simple act of saying something. A locutionary act that also performs an action, such as asking or answering a question, giving some information or issuing a warning is an illocutionary speech act. A locutionary act, which produces certain consequential effects on the feelings, thoughts or actions of the one hearing the speech or in the one making the utterance, is perlocutionary. In other words, in perlocutionary speech, what is spoken about is known in the act of speaking it. For example, if I instruct someone to 'Close the door', I am performing an act by giving the order. The action is contained in the statement and thus is perlocutionary, or performative (Cox 1998a: 71).

Austin added that language to be perlocutionary does not require an explicit statement of the act to be performed, but could employ 'in place of the explicit formula … a whole lot of more primitive devices such as intonation, for instance, or gesture' (Austin 1963: 25–6). Simply saying 'Dog' with the proper intonation and gesture could warn a would-be victim of an imminent attack. Austin explains: 'Our explicit performative formula ("I promise … ", "I order you … etc.") serves to make explicit and at the same time more precise, what act it is that the speaker purports to perform in issuing his utterance' (Austin 1963: 26).

That identity and alterity are best understood as performative and thus similar to perlocutionary speech acts is evidenced through the psychological dimensions of experience. Van Alphen (1991: 5) argues that Freud's psychoanalytic theory demonstrated that the self and the other are not distinct but one and the same: 'The other is part of the self. We are our own others. The other is always the other within.' Thus, when we speak of identity and alterity, we refer to that which directly affects the self. Freud's concern was not with the 'integration of the other' but with the 'disintegration of the self' (Van Alphen 1991: 11). In his description of the technique of psychoanalysis, for example, Freud (1949: 46) described the neurotic ego as one that 'is no longer able to fulfil the task set to it by the external world (including human society)'. It is so disturbed that 'its organization is impaired, it is internally split apart, it is no longer capable of any proper synthesis, it is torn by discordant impulses, unappeased conflicts and unsolved doubts' (Freud 1949: 46). By focusing on how psychoanalysis raises 'the mental processes' in the ego 'to a normal level' and returns to the patient 'once more … the possession of his ego', Freud showed how ego states affect the perception of the other and function to interpret the other for the self (Freud 1949: 47). This leads Van Alphen (1991: 15) to conclude: 'Identity and alterity are not "givens", they are not presences behind the self or the other, but changeable products of the ongoing process of constituting a self-image.'

Implications of identity and alterity for innovations in religious method

What does Van Alphen's analysis of identity and alterity imply for innovations in religious methodologies generally and for identifying African identities specifically? Van Alphen (1991: 15) himself suggests the answer: 'The only way to know the other is by letting the other speak about me, by giving the other the position of "I"'. The reason for this is that when I speak about the 'other', I am immediately involved in demarcating my own self-image. By extension, when the 'other' speaks about me, the other also is engaged in a process of self-definition.

For methodologies aimed at examining cultures and identities, this implies that research proceeds legitimately only when contracts of understanding are formed between the researcher and the researched communities. The contract entails dialogue in the fullest sense of the term where the researcher outlines the purpose and speaks performatively (with effect) to what traditionally would be regarded as the objects of the research. This reveals to members of the researched community nothing about themselves, but a great deal about the researcher. Particularly when researchers speak of the objects of research (alterity), they transport the 'other' into themselves and thereby make their own identities transparent. The counterpart to this occurs when a researcher invites (not compels) members of the researched community to speak about their perceptions of the researcher and the research project. Based on the premise that the other is always the self within, and that the self within can be known only through affect and effect, this methodology provides the only sure way to attain understanding of the other.

This method, moreover, confirms what anthropologists, ethnologists and empirical scholars of religion have argued persistently, that reliable studies of the 'other' emerge only after a researcher has experienced a long exposure of living within and among the people under study. What is innovative in this approach is not the time and commitment involved in the research, but the epistemological process of discovering the other in the self, of knowing alterity through identity.

In the end, the distinction between researcher and researched becomes blurred, if not destroyed altogether, by this methodology. This is why the 'other within' position can be depicted as incorporating both Panikkar's diatopical hermeneutics, which steps outside of boundary discourse and power relations, and Krieger's fourth stage in methodological conversion, which turns the identity of the inner self into that of the other. The knowledge that results from these innovative methods cannot convey knowledge of the 'other' in some objectified and reified understanding of knowing. The findings of this kind of research depend on the specific interactions between identities and others, what Van Alphen (1991: 5) calls the 'interlocutionary situation'.

This approach to the study of religions overcomes the polarity created by the classic insider and outsider distinction in research, and thereby defuses the controversy between religionist and reductionist methodologies. It also advances the Panikkar-Krieger methodology beyond its close alliance with models of inter-religious dialogue and their clearly articulated theological aims. The 'insider within' method assumes that the researcher remains always the insider because what is outside is projected from the inside. The researched communities also always remain insiders with respect to the one conducting research. The two meet only when they incorporate their respective others within.

Any uniquely African identity in this context will emerge as a form of alterity to Western research initiatives. What the African says about the West, its history of colonialism and its intellectual domination will reveal far more about the Africans sense of self than it will about the Western imperialist agenda. I am suggesting, therefore, that the best way to understand academic descriptions and interpretations of African religious communities is to read them as projections of the self-perceptions of the authors, that is, as reflections of identity through discussions of alterity.

Chapter 6

PHENOMENOLOGICAL PERSPECTIVES ON THE SOCIAL RESPONSIBILITY OF THE SCHOLAR OF RELIGION

Jack Nelson-Pallmeyer (2003: xi) begins his controversial book, *Is Religion Killing Us?*, with the assertion that 'religion kills, or more accurately, religion is used to justify killing precisely because issues of ultimate consequence and meaning are understood to be at stake'. Nelson-Pallmeyer focuses on the three main monotheistic religions, Judaism, Christianity and Islam, and argues that the sacred texts of each are '*dominated by violence-of-God traditions*' (2003: xii) (emphasis in original). He devotes the remainder of his book to exposing how God is depicted in the Hebrew Scriptures, the New Testament and the Qur'an as a vengeful deity, who punishes those who oppose him in both this life and the next, and who urges his followers to commit acts of aggression in his name. Nelson-Pallmeyer asserts in the final three chapters of his book that followers of the great monotheistic religions can be saved from their devotion to a God of violence by learning to see their enemies in a new light as fellow humans and by doubting the authority of the sacred texts themselves.

A similar argument has been developed by Mark Juergensmeyer in his book, *Terror in the Mind of God* (2001: 6), in which he contends: 'Within the histories of religious traditions – from biblical wars to crusading ventures and great acts of martyrdom – violence has lurked as a shadowy presence.' The aim of his book is to investigate 'public acts of violence at the turn of the century for which religion has provided the motivation, the justification, the organization, and the world view' (Juergensmeyer 2001: 7). As a sociologist, Juergensmeyer (2001: 7) seeks to 'understand the cultural contexts that produce these acts of violence', but adds that 'religious activists' have gone about 'their business of killing with the certainty that they were following the logic of God' (Juergensmeyer 2001: 218). Juergensmeyer concludes his book, not with a programme for curing religious violence, but by describing various scenarios that could dominate world affairs and that may help to clarify why 'bad things are done by people who otherwise appear to be good – in cases of religious terrorism, by pious people dedicated to a moral vision of the world' (Juergensmeyer 2001: 7). He cites with approval the views of the French thinker Marcel Gauchet who, according to Juergensmeyer, urged 'Western society to recover the spiritual roots that it abandoned when it transferred the sense of sacrality from God to the nation' (Juergensmeyer 2001: 240). On this point, Juergensmeyer concurs with the American theologian Reinhold Niebuhr whom he commends for describing religion as providing society with 'a concern with the quality of life' (Juergensmeyer 2001: 240).

Juergensmeyer reconciles this description of the positive role of religion in society with violent acts committed in the name of religion by urging his readers to understand the mind of the terrorist and to take into account the social conditions that cultivate attitudes of hatred. He admits that violence 'has much to do with the religious imagination, which always has had the propensity to absolutize and to project images of cosmic war' (Juergensmeyer 2001: 242). He contends that religiously inspired violence also results from conditions dominating the larger society in which 'tensions of this moment of history ... cry out for absolute solutions' to what people experience as 'personal humiliation' (Juergensmeyer 2001: 242). This helps explain why many religious activists possess an intense and sincere desire 'to restore an integrity they perceive as lost in the wake of virtually global social and political shifts' (Juergensmeyer 2001: 242). Juergensmeyer thus interprets religious violence in ways that promote public understanding without at the same time condoning acts of terrorism. His project ultimately aims at re-interpreting religion in the public sphere in order to promote well-being and communal understanding, what he labels in one of the sub-themes of his concluding chapter, 'Healing politics with religion' (Juergensmeyer 2001: 238).

Throughout his book, Jack Nelson-Pallmeyer employs a method based on a scholarly analysis of texts with the aim of influencing the behaviour and practices of adherents within Judaism, Christianity and Islam. By exposing them to the atrocities their sacred scriptures urge them to commit out of obedience to the demands of God, he intends to uproot religious intolerance and replace it with understanding, cooperation, dialogue and peace-making. Although the methods he uses are different, in the end, Juergensmeyer seeks to achieve a similar goal. If politics can be healed by religion, religious activists can be placated by coming to understand the social contexts out of which they have experienced feelings of humiliation and, at the same time, they can reconnect with the positive goals enshrined in their religious traditions.

By combining critical analysis with calls for social action, Nelson-Pallmeyer and Juergensmeyer exemplify precisely the type of approach that has generated a sometimes acrimonious debate amongst scholars in the academic study of religion. I call this the debate over the socially engaged scholar of religion, which has been created by the contexts in which the study of specific religions occurs, where scholars often are called upon to make personal decisions as to whether or not they should become involved *as scholars* in the social, political and economic issues that affect directly the religious communities they are studying. In order to understand the background and significance of this debate for academics working in the field of religious studies, it is necessary that I discuss the main features within the academic study of religions, which was dominated by the phenomenology and history of religions during the early to middle part of the twentieth century.

Academic neutrality and understanding

At the outset, it is important to underscore that one of the primary reasons phenomenologists and historians of religion developed methods for studying religion was in reaction to the theological motives that stood behind the emergence of the comparative study of religions in the late nineteenth century. Confronted by a growing awareness of the plurality of religious traditions, theologians sought to develop comparative methods in order to demonstrate the superiority of Christianity over all the other religions of the world. For example, the German theologian Ernst Troeltsch (1991: 78), writing at the turn of the twentieth century, contended that Christianity had lost its 'exclusive-supernatural foundation' and had become 'perceived as only one of the great world religions, along with Islam and Buddhism'. Troeltsch maintained that all religions respond to common human aspirations, such as the search for meaning and the attainment of a sense of inner peace. He concluded that only a religion of redemption can satisfy the deepest needs of humanity, which 'Christianity alone among the religions completes' (Troeltsch 1991: 84).

I have argued in a previous publication that scholars, such as W. Brede Kristensen, who was appointed Chair of the History of Religion at the University of Leiden in 1901 and Gerardus van der Leeuw, who held a comparable post in Groningen in The Netherlands from 1918 to 1950, sought to distance the study of religion from its close association with theology by promoting a non-theological, non-confessional approach, which situated the phenomenology of religion as a discipline among the historical and social sciences (Cox 2006: 108–38). This scientific or objective approach, which to this day is maintained by many academics working in the field of religious studies, has obvious relevance to the question of what social responsibility researchers owe to those communities that constitute the objects of their research. Scholars, writing in the phenomenological and historical traditions, refused to make normative statements about the truth of religion or to pass judgement on the actions performed in response to what religious adherents regarded as sacred obligations. The primary aim of proponents of the academic study of religion was to achieve understanding based on objectively neutral descriptions, which, at the same time, would fairly represent the believers' own perspectives. Fairness would be ensured by the carefully constructed method of empathetic interpolation, which was made possible by cultivating a feeling for what it would be like to be an adherent within a particular religious community (Cox 2010: 52–5).

The British phenomenologist of religion, Ninian Smart, exemplified just this approach when he invited his readers to consider the life and behaviour of Adolf Hitler, who for most people represents a historical figure with whom it would appear impossible to empathize. Smart (1984b: 264) asks, 'Does it mean that I need to be a Hitler-lover to understand him?' In one sense, Smart answers this question affirmatively: 'If we are indeed to get into his soul we have to drop our preconceptions, and treat Hitler as a human being who had his own thought world' (Smart 1984b: 264). This involves following him 'through his Austrian childhood and relationship to his father and dear mother; through his scholastic failures and outcast status in Vienna; through his years in the trenches fighting in France' (Smart 1984b: 264). In other words, Smart calls on us to treat Adolf Hitler as a human being, but, he adds, 'all this is strictly *empathy*, "getting the feel of"' (Smart 1984b: 264) (emphasis in original). Empathy, he argues, does not require a person to condone Hitler's actions or approve 'in any way the rightness of his creed' (Smart 1984b: 264). Smart concluded that under such procedures developed within the phenomenological and historical approaches to the study of religion, it was deemed irrelevant whether or not the beliefs of any community were true or false or whether their practices could be fitted into morally acceptable categories. Questions of truth and value are 'bracketed out', suspended, and hence they play no role in the scholar's task *as scholar*.

This position was endorsed in 1960 at the Congress of the overarching international body of scholars of religion, the International Association for the History of Religions (IAHR), held in Marburg, Germany, in a statement signed by such notable thinkers as Mircea Eliade, a leading historian of religions at the University of Chicago. The communication contended that students of religion may wish to 'join with others in order to contribute their share towards the promotion of certain ideals – national, international, political, social, spiritual and otherwise', but, it warned, 'this is a matter of individual ideology and commitment, and must under no circumstances be allowed to influence or colour the character of the IAHR' (cited by Geertz and McCutcheon 2000: 15–16). This principle was supported at the Turku Regional Conference of the IAHR held in 1973 by its then General Secretary, C. J. Bleeker (1979: 174), who noted that some people 'think that the history of religions and the phenomenology of religion should mainly serve to foster world-peace and social harmony, by creating mutual understanding among the adherents of the different religions'. However noble such ideals may be, he reminded the conference, the history and phenomenology of religion 'are a purely scholarly affair' (Bleeker 1979: 174).

These issues have persisted since Marburg and Turku as underlying concerns for students of religion, but they have re-emerged recently, as evidenced by Nelson-Pallmeyer's and Juergensmeyer's books, most notably under the influence of religiously inspired acts of terror culminating in the attacks on the World Trade Center in New York on 11 September 2001 and by other atrocities such as those perpetrated on Madrid trains in March 2004, on London buses and tubes in July 2005 and more recently in May 2013 by the murder in Woolwich, England, of the soldier Lee Rigby, which the British government labelled an act of terrorism. Although these acts are often condemned as evidence of Islamic extremism, concerns over religiously motivated violence in academic and popular contexts extend far more widely. For example, Juergensmeyer, who published his book just around the time the World Trade Center was destroyed, cited numerous instances of religious violence committed during the 1990s by 'the Christian militia, the Christian identity movement and Christian anti-abortion activists' (Juergensmeyer 2001: 3–4). Such events have inspired increasingly contentious debates that challenge the customarily neutral, but empathetic, stance promoted by phenomenologists and historians of religion.

Challenges to phenomenological neutrality

Although, as I noted, the intellectual tradition out of which the academic study of religion emerged advocated a neutral stance with respect to the truth claims and social actions of believing communities, more recently, dissenting voices to this dominant view have begun to emerge. To demonstrate this, I review the positions maintained by three scholars of religion, writing from quite different social and historical perspectives: Paul-François Tremlett, a lecturer in Religious Studies in the Open University, UK, in an article first delivered to the 2006 Annual Conference of the British Association for the Study of Religions held in Bath, England; Russell McCutcheon, who is Professor of Religious Studies in the University of Alabama, in his book *Critics Not Caretakers* (2001); and David Chidester, who is Professor of Religious Studies in the University of Cape Town, South Africa, in his volume *Savage Systems* (1996).

In his article, which carries the title 'The Ethics of Suspicion in the Study of Religions', Tremlett, who is an anthropologist of religion, sets the context for his stinging critique of phenomenological neutrality by referring to research he conducted in the early 2000s in the Philippines.

> Any visitor to the Philippines willing to spend a little time each day to watch local television, read newspapers and comics, catch a movie or live with a family will soon come to be aware of stories about sorcery and witchcraft (*kulam*), of blood-sucking flying bats (*aswáng* and *mananangal*), dwarves and elves (*duwende*), spirits that enchant the unwary such as the *engkanto* and *tikbalang*, ancestral spirits (*anito*), as well as the pervasive use of creolised prayers that combine Tagálog and Latin (*orasyón*) and amulets (*anting-anting*) through which to guard against the mischief or possible malevolence of these alleged supernatural agents or for the accumulation of spiritual power and potency (*kapangyarihan*). (Tremlett 2007: 5–6)

Tremlett then endorses what he calls:

> a distinction between two kinds of knowledge: a rational-scientific corpus of statements and propositions that are held to accurately describe reality and which encourage forms of social action that are efficacious precisely because of that correspondence, and a religious or traditional corpus of knowledge which while signifying a cultural richness that must be preserved, is out of synch with the real. (Tremlett 2007: 12)

The implication of the second point, he says, is that the proper place for religious knowledge is the library and museum, since 'it cannot serve as an effective guide for living' (Tremlett 2007: 12). Tremlett admits that advocates of the phenomenological method would no doubt argue that the rational account 'is at best uncharitable and at worst unethical, precisely because of its orientation towards generating cognitive change in the believer' (Tremlett 2007: 12). But his own field studies demonstrated quite the opposite:

> Filipinos are broadly ignorant of basic standards of health and nutrition and their links to disease and ill health. Surely, the ethical response to this situation is precisely to challenge beliefs when and where they clearly obstruct or prevent people from understanding the causes of sickness. In which case, for analysis to cease at the believer's point of view as phenomenologists of religion suggest emerges not as ethical, sympathetic or empathic, but as the abdication of responsibility towards those whom one is engaged in representing. (Tremlett 2007: 12)

Russell McCutcheon considers the issue of scholarly social engagement from a more theoretical perspective than Tremlett by defining the public role of the student of religion as that of a critic. This applies in the first instance to the way religions themselves are described and analysed, and hence refers to a critical self-examination of theory and method in the study of religion. McCutcheon (2001: 141) says, 'Our role is unfailingly to probe beneath the rhetorical window dressings that authorize conceptual and social constructions of our own making'. This involves not only critically assessing institutions that study religion but more broadly entails challenging what McCutcheon (2001: 140–1) calls '"mechanisms of power", which the scholar of religion uncovers, brings to light and where appropriate challenges'. In the public sphere, this requires questioning unexamined assumptions, promoting 'intellectual freedom' and, by cooperating 'in a cross-disciplinary way' with other scholars who employ methods drawn from their own fields of study, identifying 'those homogenizing, ideological strategies so necessary for the manufacture and management of human communities' (McCutcheon 2001: 142).

Armed with this information and using well-honed analytical tools, McCutcheon (2001: 142) describes the appropriate engagement of the scholar of religion with institutions in society as 'cultural criticism'. This implies that in their roles as academics, intellectuals are not called on to participate in activities aimed at eradicating practices that they might find reprehensible, but should instead raise critical questions about such practices, uncover the motives that inspire institutional support for socially destructive behaviours and expose how authority figures benefit from them. This strategy is explained in McCutcheon's (2001: 142) concluding comments where he prescribes for scholars of religion 'the role of critic … rather than savior'.

If McCutcheon's discussion tends towards a highly theoretical analysis of the public role of the scholar and Tremlett bases his analysis on field studies, David Chidester roots his argument squarely in the historical context of South Africa and its sordid policy of apartheid. Chidester does not directly confront the problem of the socially engaged scholar of religion, but he demonstrates how social, historical and political contexts in the study of religions affect what appear to be empirically-based interpretations and dictate the categories through which those interpretations are filtered. He cites with approval Jonathan Z. Smith's (1990: 34) observation that the history of the study of religions 'has been by no means an innocent endeavour'. Chidester's opening line in his book makes this point absolutely clear: 'This book is ... a critical analysis of the emergence of the conceptual categories of *religion* and *religions* in colonial frontiers' (Chidester 1996: 1) (emphasis in original). The analyses which follow underscore repeatedly the fact that the study of religion looks very different when seen from the perspective of the marginalized than it does from within academic structures of power operating in Western universities. The main point I draw from his line of reasoning is this: if interpreters of religion have produced their analytic categories historically by siding with powerful political and social interests, the argument cannot be maintained today that the scholar, for reasons of academic neutrality, should remain aloof from engaging with the pressing social problems that affect the lives of those who constitute the subject matter of religious studies.

Chidester (1996: 2) supports this contention by showing in a detailed historical account of missionary and colonial activities in South Africa that the findings of 'comparative religionists' became powerful tools of colonialism to establish and exercise 'local control' by constructing a 'discourse about others that reinforced colonial containment'. He demonstrates how attitudes towards Indigenous people changed from declaring initially that they had no religion, through ones with their roots in ancient religions, usually degenerated from ancient Judaism, to a religion that could be compared with Western religion. In each case, he argues, these interpretations served colonial interests. For example, sixteenth and seventeenth-century travel literature describing the Africans as having no religion resulted not just from ignorance, but served to justify 'an intervention in local frontier conflicts over land, trade, labor and political autonomy' (Chidester 1996: 14). By the eighteenth century, when trade routes had been established with Portuguese, Dutch and English traders, the usefulness of referring to African religion as 'fetishism' is seen, since it reinforced the idea that Africans 'overvalued trifling objects ... but they undervalued trade goods' (Chidester 1996: 15). Chidester points out that by the nineteenth century, when European colonization was gaining momentum, the denial that Africans had religion perpetrated the notion of the 'lazy savage', one who lacked initiative and industry. Finally, when religious 'systems' were acknowledged in Africa, they were asserted in order to establish boundaries, to fix the parameters between the religion of the white and that of the savage. This reification of religion created frontiers, whereby the 'other' could be contained, but at the same time, where negotiations across frontiers could occur (Chidester 1996: 21).

If Tremlett, McCutcheon and Chidester are correct, phenomenologists of religion can no longer pretend that they maintain a position of neutrality towards the truth claims or values of the communities they are studying. If we follow Tremlett, it is impossible for researchers to ignore their fundamental ethical responsibility to attempt to correct or even oppose religious beliefs or practices that are damaging to local communities and/or harmful to the wider society. Certainly, Tremlett, McCutcheon and Chidester each would agree with the argument that students of religion need to be understood as participants, or players, in the larger social and historical processes in which they are inevitably entangled. I test this argument in the remainder of this chapter by describing one of my own experiences in Zimbabwe, where as a researcher I was confronted with a decision whether to remain committed to a position of impartiality or to attempt to influence beliefs and actions that I personally regarded as wrong and injurious to the members of the religious community I was studying.

Social responsibility in Zimbabwe: Religion and AIDS

In July and August 2004, I made field visits to south-central Zimbabwe near the village of Mberengwa with my colleague from the University of Zimbabwe, Professor Tabona Shoko. During our research, we encountered several instances in which individuals were being treated for illnesses (and in one case confirmed as full-blown AIDS) by use of traditional or Christian healing practices. In his book, *Karanga Indigenous Religion in Zimbabwe: Health and Well Being* (2007), Shoko discusses the development of an African Initiated Church (AIC) called St Elijah Chikoro Chomweya (School of the Holy Spirit). This church was founded by Steven Shava, whom Shoko (2007: 116) describes as having been a prominent evangelist in the Lutheran Church throughout southern Zimbabwe, but after having experienced a series of visions, in 1991 formed his own church, which he developed into a ministry of healing. After determining the causes of illness, Shava alleged to have cured illnesses and resolved a series of other misfortunes through prayer, laying on of hands and casting out evil spirits. Shoko (2007: 120) notes that, according to the teaching of the church, 'illness and disease in this world can be traced to Satan, the arch-enemy of God, malignant spirits and witchcraft'.

On our field visits in 2004, Shoko took me to the home of Steven Shava, whom I met along with his son, Venson Shava, who had succeeded his father as bishop and had given the church a new name: The Apostolic Enlightenment Mission. Shoko explained that under the leadership of Venson Shava, the church had spread throughout Zimbabwe and increased its membership, particularly around the capital Harare. Shoko (2007: 117–8) observed that the reorganized and renamed church 'has devised new structures, and ... grasped modern techniques of evangelization', which largely explains its rapid growth throughout the country.

In an interview I held with Venson Shava at the compound of his father in Chatira village in the Mberengwa District on 1 August 2004, he explained to me that the St Elijah Church began

> when my father, a Lutheran, had a vision to prophesy. He was able to foretell not only the resolution to personal problems but larger problems affecting people

through the power of the Holy Spirit. We do not believe in ancestral spirits as helpers. These are evil spirits, demons.

He then made the important comment:

People have many problems. They cannot afford to go to hospital. We are able to know what causes the illness. We know even before they come to us what the problem is. Africans believe in spirits and spiritual causes for illness. Witches and evil spirits can afflict people. We cast out the evil spirits by the power of the Holy Spirit. People come to us and those with the gift of prophecy are able to tell them what they need and how to solve problems.

Shava was indicating that for the faithful there is no need for doctors, hospitals or other forms of Western medical intervention. The Apostolic Enlightenment Mission teaches that through the gift of the Holy Spirit prophets can determine the causes of illness and treat patients by prayer and the laying on of hands.

I saw this belief put into action when Tabona Shoko and I attended an Apostolic Enlightenment Mission church service on 15 August 2004 near the Kutama Mission around 80 kilometres west of Harare. The service was held outdoors on the communal lands at the homestead of a member of the Apostolic Enlightenment Mission. The programme followed a pattern of prayers, hymns, Bible readings and culminated with a sermon by Bishop Shava. After the sermon had been delivered, the remainder of the service was devoted to prophesying and healing. One prophet, in particular, a man who appeared to be in his thirties, came forward and drew attention to several people. One woman he identified was holding a baby. The prophet disclosed to the congregation that 'the witch's familiars are hovering around the baby trying to make her ill'. Another woman, who was elderly, was singled out by the prophet and informed that, although she was ill, it was 'very hard for the Holy Spirit to help her because she is not a member of the church. She was advised that she must join the church and then she could be healed. The prophet then called forward people who had 'a secret sin or had done something in the dark' to receive a blessing from the Bishop. Six men came forward and knelt before the Bishop while ten women knelt immediately behind the men. The Bishop laid his hands on each person and offered a prayer.

Then those who were ill were instructed to come forward. Approximately thirty people responded, most of whom were women. Around ten who came forward were children, and a few men also approached the front. The ill members of the congregation sat on straw mats. The Bishop was joined by three other men who laid their hands on the heads of those seated on the mats. Many rolled their heads around under the pressure exerted by the healers. No water or ointment was applied. Two women swooned as if in ecstasy or trance. Of course, it is impossible to determine how many of those who came forward suffered from AIDS or were HIV positive, but, if statistics are to be believed, many would have been.[1]

After the service concluded, I again interviewed Bishop Shava, who reiterated the fact that the members of his church were poor and could not afford hospitals or medication. In place of expensive Western medical interventions, the church ministers to them by healing the sick. Then, in a clear indication of the underlying doctrinal stance of his church, the Bishop indicated that he was raising funds to build a new, modern and extensive healing centre near his father's home in the region of Mberengwa. This suggested two points on which I could have challenged the Bishop on empirical and ethical grounds: (1) the church discourages the use of Western medicine claiming it is too expensive, while raising money for its own alternative healing centre; (2) in opposition to what we know scientifically about the causes of illness, as we have seen, prophets frequently attribute illness and misfortune to witchcraft or evil spirits, even before the person asks for help, and then tells the patient what to do, with the possible consequence in some cases that the Apostolic Enlightenment Mission itself could benefit financially.

What I have just described, of course, is a quite practical, and personal, account of the problem I faced as a scholar of religion, but it confirms that issues surrounding the social responsibility of a researcher are not merely theoretical. Rather than confronting the Bishop with the moral problems entailed in his approach to treating illness, which certainly would have resulted in the deaths of many HIV-infected people, I responded in a way that was typical of a researcher trained in the phenomenological tradition. I made no comment or judgement on the beliefs or practices of the church or its leaders. I was an empathetic participant in the church service and treated with respect the practice of laying on hands as a method of healing. On reflection afterwards, I asked myself if I was right to remain a silent, empathetic participant observer, or if I should have pointed out the fact that the Bishop was putting members of his congregation at risk, particularly those suffering from AIDS or other life-threatening illnesses that could have been treated by drugs or other forms of Western medical intervention. If I were to follow Tremlett's lead, I should have acted as an agent promoting 'cognitive change' out of ethical and humanistic motives.

A defence of the phenomenological approach

According to traditional phenomenological methods, direct interventions by a researcher to promote change or correct perceived cognitive errors would prove to be highly offensive to most religious groups. This, in turn, would distort the results of research and militate against achieving understanding which, according to phenomenologists, defines the goal of humanistic research (Waardenburg 1978: 224–5). If I were to leave the issue there, this would appear to entail a retreat into a position of academic neutrality, detached objectivity and a denial that the researcher has a social responsibility to the community under study and to the wider society. This conclusion entails a fundamental misunderstanding of the phenomenological method that falsely represents its research aims. According to phenomenologists of religion, the primary role of the observer is defined as describing and interpreting religious beliefs and practices accurately, fairly and empathetically (Cox 2010: 49–58). This limited research agenda possesses a certain potency by informing outsiders about the beliefs, practices, perspectives and values of specific religious communities and in the process by bringing to public attention the dynamics operating as the religious group interacts with norms and expectations maintained within the wider society. As one whose particular skills produce critical analyses of religious contexts, the academic bears a responsibility to apply intellectual reflection to the vital issues affecting contemporary society. On this reading, the phenomenology of religion affirms the maxim that scholars as public intellectuals are obliged to engage with the social contexts out of which their studies emerge.

An example of how I have interpreted appropriate scholarly social intervention is found in a paper I contributed to a conference on the religion–secular dichotomy in colonial contexts, which was later published as a separate chapter in a volume edited by Timothy Fitzgerald. In the published article (Cox 2007b: 71–92), I outline how the capitalist reinterpretation of land in the state of Alaska in the United States, where I lived and worked from 1981 to 1986, under the terms of the Alaska Native Claims Settlement Act (ANCSA) has placed ownership of traditional lands under the control of Indigenous shareholders in Native corporations. Although I did not directly criticize the Act, I attempted to show how its enactment completed a long process of assimilation of Indigenous peoples in Alaska and how it was conceived by those who framed it as a means of finally making Alaskan Natives fully 'Americanized'. I noted that the Indigenous transmission of authority, which resided traditionally in a loosely organized social structure that employed numerous specialists, including shamans, was constructed to guarantee the means of subsistence through elaborate rituals, which dramatized and enforced societal rules. I argued that through ANCSA, the customary patterns of life had become subject to the radically homogenizing power of the capitalist system, which paradoxically had created an equally radical heterogeneous system in the form of individual shares in corporations. My aim in this article clearly was to act as a critic of a system that in many ways has had devastating effects on the Indigenous populations of Alaska, but I made no specific proposals for change or for social action. I portrayed the scholarly role as one of informing policies for change, but not as devising recommendations for changes to the law.

When applied to the case of HIV/AIDS in Zimbabwe, and to my encounter with the beliefs and practices of the Apostolic Enlightenment Mission, my role as a researcher in the phenomenological tradition was not to act as an evangelist for Western rationality. Nor was it to remain silent over the problems entailed in the position maintained by leaders of the church. As a scholar of religion, my role was to analyse data, make the results of my analysis widely available and, where relevant and appropriate, engage in debates that my analysis might generate within society. I do not believe personally that HIV/AIDS is caused by witchcraft or evil spirits, but many people do. My obligation is to make public my descriptions and analyses, which draw attention to the fact that a large number of people in Zimbabwe do attribute illness to spiritual causes, so that those constructing policies can act in a more informed manner than they might otherwise do. This is one step removed from direct action, but it is intended to inform action. This is an appropriate way for the scholar to be socially engaged, but it differs markedly from actions I might undertake in other contexts as an individual citizen by participating in various causes, protests or political party meetings.

Conclusion

Following McCutcheon and Chidester, I conclude that the role of the academic is limited to describing social and historical processes that have resulted from institutions of power (both religious and secular), to identifying what effects these processes are having on religion in contemporary contexts, and using these insights to inform the general public – including religious practitioners – about issues relevant to the function of religion in modern society. I disagree with Tremlett that it is the responsibility of the researcher *as researcher* to attempt to correct the errors of those he or she is studying, even when the community uses religion to justify acts of violence. In a much more restricted sense, by interpreting religious beliefs and practices in social contexts, scholars of religion are provided with a key method through which they can offer informed, accessible general comments, while submitting incisive analyses that could assist those responsible for devising and implementing policies.

This, of course, explodes the myth of pure neutrality, but it does not erase the position maintained by those writing in the tradition of the phenomenological study of religion, such as Kristensen, Van der Leeuw and Bleeker, who resisted the persistent threat posed by theologians of reducing religious studies to a branch of Christian theology. My suggestion that the scholar of religion should accept a quite limited role with bounded responsibilities within social contexts avoids the twin errors, on the one hand, of maintaining the indefensible idea that the academic can somehow operate from a position of detached objectivity, and on the other, of confusing political and social actions with critical analysis. My solution has the beneficial side effect that by clearly delineating and demarcating what constitutes the social responsibility of the scholar of religion, religious studies is protected from yet another attempt to conflate its academic mission with theological motivations.

Part III

CLASSIFICATIONS AND DEFINITIONS: ON DELIMITING
THE FIELD OF INDIGENOUS RELIGIONS

Chapter 7

THE TRANSMISSION OF AN AUTHORITATIVE TRADITION: THAT WITHOUT WHICH RELIGION IS NOT RELIGION

Setting the context

The backdrop for this chapter is a debate that is not new, but which persists to this day among students of religion concerning the appropriate relationships between religious studies, theology and the social sciences. Scholars of religion, particularly those writing in the phenomenological tradition, including the seminal Dutch phenomenologist, Gerardus van der Leeuw (1938: 655–8), the historian of religions Mircea Eliade (1969: 6), and Ninian Smart (1984a: 54–8), who founded the first department of religious studies in the United Kingdom at Lancaster in 1967, repeatedly insisted that religion exists as an entity in itself, or as a classification sui generis, which requires specific methodological tools unique to its subject matter that are quite separate from any operating within either theology or the social sciences. It is this claim that has brought charges from numerous contemporary scholars, such as Russell McCutcheon (1997: 23), Robert Segal (1999: 139–63), Donald Wiebe (1999: 141–70) and Paul-François Tremlett (2008: 47), that much academic work that goes under the guise of a 'science' of religion is more akin to theology than to genuine scientific disciplines. For example, Segal (1999: 142) accuses Eliade of adopting a faith stance through his contention that the central component in religion is the sacred, which believing communities apprehend through hierophanies, while Wiebe (1999: 198) argues that Eliade's hermeneutical approach 'is indistinguishable from the religio-theological'. This same point, aimed at the phenomenology of religion in general, has been made by Armin Geertz and Russell McCutcheon, who assert that 'because many of its earlier practitioners were educated in theology ... the phenomenology of religion became a useful discipline that allowed students of religion to pursue their theological interests' (Geertz and McCutcheon 2000: 17)

One of the most biting critiques of the way religious studies emerged as an academic discipline, particularly in the mid-to-late twentieth century, has been expounded by Timothy Fitzgerald in his book, *The Ideology of Religious Studies*, which, although published in 2000, still remains controversial. The most radical part of Fitzgerald's thesis is his contention that the term 'religion' as an analytical category should be abandoned as an essentialist, ideological concept created by theologians for theological purposes. Fitzgerald identifies Ninian Smart as a chief culprit in smuggling theology into the academic study of religions. According to Fitzgerald (2000: 55), Smart is guilty of maintaining 'an essentialist, reified concept of religion and religions' based on the idea that religion is 'a distinctive and analytically separable kind of thing in the world that can be identified and distinguished from non-religious institutions throughout the vast range of human cultures'. This becomes particularly clear when Smart applies his famous dimensional categories to religions, whereby the core of religion is expressed in various observable forms, such as myths, rituals, art and legal institutions. Fitzgerald (2000: 56) claims that 'the imagery is of a primary substance, an essence, taking on some of the secondary properties of the institutional media through which it manifests itself'. This essentialist notion of religion is also implied in Smart's distinction between religious and ideological world-views (Smart 1981: 19–21), or what he refers to as the difference between 'secular ideologies' and 'sacred world-views' (Smart 1995: 14). Fitzgerald (2000: 56) describes this as drawing a line between 'religions proper (Islam, or Buddhism for instance) and religionlike ideologies such as nationalism, Marxism, Maoism, and Freudianism'. Maoism, as a secular ideology, in Smart's thinking, can be analysed according to the dimensional model, just as can Buddhism, but only Buddhism can be regarded as encompassing a genuinely religious world-view because, in Fitzgerald's words, 'it is centred on the transcendent', which defines its core or irreducible essence (2000: 58). This, according to Fitzgerald, demonstrates that Smart's methodology depended on the assumption that a transcendent reality lies at the core of religion. This leads Fitzgerald to conclude, by implication at least, that many scholars working in departments of religious studies continue not only to interpret religion theologically but actually endorse, although at times unwittingly or even surreptitiously, a theological interpretation of religion.

Since I consider myself one who falls within an academic tradition represented broadly by Smart, I have attempted in some of my most recent writings to respond to such critiques by disengaging the concept of 'the sacred' or 'divine' from the core of religion and instead locating the study of religion squarely within social and cultural contexts (see, for example, Cox 2004: 259–64; Cox 2008: 45–57; Cox 2009: 99–116). In pursuit of this aim, in this chapter, I revisit a book by Walter Capps, entitled *Religious Studies: The Making of a Discipline* (1995), which now has attained almost classical status among students of religion. In particular, I am interested in following Capps's discussion of what he calls the sine qua non of religion – that without which religion is not religion. He argues that methodologically the scholar 'must adopt a kind of reductive analytical technique, probing one's way ... to "that without which the subject would not be what it is"' (Capps 1995: 1). He cites examples of attempts to isolate the sine qua non of religion, such as the Kantian emphasis on morality, Schleiermacher's identification of the religious impulse as feeling, and Rudolf Otto on religion as the human relationship to the holy. Capps is relaying what these scholars regarded as the lowest common denominator or the indispensable condition which must be present for anything to fit into the classification 'religion'. In this chapter, I am taking up Capps's challenge that scholars locate the sine qua non of religion as a starting point for my attempt to separate the sacred from religion and thereby disarm the host of recent critics of the role of the phenomenology of religion within the field of religious studies. I hope to establish a theoretical framework whereby we can lay to rest once and for all the dubious connection between the academic study of religion and theology and at the same time maintain a place for religious studies as a broadly based but distinct scholarly discipline.

The idea of a sine qua non of religion

The notion of the sine qua non of anything is related to the philosophical distinction between accidental characteristics and the necessary and sufficient conditions for something to be what it is. In their helpful introduction to philosophy, Popkin and Stroll (1986: 51–2) clarify the differences between accidental, necessary and sufficient conditions by asking what components are necessary for an individual to fit into the category 'brother'. They explain someone who is a brother might have blond hair, but this is not a necessary condition, since many people or even things have blond hair and are not brothers, such as women or dolls. Aristotelian logic would call, in this instance, having blond hair an 'accidental' cause, neither necessary nor sufficient (Sainsbury 1995: 4). A necessary condition for being a brother is that a brother must be male. Of course, that is not sufficient, since a male may have no siblings. A second necessary condition of being a brother is to have at least one sibling, but being a sibling is not sufficient, since women have siblings. Thus, the necessary and sufficient conditions for being a brother are that the person must be male and have at least one sibling.

Locating the sine qua non of religion can be distinguished from defining religion because definitions may extend beyond identifying indispensable conditions and include other characteristics (some of which may be accidental), which augment, clarify or exemplify the necessary conditions. For example, a definition suggested by the American scholars Hall, Pilgrim and Cavanagh (1985: 11) that 'religion is a varied, symbolic expression of, and appropriate response to, that which people deliberately affirm as being of unrestricted value for them', contains what we might call an overly extensive list of necessary conditions, but also includes 'accidental' characteristics, similar to a brother having blond hair. The overly broad nature of this definition is demonstrated by the authors' requirement that religions express themselves symbolically. Of course, this is true, but so do all human activities, including the use of language itself. The presence of symbols might be called a necessary condition for any human activity to occur and as such, when described as indispensable for religion, is so obvious as to be meaningless, or even tautological. Some religions emphasize 'deliberate affirmations', but certainly not all do. Deliberate affirmations in this sense are accidental characteristics of religion since they belong only to some religions.

These distinctions suggest that by calling for a reductive analysis of religion under the banner of the sine qua non of religion, Capps was urging scholars to isolate the most essential characteristic or characteristics of religion which, although necessary, are not necessarily sufficient, for religion to exist. If we consider E. B. Tylor's (1903 [1871], 1: 424) famous 'minimum' definition of religion as 'the belief in Spiritual Beings', we can see immediately that this is not sufficient, since it does not include identifiable communities. I might believe personally in supernatural agents, but I am not a religion. Belief in gods, spirits and deities arguably may constitute a necessary condition on some, but certainly not all, accounts, and therefore cannot operate as a sufficient condition for religion to exist (Cox 2010: 12–13). Definitions of religion, in other words, may be expansive, including far more than is implied by the sine qua non of religion, or they may be restrictive, excluding the necessary and/or sufficient conditions requisite for religion to be religion.

I am aware that by referring to accidental, necessary and sufficient conditions I am entering into a complex philosophical and linguistic discussion (even a minefield), which extends beyond my intention in this chapter. I simply want to identify, following Capps's reductive analysis, what I believe must be present necessarily for religion to exist. The sine qua non of religion on this interpretation must satisfy the necessary conditions for religion to be present, but it is not required to show that the bare minimum of religion also meets the sufficient conditions for something to be called religion. In other words, this is like identifying one of the necessary conditions for a brother to be a brother, either a male or a sibling, but the sine qua non does not have to meet the sufficient conditions. A brother must be a male. Without the condition of maleness, a brother cannot be a brother. In this chapter, I am isolating one condition which must be satisfied without which religion would not be religion, but I am not claiming for this an exclusive condition. Other conditions may be necessary, but I am focusing on one which I regard as an essential, irreducible characteristic necessary for religion to be present in any human activity. Following the lead suggested by the French sociologist Danièle Hervieu-Léger (1999: 88) that 'there is no religion without the explicit, semi-explicit, or entirely implicit invocation of *the authority of a tradition*' (emphasis in original), I contend that the sine qua non of religion is best expressed by the phrase, 'the transmission of an authoritative tradition'. Without a community that is defined by and responds to a tradition that is passed on with authority from generation to generation, religion is absent.

An authoritative tradition is most visible in ritual contexts, where its authority is underscored most forcefully and through which it is transmitted with an overwhelming power. This is because in rituals the transmission of the tradition is symbolized by direct contact with its authoritative source. In rituals, the symbols of the tradition are visible, and sometimes capable of being touched, tasted, smelled or heard. The ritual reinforces the tradition, which it conveys with an authority that stretches back to its source and which is repeated usually in the exact or nearly exact forms that it has been practised for generations – subject to a few alterations, changes or modernizations. In the case of new religious movements, the new tradition is related to an older tradition, either as a reform movement or as a re-invention of that which preceded it. In what follows, I will exemplify my interpretation of the sine qua non of religion by examining two quite different rituals, one drawn from the Indigenous Religions of Zimbabwe and the other from a neo-shamanic group operating in the north-eastern United States.

A case from Zimbabwe

I begin by referring to a rain ritual I have written about previously in research I conducted in the 1990s in Zimbabwe (1998: 87–9). My original discussion of the ritual was in the context of explaining how it could be interpreted by and placed within classifications consistent with the phenomenological method in the study of religion. I want to re-visit the rain ritual in this chapter in light of my claim to have isolated a sine qua non of religion.

The context for the ritual was the severe drought which was occurring throughout southern Africa during the 1991–2 rainy season. The rains had not come in sufficient amounts to sustain the crops and the cattle on which the people depended for their well-being. The normal time to conduct rituals for rain was in September or October, just at the beginning of the rainy season. The ritual I attended was unusual in this regard, since it was held in March, when the rains were due to end. So, in this sense it could be called a crisis ritual rather than a calendrical ritual – one in which the people were appealing to the ancestors to intervene and supply rain, even at such a late date, which would rescue the crops and save the dying cattle.

The ritual occurred in the region of Chief Chingoma in the Mberengwa District of south-central Zimbabwe. The Chief had announced that the ritual would take place prior to my arrival and already had begun preparing for the ceremony. This entailed informing the headmen within his chieftaincy about the forthcoming ritual. Each headman selected dried *rapoko* (millet) seed to contribute to the brewing of traditional beer and brought it to the Chief's residence about a week before the ritual was to be held. It was brewed until it reached a satisfactory level of fermentation under the supervision of women of non-childbearing age.

On the day of the ritual at around 9:00 am, the Chief gathered together his headmen and other elders (around twenty-five men in total) at the place where the ritual was to take place, on a granite outcropping which sloped down to a large *mukamba* (shaped like a tortoise) tree, under which rain rituals were normally performed. Around ten women were also present, but these were seated to the left of the Chief and did not participate in the dialogue he was having with his headmen and the elders. The gist of the Chief's conversation with the headmen and elders concerned the undermining of his authority by Village and Ward Development Committees, which were appointed by the ruling ZANU-PF party. Decisions normally falling to a chief, such as where to construct dams, where to build roads and permission to conduct mining were being overridden by the political appointees in the Village and Ward councils. Of course, for many decades, chiefs had been required to cooperate with various governments over such decisions, but at the very least, they were consulted and made central to the process. Chief Chingoma was complaining about the erosion of his power in his region, even to the point of having to abandon traditional courts, whereby he had customarily settled disputes among various parties living in his chieftaincy.

After around an hour of these discussions, the Chief called for selected women representing each headman to go to the place where the beer had been brewed. A few minutes later, nine women appeared carrying pots of beer on their heads. Each one placed her pot beneath the tree. The participants in the ritual, by now numbering around fifty, moved closer to the tree. Tobacco snuff (*bute*) was passed from person to person, and each one took a deep sniff of it. Some of the people sneezed after breathing the snuff, which traditionally indicates that the ancestor spirits are present. Following this, an old woman dipped a gourd into one of the pots, poured beer at the base of the tree and announced:

> Here is your beer we have prepared for you. Our people are suffering. Our cattle are dying. The crops are failing. There is no rain.

While she was saying this, the men clapped their hands rhythmically and the women ululated (a traditional high-pitched sound uttered by women while they move their hand over their mouth rapidly).

A man who was in charge of distributing the beer then called out the names of the headmen, who came forward and picked up a pot of beer and poured some into smaller containers. Gatherings of people formed and the beer was passed from person to person in the small groups. This beer drinking, which was quite informal, went on for several hours while the people conversed among themselves and some smoked cigarettes. The entire atmosphere was light-hearted and friendly. After a few hours of this informal, relaxed beer drinking and socializing, a few men formed a line to the side of the tree and began dancing to the beating of drums, the shaking of rattles and the occasional blast of a kudu horn.

After the dancing had been going on for around an hour, an old woman began to cry and wail. Someone said, 'She is becoming possessed'. She was taken away from the sight of the participants and re-appeared in dress traditionally worn by a person acting as a medium. She had a headdress with eagle feathers extending out of the top, a black cloth wrapped from her shoulder to her waist, a skirt made from animal skins, and was holding a rattle. She carried a walking stick (*tsvimbo*), which throughout most of Zimbabwe symbolizes the tradition of the ancestors. She joined the group, which had formed a line, and began dancing alongside them in front of the people, parallel with the tree. She was accompanied by the Chief and another man, who I was told later was her ritual assistant. The woman under possession quite noticeably had assumed the characteristics of a man – walking, talking and moving like a man. After around thirty minutes spent dancing, the possessed woman sat down on a natural protrusion extending from the base of the tree, which someone told me was her 'stool'. Around ten people formed around her as she sat on her 'stool', each of whom, I was informed, was a member of the Chief's family. Each member of the Chief's family either knelt or squatted in front of the woman and shook her hand while she said something to them which I could not hear. She then went with the members of the Chief's family around twenty-five metres to the west of the tree and conversed with them for around forty-five minutes. In the meantime, others continued to dance to the drumming, shaking of rattles and blowing of the kudu horn. During the entire ceremony, the beer was continually passed from person, with the containers being replenished from the larger pots beneath the tree. After the meeting with the Chief and his family concluded, the old woman returned, but was dressed in her normal attire – a yellow sweater and a black head bandana. The dancing and beer drinking continued until the beer was finished, about sunset, and the Chief announced that the ritual had come to an end.

In interviews I conducted after the ritual had concluded with Chief Chingoma and his son, who was my MA student in the University of Zimbabwe, I learned that the spirit medium was possessed by the Dunda spirit, one of the Chief's ancestors. According to Chief Chingoma, Dunda told him and his family that the drought was a result of the unhappiness of the ancestors with the undermining of traditional authority by the ZANU-PF government, and that until the Chief's traditional authority was restored, the drought would continue and no rain would fall. The next day I interviewed the spirit medium who had been possessed by Dunda, whose name I learned was Va Empty (so named because she had never been able to bear children). When I asked her the meaning of the ritual, she responded in a terse, almost aphoristic phrase: 'The ancestor never settles on the cockerel, always on the bull.' At first, I did not understand her meaning, but soon it became clear. In traditional Zimbabwean society, the spirit of a senior ancestor, such as an elder in the family, has a bull dedicated in his honour. At certain times, rituals are performed to remember and pay respect to the ancestor, which usually culminates with the sacrifice of the bull dedicated to him (Bourdillon 1987: 27–8). The symbol of the nationalist leader Joshua Nkomo's ZAPU party, prior to its union with ZANU, was the bull. The symbol of the current ZANU-PF ruling party was the cockerel. Nkomo had been regarded by the people in the region as a much more traditional leader than Robert Mugabe, who by that time was president and virtual head of the ruling party. Nkomo, who had been one of the contenders for heading the new government after Independence in 1980, had been marginalized politically in the government headed by Mugabe. Nkomo's visit to the traditional Mwari shrines in 1953 in south-west Zimbabwe, according to Ranger and Ncube (1996: 42), 'became legendary in ZAPU circles'. They explain that 'ZAPU's nationalist ideology had come to incorporate – and to incorporate at many levels – the power and the discourse of African religion' (Ranger and Ncube 1996: 43). As evidence of this, Nkomo was rarely seen without his walking stick (*tsvimbo*), which symbolized his connection as a leader of the nation to the founding ancestral traditions. By contrast, Mugabe was a modern socialist, had spurned the traditions as backward and usually dressed in Western clothing in a suit with a tie (Worby 2003: 49–50). Va Empty's message was clear. The ZANU-PF government had neglected the authority of the chiefs, had side-lined Nkomo and was populating rural areas with decision-making bodies comprising representatives of the ruling party. The ancestors of the chiefs, who extended in a genealogical line all the way back to the founding ancestor and had brought the people into the region in the first place, were offended. In order to relay their displeasure to the government and party rulers, who had usurped the legitimate role of the chiefs as representatives of the ancestors, they had withheld rain and would do so until the rightful authority of the chiefs had been restored.

A neo-shamanic trance dance

I turn now to exemplify my interpretation of the sine qua non of religion from an entirely different context and cultural setting, that of a neo-shamanic trance dance organized by the Lightgate Learning Center in Thetford, Vermont (see also, Cox 2007a: 155–8; Cox 2003: 69–87). In the summer session 2001, I taught a course on shamanism at Dartmouth College in Hanover, New Hampshire as part of an ongoing exchange programme between Edinburgh University and Dartmouth College. I came across literature on the Lightgate Learning Center in a local supermarket in which the Center described itself as 'a gateway to enlightenment for body, mind and spirit' by providing various activities including 'a shamanic journey through soul hunting', 'meditative stretching' and 'trance dance'. The literature from the Center described trance dance as replicating a practice that 'has existed for over 40,000 years' and suggested that people all over the world, independent of religion and culture, engage in trance dance 'to get in touch with greater wisdom and mysteries'. The organizers of the event promised that the dance would have numerous effects on those who participated in it, including purifying the 'body, mind, soul and feelings'. The brochure that described the trance dance experience claimed that it 'is one of the oldest healing rituals we know today'. After reading the literature from the Lightgate Learning Center and reviewing their website, I arranged for my class to participate in a trance dance as part of an experiential learning exercise. This occurred on the evening of 9 August 2001. The trance dance was led by one of the Lightgate staff members, Rahel Kuhne, who was described in the literature as having been 'a passionate Trance Dance presenter since 1994'.

Eight students and I shared in the dance, which took place outside on a lawn behind the Center's house, bordering large grassy fields in a peaceful, rural setting. We sat down on blankets that had been arranged to form a square with candles and burning incense in the middle. Soft instrumental music was playing in the background from a large, sophisticated sound system with multiple speakers. Two other people joined the group, one of whom was an experienced practitioner of trance dancing. After introductions were completed, Rahel explained that dancing is an ancient form of getting in touch with one's inner self, with spirits of animals and nature. She emphasized that entering into trance to experience ecstasy was 40,000 years old, as testified by rock paintings all over the world. She added that trance dance has great healing power by combining body and spirit in a way that produces a deep sense of calm and serenity. She told the group that during the dance, we would encounter various animals, some of which, like the snake, might frighten us. We were assured that we should not be afraid if this happens, since the snake possesses healing properties. Rahel insisted that the entire experience is safe and urged us simply to trust the experience and forget our egos. We were then taught a breathing technique to help us concentrate and to foster the conditions which would enable us to enter a trance. We were instructed to take two deep breaths through the nostrils in quick succession and then exhale through the mouth. In order to avoid feeling self-conscious and to prohibit us from staring at our fellow participants, we were issued with scarves to use as blindfolds. She indicated that when the music begins, we should dance in any way that feels comfortable to us and not to worry about bumping into others, since she would be observing the group's movements and would protect us.

The first noise I heard after standing up and putting on my blindfold was the deep, resonating sound of the sacred Hindu syllable, OM. The 'OM' reverberated over the speakers creating vibrations that I felt throughout my body. After this, various types of music were played, each of which seemed to represent sounds from various parts of the world. I identified the early tracks as African music, with its typical drum beating and shaking rattles. I moved with the rhythm until the music slowed and sounded more ominous with deeper and more powerful beating of the drums, which was accompanied by animal-like sounds. After the music, drum beating and animal sounds had been going on for what I judged to be around thirty minutes, a deep male voice came over the loudspeaker and announced in a slow, sonorous way: 'Trance Dance is 40,000 years old. It has been practised by our ancient ancestors all over the world.' I recall the voice listing as examples of the universal practice of trance dance Australian Aboriginal peoples, the Yoruba of West Africa, Umbanda, Vodou, Native Americans and Siberian shamans. The voice declared, 'They worshipped animals', and then commanded, 'Now, place your feet solidly on the ground and dance as you enter into trance.' This was followed by the sounds of breathing coming over the tape consisting of two quick sniffs and a loud exhaling of breath. The music then began again, comprising variations of Latin American, African and black American melodies. The rhythm would build up to a fast beat and then slow, often with a quiet pause inserted before resuming. Rattles could be heard in the background and animal sounds could be detected, including hissing like a snake. Someone began keeping time with the rhythm by clapping, which was then emulated by others in the group. Suddenly, a very serene choral music was played, which was followed on the tape by the noise of children laughing. The final sound repeated the sacred, vibrating 'OM', which many of the participants joined in saying. Then, there was absolute silence. At this point, Rahel invited us to remove our blindfolds and asked us to be seated again on the blankets. I looked at my watch and noted that we had been dancing for two hours. Rahel explained that we needed a little time to re-enter the world and gather our thoughts before leaving for home.

Implications for the sine qua non of religion

In the examples of the rain ritual in Chief Chingoma's region in south-central Zimbabwe and in the trance dance held in the north-eastern part of the United

States, several components operating together can be identified which support my interpretation of the sine qua non of religion. In both, there was an appeal to a legitimizing tradition, stretching back in time to preceding generations, constituting what Danièle Hervieu-Léger (2000: 65–100) calls a 'chain of memory'. The authority was dramatized and reinforced in each case by the ritual performances.

In the ritual organized by Chief Chingoma, the Chief's ancestor spoke directly to the people, was seen and heard, and could even be touched. The ancestor's message was conveyed with an overwhelming authority which bound the community together and was used to explain events directly affecting the community. The Chief's role as one who represents and preserves traditional authority was reinforced in the ritual and shown to be superior to the authority of the political appointees whose decisions were deemed illegitimate because they did not stem from an authentic tradition that can be traced to quasi-legendary stories relating the feats of the founding ancestors. Without this reference to an overpowering authoritative tradition on which the ritual was based and which was transmitted through the ritual directly, the events occurring within the ritual could not be classified as 'religion'. This is because without the legitimizing authority conveyed in the tradition, which had been passed on from generation to generation, the ritual would not have been binding on the community nor would it have supported the belief-system that gave it meaning and explained events which were causing them suffering. It is only because the message was delivered in the ritual with the force of the authoritative tradition rooted in and reinforced in the memory of the community that it could provide a frame of reference through which the community could make sense of the events which were confronting it. Without the tradition, which legitimated the authority of the ritual, the ritual itself would have been reduced to individual interpretations of its meaning and relegated at best to a kind of entertainment or play-acting. The fact that the authority transmitted could be traced back in time to the source of the tradition is what gave the ritual its irreducibly religious element.

In the case of the trance dance led by a neo-shamanic practitioner, the authority of the ritual event was legitimated by an appeal to a postulated ancient, universal tradition that was alleged to be 40,000 years old. Rahel Kuhen and the voice transmitted during the dance claimed the authority of humanity's Indigenous ancestors, who everywhere entered ecstatic trances, encountered various animal spirits and experienced renewal as a result. Without the 'chain of memory' linking what went on in an isolated field in rural Vermont with an archaic, primordial and universal healing ritual, for the organizers of the trance dance, the meaning of the event would have been reduced to a kind of modern therapy. By appealing to a postulated legitimizing authority, the leaders of the dance could claim a power over the participants that had been transmitted not simply by an experienced and trained leader but by generations of humans whose presence was invoked in the trance dance itself.

It should be noted that for the trance dance to function as it did with its postulated authority over the participants, it was not necessary to affirm beliefs in supernatural agents, gods or deities. The participants engaged with animals, children, drums and music, but these were more like accidental conditions which were used in a utilitarian fashion to create the atmosphere for individuals to enter into trance. The important factor in the entire event, that which gave the dance its force, was its claim to unite the participants with age-old practices of human communities. The dancers were assured that by moving towards the experience of trance, they were tapping into a power that had been present since the dawn of human life itself. It does not matter that this appeal to tradition was entirely alleged, one might even say 'invented'. For our purposes, the claim to legitimization by appealing to the transmission of an authoritative tradition was the focal point of the entire ritual and what gave it its 'religious' dimension.

Conclusion

If we return to where I began this chapter with the example of the necessary and sufficient conditions required for a brother to be a brother, we saw that it is necessary for a brother to be a male, but not sufficient, since not all males are brothers. In the case of religion, I have argued that a necessary or indispensable condition for religion to be present in any human activity requires the existence of a community that is bound by an authoritative tradition. Yet, I have not established that this is a sufficient condition. Since I have not done this, it could be argued that other conditions can be identified which are also indispensable for religion to be religion. Nonetheless, by calling the transmission of an authoritative tradition at the very least a principal sine qua non of religion, I have avoided identifying just one among numerous candidates for this label and thus have side-stepped the error of overly expanding the necessary conditions. My case studies of the rain ritual in Chief Chingoma's region in Zimbabwe and the trance dance conducted under the auspices of the Lightgate Learning Center in Thetford, Vermont confirm Danièle Hervieu-Léger's conclusion that there is no religion without the 'invocation' of the authority of a tradition (1999: 88), the force of which I have shown for any religious community legitimizes or authenticates its tradition. By arguing that without an overpowering authoritative tradition what otherwise might appear to be a religion is not religion, I have met the requirements implied in Capps's challenge to scholars that they analytically reduce the necessary conditions required for religion to exist by heuristically searching for the sine qua non of religion.

If I am correct in my analysis, three conclusions follow which bear directly on the debate to which I referred at the beginning of this chapter concerning the appropriate relationships between religious studies, theology and the social sciences:

1. It still has to be established that religion to be religion also requires as a necessary condition belief in supernatural beings or some kind of spiritual

force; my example of the trance dance suggests that such a belief does not constitute a necessary condition.

2. Religion must involve a community which at the very least asserts its power over individual participants by appealing to an authoritative tradition, even if the community is loosely bound in space and time, and the authoritative tradition is entirely postulated.

3. Religion in its most irreducible form is implicated in other disciplinary studies, as exemplified in my cases, including politics, economics, studies of social structures and linguistic analysis. In this sense, my sine qua non of religion, as a form of reductionism, is set alongside other reductions of human behaviour and, rather than creating an academic competition for the 'best' explanation, complements other explanations – making the study of religion genuinely interdisciplinary.

Chapter 8

REFLECTING CRITICALLY ON INDIGENOUS RELIGIONS

This chapter offers perspectives on the academic study of Indigenous Religions with the aim of identifying, clarifying and exemplifying important theoretical issues in this emerging field in religious studies. I call this an emerging field because the academic study of the religious practices of Indigenous populations, which began in the latter part of the nineteenth century, initially fell to anthropologists, who applied evolutionary theories to interpret the development of human cultures, beginning with the lowest, most primitive peoples, found in small-scale societies with rudimentary means of production and gradually extending to the highest forms of civilization, exemplified in their minds by European culture. Classic examples are found in E. B. Tylor's *Primitive Culture* (1903 [1871]) and J. G. Frazer's *The Golden Bough* (1911–15). Other early studies of Indigenous Religions were found in reports by Christian missionaries, who often gained an intimate knowledge of the languages of the peoples to whom they were delivering the Christian message, but often maintained a somewhat negative attitude towards Indigenous religious practices. The different approaches adopted by early anthropologists and missionaries are exemplified in the case of Australia. During the latter part of the nineteenth century Baldwin Spencer, along with his colleague F. J. Gillen, applied evolutionary theories in their analysis of the central desert peoples of Australia, whereas the Lutheran missionary Carl Strehlow, who learned the languages of the peoples of Central Australia and worked among them for nearly thirty years at the Hermannsburg Mission, never attended an Indigenous ritual and worked hard to discourage his Christian converts from retaining any ties with traditional beliefs and practices (see Spencer and Gillen 1899; Spencer and Gillen 1927; Kenny and Mitchell 2005: 54–70; T. G. H. Strehlow 1971a: xvi).

Anthropological and missionary writers dominated the study of Indigenous Religions well into the twentieth century, although later attitudes differed markedly from those expressed initially in these fields. For example, E. E. Evans-Pritchard, who conducted important studies of the Azande and Nuer peoples of southern Sudan, adopted an empathetic approach to the subjects of his study and, unlike many earlier so-called armchair anthropologists, like Tylor and Frazer, actually lived among African societies for a number of years. Evans-Pritchard attempted to interpret Azande beliefs in witchcraft for a Western audience by showing how, given the world-view and assumptions of the Azande, beliefs in witchcraft and magic were internally consistent and rational. He suggested that the Azande belief in witchcraft 'provides them with a natural philosophy by which the relations between men and unfortunate events are explained and a ready and stereotyped means of reacting to such events' (Evans-Pritchard 1976: 18).

In a similar manner, missionaries, like Edwin W. Smith (1950), who worked in what is now Zambia, and Geoffrey Parrinder (1974), who served in West Africa conducting research in Dahomey (now Benin), identified the Christian God in the pre-Christian beliefs of the Indigenous peoples of Africa and thus sought to reverse the earlier tendency of Christian missionaries to describe Indigenous religious practices as pagan and superstitious. The offshoot of field studies undertaken by those like Evans-Pritchard was a branch of anthropology, called the anthropology of religion. What followed from Smith and Parrinder, and their African followers, like J. S. Mbiti (1970) and E. B. Idowu (1962), was a Christian theology of Indigenous Religions. Although Parrinder pioneered a religious studies department in Ibadan in Nigeria, his approach always followed closely a Christian theological scheme outlining the study of Africa's three religions (Christianity, Islam and African Traditional Religion) in terms of systems, including, and perhaps most importantly for him, belief in a Supreme Being (Parrinder 1976).

The academic study of Indigenous Religions as a separate subject within a department of religious studies was initiated in the 1970s by Andrew Walls and Harold Turner at the University of Aberdeen (Cox 2007a: 22–6). They inherited earlier terminology, which referred to Indigenous Religions as 'primitive', but transformed this into the study of 'primal' religions. Turner (1971) initially employed the phrase 'tribal religions', but soon joined Walls in opting for the nomenclature, 'primal'. The study of Primal Religions as a distinct tradition in a department of religious studies was in the first instance a practical measure. Both Walls and Turner had worked in West Africa, where they encountered numerous Indigenous peoples, some of whom practised variations of traditional rituals, whereas others had adopted missionary forms of Christianity and still others had seemingly blended tradition with Christianity to form new religious movements. This rich field of religious activity could not be covered adequately under the 'world religions' rubric and thus called for a dedicated topic for study in its own right. If students could focus on Buddhism or Hinduism or Islam in departments of religious studies, they ought to be given the opportunity to concentrate their studies on the Primal Religions of the world, and their interactions with global religious movements. Walls (1987: 252) developed the specialized study of Primal Religions to describe what he called the religions of 'circumpolar peoples, ... various peoples of Africa, the Indian sub-continent, South East Asia, North and South America, Australia and the Pacific'. In 1976, a postgraduate course entitled 'Religion in Primal Societies' was launched in the Department of Religious Studies in Aberdeen with the stated aim of:

> providing instruments for the study of the 'primal' (or 'ethnic' or 'traditional') religions characteristic of many societies in Africa, the Americas, Asia and

Oceania, the effects on belief systems, practices and religious institutions of the meeting of these religions with 'universal' religions (notably Christianity and Islam) and the new religious movements arising after contact with Western influences. (Cox 2007a: 22)

The choice of the term 'primal' in place of 'primitive' or 'tribal' on the surface was intended to overcome what Walls (1987: 252) called the 'evolutionistic' connotations associated with 'primitive' and the close connection of 'tribal' to what earlier anthropologists had called 'savage' peoples. Turner (1971: 7) rejected the connotations associated with the word 'primitive' since, he explained, 'it is a great mistake to think that because a tribal society is ... poor in scientific knowledge, tools or agricultural methods, it must also be primitive mentally and in its thinking about human life'. By the mid-1970s, the expression 'primal religions' had even been accepted within the Christian ecumenical movement as a partner in dialogue with Christianity. John B. Taylor, who headed the Unit on Dialogue with People of Living Faiths and Ideologies in the World Council of Churches from the late 1970s to the early 1980s, argued that 'primal' should be substituted for a whole series of other less acceptable terms such as 'pre-literate, primitive, pagan, animistic, primordial, native, ethnic, tribal and traditional' (Taylor 1976: 3–4).

From the academic study of Primal Religions to Indigenous Religions

When Andrew Walls moved from his post in Church History in the Faculty of Divinity in the University of Aberdeen in 1970 to establish the first religious studies department in Scotland, quite deliberately he situated religious studies not in an ancient Scottish Department of Divinity with its close connections to the Church of Scotland, but in the University of Aberdeen's Faculty of Arts and Social Sciences. Walls did this to emphasize that the academic study of religion is a field in its own right and should not be reduced either to the social sciences, in the case of Primal Religions to a field dominated by anthropologists, or to theology. Both Walls and Turner advocated the use of the closely related phenomenological and historical approaches to the study of religion, which they thought were particularly suitable for the study of Primal Religions (McKenzie 1990: 29–33). While acknowledging that the various disciplines in the humanities and social sciences 'can be, and must be applied' to the study of religion, Walls contended that 'the study of religion is a field in its own right' (Walls 1980: 148). In line with the phenomenological method, which privileges the believers' own perspectives as the basis for interpreting religions, Walls explained that 'religion can best understand religion' by which he meant that 'religious commitment' provides the best 'entrance gate' for describing religious practices since it alone leads to understanding from the point of view of adherents (Walls 1980: 143). It was this specifically 'religious' interpretation of religion that Walls applied to the study of Primal Religions, which he argued provides the key for understanding religions everywhere. The case of Africa is illustrative, since throughout sub-Saharan regions 'the old religions' form 'the sub-structure of African Christianity' (Walls 2004: 215). In this sense, Walls believed that the study of Primal Religions was a precondition for understanding religion in all its forms everywhere.

By the 1980s, the study of Primal Religions as a subject in its own right was making inroads into academic departments internationally. This was due, in part, to the large number of postgraduate students the Aberdeen department attracted from its founding in 1970 and by the international reputation obtained by the Centre for the Study of Christianity in the Non-Western World, which Walls launched at Aberdeen in 1982. Due to severe cuts in the academic programme at the University of Aberdeen in the mid-1980s, in 1986 Walls moved the Centre for the Study of Christianity in the Non-Western World to the University of Edinburgh where he, along with his colleague John Parratt, introduced the study of Primal Religions into the Edinburgh Religious Studies curriculum (Cox and Sutcliffe 2006: 9–10). When I arrived at the University of Edinburgh in 1993 from the University of Zimbabwe, I taught the Primal Religions section in the introductory undergraduate course on world religions and taught sections of the African Primal Religions postgraduate course in the Centre for the Study of Christianity in the Non-Western World. I also worked closely with Kwame Bediako, who was the African Christianity Lecturer in Edinburgh each year for three months from 1993 until 1998, and who was a leading exponent of a theological interpretation of Primal Religions in Africa (Cox 2007a: 26–9).

In 1996, I published an article in the newly founded Edinburgh journal, *Studies in World Christianity*, in which I criticized the term 'primal' for veiling theological assumptions (Cox 1996c: 35–56). My reasoning was based on the conviction that, as it was conceived originally by Walls and Turner, 'primal' did more than fill an academic gap in religious studies by using a descriptive category phenomenologically and historically; it clearly conveyed an ideological message. Primal Religions were presented as antecedent to universal religions and as providing the foundation on which all the world's religions are based. Turner defined primal as referring to the 'most basic or fundamental religious forms in the overall history of mankind' having 'preceded and contributed to the other great religious systems' (Cited in Shaw 1990: 341). Walls (1988: v) argued that 'primal religions ... underlie all other religions', adding that 'though we think of ourselves as Christians, Buddhists, Muslims or unbelievers, we are all primalists underneath'.

The assertion that all religions share an original primordial base has clear connections to the Christian missionary theory of fulfilment. It is but a short step from the notion that all religions share a common primal base to the Christian idea that Christ sits at the pinnacle of all the world's religions and fulfils their highest strivings. This is just what Bediako implied when he described Africa as the 'receptor culture' for the Christian message. It is a 'receptor' in the sense that 'African pre-Christian religious cultures' not only provide 'a valid carriage for the divine revelation', but they also provide 'the idiom for Christian apprehension' (Cited in Cox 1998a: 28).

When I was appointed convener of Religious Studies in the University of Edinburgh in 1999, I worked to change the nomenclature used in the Department from Primal Religions to Indigenous Religions. I set up a cluster of courses which enabled undergraduates to study Indigenous Religions as a discrete religious tradition. I followed the lead of Andrew Walls at Aberdeen in three respects. First, I envisaged the importance of Indigenous Religions as a part of a religious studies programme very much in the same way he had done, including the manner by which Indigenous religious practices had interacted and continue to interact with universal religions. In other words, I sought to fill a gap that was evident in most religious studies departments, which continued to be dominated by their emphasis on the study of 'world religions'. I also followed Walls by arguing that the study of Indigenous Religions in departments of religious studies is quite distinct from how it had been and still is treated by anthropologists or other scholars in the social sciences. I emphasized that the phenomenology of religion, accompanied by the history of religions, offers an approach not replicated in other parts of university programmes. Finally, I maintained with Walls that the study of Indigenous Religions is separate from Christian theology by insisting that Indigenous Religions be taught in an empathetic manner, while at the same time developing descriptive, non-judgemental and hence non-normative interpretations of Indigenous beliefs and practices. I differed from Walls over his argument that Primal Religions provide the foundation for all religions and that 'we are all primalists underneath'. I contended that this interpretation, although not strictly a theological statement, was highly useful for theology and thus would be better replaced by a term that was completely free from theological connections. I suggested that the term 'indigenous' provided a far better descriptor than primal as being consistent with phenomenological and historical methods.

Problems of definition

At first, the substitution of 'indigenous' for 'primal' in the academic programme at Edinburgh was done rather uncritically, apart from clearly separating the study of Indigenous Religions from associations it might have with theological or missionary assumptions. In introductory lectures on Indigenous Religions, I relied, at least in part, on the list of characteristics developed at Aberdeen by Philippa Baylis in her booklet, *Introduction to Primal Religions*, which she produced for her students based on Harold Turner's earlier publication, *Living Tribal Religions*. Following Turner, Baylis (1988: 3) identified six main characteristics of Primal Religions:

1. They cannot be separated from society as a whole. Everything, including work, family relationships, eating, sexual activity and so on are all 'religious'.
2. Primal Religions are local as opposed to universal.
3. Primal Religions are tolerant of other religions and readily adapt aspects of other religions into their own world-views.
4. Primal Religions are ethnocentric and non-missionary; they never seek converts.

5. Primal Religions are non-literate; they convey their beliefs and practices orally.
6. No creeds or statements of faith are found in Primal Religions; they are non-systematic in Western terms.

It soon became apparent to me that some of these characteristics were secondary to what I meant by an Indigenous Religion and that clarification was required if we were to maintain a sensible approach to the study of Indigenous Religions as a generic category. Many of the features on Baylis's list could be applied to other 'non-Indigenous' religions. For example, it could be argued that all religions, in their pure form, urge their adherents to integrate every activity of life with the central tenets of faith. The separation of 'religion' from 'non-religion' only makes sense in Western, secularized societies. Or, all religious traditions, even those traditions of the 'book', like Judaism, Christianity and Islam, originally were oral in nature. And certainly, not every religion with a universal cosmology, such as non-dualistic philosophical Hinduism, is dogmatic in nature by insisting that a particular belief is exclusively true and necessary for salvation. Being non-missionary is not a characteristic exclusive to Indigenous Religions.

Andrew Walls was aware of the overly simplistic characteristics conveyed in some of the items on Baylis's list and offered an interpretation of how Primal Religions could be fitted into a universal phenomenological scheme. He divided religions into the following classifications:

1. God-dominated systems, which by definition are theistic, represented quite obviously by the great monotheistic religions, but also found in many African religions.
2. Divinity-dominated systems, in which numerous deities are addressed in rituals, as is evident in many West African religions.
3. Ancestor-dominated systems, where religious attention is paid primarily to kinship spirits.
4. Power-dominated systems, where ritual attention is focused on objects of power, normally impersonal, as might be found in some African societies in which manipulation of power (sometimes called magic) prevails, rather than appeals to personal or living spirits (Walls 1987: 254–5).

It is clear that these typologies are ranked by their relative proximity to beliefs about God, where the transcendent is paramount, with impersonal power the furthest away, as Walls (1987: 255) puts it, where 'the hypostatization of the transcendent ... is slight'. On this scheme, Primal Religions are classified not according to rather vague criteria as demonstrated, for example, by the ideas that they do not separate religion from other aspects of life or that they are non-missionary in nature, but by the variations they demonstrate in their beliefs about transcendence. This has the advantage of refusing to classify all Primal Religions by placing them within one category (such as non-literate) and it is highly useful for understanding changes affecting those Primal Religions that are ancestor or power-dominated when they encounter religions that are God-dominated. It suffers from the distinct disadvantage that it measures religions according to criteria dictated by the category 'transcendence' and hence can be accused of a Christian bias. In this sense, Walls's typologies offer little improvement over Parrinder's earlier systematic categories organized with African beliefs in God at the pinnacle.

These early attempts to identify the principal characteristics of Primal Religions, and as they were rather uncritically assimilated by substituting the term 'indigenous' in the Religious Studies course in Edinburgh, led me to work on narrowing the definition of Indigenous Religions to achieve clarity about what key properties differentiate an Indigenous religion from other types of religion. I regarded this as a necessary prerequisite for empirical studies to be undertaken among Indigenous societies, and essential if the results of such studies were to be tested scientifically. I sought to do this in my book published in 2007, *From Primitive to Indigenous: The Academic Study of Indigenous Religions.* In the remainder of this chapter, I want to reaffirm how I defined Indigenous Religions in that book, and then consider competing definitions, which I did not address specifically there. I will conclude with some further reflections on why we need a classification in the first place and try to address the still unanswered problem as to why 'indigenous' offers a clear improvement over the expression 'primal', or indeed other terms that have been used or suggested as alternatives.

An empirically testable definition of Indigenous Religions

In *From Primitive to Indigenous*, I identified two principal characteristics of Indigenous Religions: (1) Indigenous religious beliefs, rituals and social practices focus on ancestors and hence have an overwhelming emphasis on kinship relations; (2) they identify exclusively with a specific geographical place (Cox 2007a: 68–71). These primary characteristics demonstrate that Indigenous Religions are localized rather than universal and that their religious beliefs and practices apply only within a particular and quite restricted cosmological framework.

The first identifying characteristic of Indigenous Religions accentuates the point that Indigenous belief systems and social structures revolve around ancestors. Myths of origin often relate, in quasi-legendary language, tales about how the people were established in the land in the first place, either by autochthonous ancestors, who brought the people into being often by miraculous feats, or by founding ancestors, who led the people to the land they now occupy. Contemporary beliefs, which are derived ultimately from the foundational myths, focus on how ancestors relate actively to living communities by maintaining a reciprocal relationship with them. The descendants must regularly honour their ancestors ritually and follow the social regulations they originally established. In exchange, the ancestors protect their descendants from misfortunes and the potentially malignant interference of alien spirits or witches. Ancestral traditions stretch back beyond the memory of living communities, but even those who are long forgotten are remembered in rituals, since the more recently deceased are honoured by name and are able to convey the respect of the people in a chain stretching all the way back to the original ancestors.

In this sense, Indigenous Religions are restricted by kinship relations. One is born into an extended family or one marries into it. Marriage regulations are carefully controlled to ensure that kinship ties are preserved and that traditional relationships between different kinship groups are observed. The particular social role ancestors occupy in the tradition varies according to the way the Indigenous society is organized, some being hierarchical, others more egalitarian, some patrilineal, others matrilineal, but the one factor they share in common is that they are all defined by and limited to patterns of kinship. This means that, unlike religions with universal cosmologies, one can never be converted into an Indigenous society, since ancestors belong only to precise kinship groups (Platvoet 1993: 29–48; Cox 2007a: 61–71).

The second primary characteristic of Indigenous Religions stresses that they are restricted not only by kinship ties, but to a particular place fixed in the tradition by their quasi-legendary myths. Foundational stories are relayed to the young and passed on from generation to generation. These local myths form the background on which rituals performed regularly in honour of the ancestors are conducted. When misfortunes occur, explanations are sought to explain why the ancestors have withheld their protection. The reasons given usually point to the failure of the descendants to remember the ancestors in rituals or they refer to some serious social infraction committed within the community that offends the ancestors. The resulting series of catastrophic events can only be rectified when the ancestors are reconciled to the community, almost always by performing rituals aimed at restoring relations with the ancestors and by making compensation to injured parties for infringing traditional social mores. The problems encountered by communities, including divining the causes and prescribing proper treatments, occur exclusively within specific geographical regions over which the ancestors are responsible and do not extend beyond the boundaries of their traditional authority.

In the contemporary world, Indigenous peoples are still defined by ancestral traditions and location, even though they may no longer reside in the place from which they originate. They continue to identify with the land out of which their ancestors mythically emerged or where according to legend they led their people and established their traditions. Frequently, Indigenous people who live in urban settings do not regard the cities in which they live as their 'home'. Often, they return to their rural homesteads or traditional centres to perform rituals and honour their ancestors. Even Indigenous groups living in diaspora, who may have moved to entirely different continents, still identify themselves with their homelands and their ancestors. They may even perform rituals from distant locations in praise of their original ancestors (Ralls-MacLeod and Harvey 2000: 4–5).

Kinship and location, as irreducible, defining qualities, provide students of religion with clear, testable and scientific criteria for denoting what is and what is not an Indigenous religion. For example, it would be clear according to these standards that the various expressions of Australian Aboriginal Religions are

Indigenous Religions. They fundamentally relate to ancestors and are limited to specific locations where their ancient ancestors travelled and settled, bringing the people who now live in these locations into being (Bell 2001: 177–92). Judaism, on the other hand, provides a more ambiguous case. It clearly identifies with a place and in the broadest sense might be considered a religion of kinship that is traceable back to the founding ancestor, Abraham. Jewish cosmology could be construed as ethnocentric, since it is restricted to the God of Israel. Nonetheless, it is more likely that in its early history the people of Israel might have been considered to have practised an Indigenous religion, since their god was a tribal god amongst other deities. Nowadays, this normally cannot be applied strictly to Jewish theology, which describes the God of the Hebrew Scriptures as the Creator of the universe (Bowker 1997: 512–14). On my analysis, in accordance with a scientific method, no matter which cases are being considered, the religious beliefs and practices of any community can be designated as Indigenous only if their central belief focuses on ancestors and their primary identity is defined by its relation to a specific geographical location.

Competing theories of Indigenous Religions and their problems

The English word 'indigenous' is derived from the Latin term *indigena* meaning 'native' and can be interpreted as referring to the religion of a people who were the original occupants or the autochthonous inhabitants of a particular location. This is precisely the way that Alan Barnard and Justin Kenrick apply the term when they refer to the so-called Bushmen of southern Africa as 'indigenous'. They write: 'Those known as Bushmen, San Basarwa, Ju'hoan, Kua, Khoe or N/oakhoe, have, according to some specialists, a cultural continuity in those lands of perhaps 400 centuries' (Barnard and Kenrick 2001: viii). If we were to restrict the study of Indigenous Religions to those who can be regarded as 'original', like the San Bushmen of southern Africa or many Aboriginal peoples of Australia or the 'first peoples' of North America, the scope of our research would be reduced significantly and, to a large extent, would become more and more marginalized as 'original' peoples are increasingly displaced by or absorbed into modern cultures. The study of Indigenous Religions then would be limited to the religions of so-called disappearing populations, or the study would be consigned to reviewing historical records of early encounters by missionaries, explorers and colonial officers with Indigenous societies, studying evidence of pre-historic cultures produced by archaeologists or, in some cases, analysing language usage.

Restricting the term 'indigenous' to autochthonous populations is neither necessary nor is it desirable for two reasons. First, it overlooks the fact that populations around the globe for centuries have migrated and have conquered lands, oftentimes displacing those who were living originally in the region. The Shona peoples of Zimbabwe present a case in point. It is estimated that the Shona formed part of the movement of Bantu populations southwards across Africa, arriving in what is now Zimbabwe perhaps as early as the second century CE

(Bourdillon 1987: 6–10). They would have found already living there the nomadic, hunting and gathering peoples referred to by Barnard and Kenrick. The Shona, who were agricultural and hence sedentary, eventually caused the original inhabitants to move south and west into parts of the current South Africa and Botswana. In the early nineteenth century, a Zulu people from South Africa, the Ndebele, invaded Shona lands in southwest Zimbabwe and either assimilated the Shona into their own culture or forced them to move north and east (Berens 1987: 288–9). Today, both the Shona and Ndebele claim Indigenous status in Zimbabwe despite neither being original inhabitants of the land. This suggests that Indigenous cannot be limited strictly to its denotative meaning as 'original' but must be applied more widely to take into account historical movements of peoples into regions, sometimes several thousands of years ago.

A second problem in defining Indigenous as original is exemplified in the case of Australia, where the meaning of the designation 'Aboriginal' has been the subject of discussion and has involved legal rulings defining the boundaries of the category. The word, Aboriginal, like Indigenous, literally refers to those who have lived in a land since earliest times, but nowadays it is not employed exclusively to refer to the original inhabitants of the land but takes into account over two hundred years of occupation by European settlers and years of ethnic mixing. This makes it virtually impossible to determine if many people who identify as Aboriginal are literally 'original' or 'autochthonous'. Demonstrating a line of descent may be difficult in some cases, and thus oral history within families may also be considered as relevant. The Australian situation demonstrates that if we mean by an Indigenous Religion the religious practices of people who are original to a location, it will be extremely difficult to delineate which groups or individuals actually can be fitted into this classification.

Another competing definition of Indigenous, largely developed out of legal rulings in Australia and emphasized by international organizations, identifies self-designation as a primary criterion for meeting the requirement for being classified as an Indigenous person or group. Australian courts have ruled that an Aboriginal person must be able to demonstrate some line of descent from pre-European peoples, but they have also included among the criteria self-designation as Indigenous and acceptance as such by an Aboriginal community (Australian Law Reform Commission: https://www.alrc.gov.au/publication/essentially-yours-the-protection-of-human-genetic-information-in-australia-alrc-report-96/36-kinship-and-identity/legal-definitions-of-aboriginality). International efforts to define what is meant by an Indigenous population, just as in Australia, have emphasized self-designation, either by an individual or a group, as Indigenous, although this has never resulted in a legally sanctioned definition. The International Labour Organization, in its Convention 169 called 'self-identification as indigenous a fundamental criterion for determining the groups to which the provisions of this Convention apply' (International Labour Organization 1989).

Self-designation as a criterion for determining communities that practise Indigenous Religions suffers from being extremely vague and, at the same time, is subject to much modern manipulation. Self-designating as 'Indigenous' makes it nearly impossible to delineate empirically what is an Indigenous Religion and who belongs to an Indigenous religious community, as is evident in numerous efforts by 'new age' groups to claim indigeneity by referring to postulated links to primordial religious practices (Cox 2007a: 155–8). In the context of Australia, problems of an overly expansive definition resulting from self-designation as a criterion for qualification as Aboriginal have been underscored by Larissa Behrendt, Professor of Law and Indigenous Studies at the University of Technology Sydney, who commented:

> If we're going to talk about treaties and recognition of rights, the question of who's in and who's out is going to be the most important issue facing indigenous Australians. If that isn't resolved, you run the risk of having the parameters stretched to the ludicrous point where someone can say: 'seven generations ago there was an Aboriginal person in my family, therefore I am Aboriginal' (Cited in Australian Law Reform Commission, section 36.32: https://www.alrc.gov.au/publication/essentially-yours-the-protection-of-human-genetic-information-in-australia-alrc-report-96/36-kinship-and-identity/legal-definitions-of-aboriginality).

A third contested theory for defining an Indigenous population and thus those who practise an Indigenous Religion refers to peoples who have been the subject of colonization and who as a result have become marginalized in society. In the second meeting of the United Nations Working Group on the Rights of Indigenous Populations in 1986, Martinez Cobo, the Special Rapporteur to the United Nations Subcommission on Prevention of Discrimination and Protection of Minorities, defined Indigenous peoples as those who 'having a historical continuity with pre-invasion and pre-colonial societies … consider themselves distinct from other sectors now prevailing in those territories'. They are distinct by being 'non-dominant' but at the same time are 'determined to preserve, develop and transmit to future generations their ancestral territories and their ethnic identity' (Cited in Australian Law Reform Commission, section 36.30: https://www.alrc.gov.au/publication/essentially-yours-the-protection-of-human-genetic-information-in-australia-alrc-report-96/36-kinship-and-identity/legal-definitions-of-aboriginality). This would mean that students of Indigenous Religions would focus on the religions (and new religions) of peoples who have been the victims of colonial expansion and cultural suppression, and who are now, often quite recently, re-discovering and re-inventing what they can know about their pre-colonial religious traditions. This could be applied, for example, to Australian Aborigines, Native Americans and in some sense to the Māori of New Zealand.

This definition of Indigenous applies in certain parts of the world, but generally not in Africa, where the 'Indigenous' population, although tracing itself to pre-colonial times, no longer is 'non-dominant' in the society. In Zimbabwe, for example, religious practices that are kinship orientated and restricted to specific geographical locations are found virtually everywhere. Although such localized religions were subjected to suppression by the European settlers and were often condemned by Christian missionaries, they were never eliminated or replaced by Christianity. In the postcolonial situation, it is not correct to say that they have been revived, but it is more accurate to indicate that they persist and continue to influence everyday life, particularly in rural Zimbabwe. Of course, the performance of traditional ancestral rituals has been affected by over one hundred years of European influence, Western education and modern economic systems, but the study of Indigenous Religions in Zimbabwe is not defined by the efforts of an oppressed minority to recover what was largely eradicated by the powerful invaders (Cox 2007a: 119–39). In other situations, however, this is the case, in Alaska, for example, where Indigenous religious practices largely disappeared by 1950 (Cox 2007a: 95–117).

Although they are not irrelevant for determining what constitutes an Indigenous Religion and what does not, definitions based exclusively on claims to belonging to an original population, to self-designating as Indigenous or to political concerns related to power and cultural revival movements make the study of what is meant by Indigenous Religions unclear, vague and difficult to test empirically. For this reason, I have argued that religions that are localized and kinship-orientated and which relate fundamentally to a place constitute the primary and essential criteria for defining Indigenous Religions. Rival definitions, as I have just discussed, and some of the secondary characteristics as shown on the list compiled by Philippa Baylis, can add to and augment the primary criteria, but they are not universally applicable, are not always empirically testable and often are so vague as to make the category largely vacuous. The study of Indigenous Religions, as I have defined them, does not consign the field to the study of limited and shrinking populations, since, as Andrew Walls and Harold Turner pointed out in Aberdeen in the 1970s, the interaction between local and universal religions and the relationships between tradition and modernity identify rich and varied resources for students of religion.

Some concluding reflections

In the end, we are still left with a term that is inadequate, partly because we are attempting to create a general and inclusive category that can apply to diverse peoples around the globe. As I have just pointed out, some groups may have legitimate claims to be original or autochthonous, others may best be defined by cultural revival movements in response to colonial oppression and still others may assert their right to be called Indigenous even if the justification for such a claim might be regarded by other self-defined Indigenous groups as spurious. This is why I have argued that any definition of 'Indigenous' must be limited, specific and clearly delineate what we mean by the term.

Given the difficulties in agreeing on a definition of 'Indigenous', it would appear reasonable to question the need for a general category in the first place. Why can we not simply discuss specific cultural groups in terms of their history, developments, transformations and responses to modernity? It is clear that no overarching universal classification can be constructed without filling it with particular entities that fit into the classification. But we need such a general category precisely in order that we can make sense of the particular entities that can be fitted into it and so, additionally, we can engage in comparative studies. This conclusion merely restates the age-old philosophical contention that naming, classifying and comparing are fundamental components of human logic and are necessary for communication and understanding to proceed (Smart 1999: 138–41). For example, if I say to you that I am sitting on a chair, it might help if I indicate that it is a desk chair, an easy chair, a wooden chair or a kitchen chair. Nonetheless, you will know in general what I mean by a chair without my having to fill in all the specific details. Because we have a general category called 'chairs', it is possible to compare and contrast examples of chairs, but also to note differences between chairs and tables or chairs and trees. Chairs, of course, could fall under a larger category, called furniture or they could be classified according to the material out of which they are formed and hence could be treated, in the example of wooden chairs, as a sub-category of trees, and so on.

By defining Indigenous Religions as kinship orientated and restricted to location, just like the classification chair, we know what we mean by the general category, but within the larger classification we find a multiplicity of specific groups that make up the whole. This also enables us to put the classification 'Indigenous' within the even broader category called 'religions', for comparative purposes, but also for describing and analysing the complex relationships that different types of religions have with one another from historical, sociological, economic, political, cultural and other perspectives. This is far different from creating a metaphysical entity or an essentialist category. Rather, it is a pragmatic way of speaking about types of communities and noting their characteristics, processes that are necessary for communication about them to proceed and for a common understanding of them to be achieved.

Finally, the term 'indigenous' as the preferred nomenclature to' primal' or any other alternative suggestion for an overarching classification into which we can fit localized ancestral traditions is confirmed by clearly delineated academic criteria. Most other designations suffer from two related problems, which have been identified and addressed thoroughly within the phenomenology of religion (Cox 2010: 24–47). The first problem results from the tendency of categories other than 'Indigenous' to impose values or biases from the outside. This in turn leads to the second obstacle that such imposed classifications cannot be affirmed by adherents as accurate and fair descriptions of their own communities. Primal, as I have shown, has been developed out of a Christian theological position and carries with it a biased perspective associated with Christian evangelization, which could never be affirmed by those who practise Indigenous Religions. Older terms like animistic, primitive, tribal, ethnic, non-literate or pre-literate have been discussed and largely rejected because they convey judgemental or prejudicial attitudes towards the groups to which they are referring, and like 'primal' generally are offensive to practitioners. Although 'Indigenous' is literally associated with original peoples, it avoids the biases or ideological connections contained in other classifications, and the term has been accepted both amongst international organizations and within groups who self-identify as Indigenous. This does not transform either the global or local dimensions of the term into a definition, as I have pointed out, but it confirms that the concept 'Indigenous' has been accepted widely among non-Indigenous international circles and at the same time has been embraced by groups claiming Indigenous status. In accordance with phenomenological principles, this makes the term both objective in the sense of finding a clear definition from the outside and subjective in that it is embraced by those from the inside who fit into the category. Although no classification is without limitations, and certainly this is the case with the term 'Indigenous', it is necessary that we employ a far-reaching concept that is generally accepted by a wide range of international constituencies, but which also proves inoffensive to the groups that fit into the category. As well as satisfying the pragmatic aim of achieving an agreed meaning on social, political, economic and cultural levels, these criteria meet the academic goal of inclusivity by reflecting both outsider and insider perspectives.

Chapter 9

KINSHIP AND LOCATION: IN DEFENCE OF A NARROW DEFINITION OF INDIGENOUS RELIGIONS

The category 'Indigenous Religions' has become widely accepted within university departments of religious studies as the preferred nomenclature to designate what Graham Harvey (2013a: 19) calls 'the majority of the world's religions', perhaps not in terms of the number of adherents, but as a persistent force, either directly or indirectly, in the majority of societies around the world. Harvey (2013a: 19) explains that Indigenous Religions 'present an elaborate and wonderful array of different ways of being human, doing ritual, inculcating ideas, dwelling in the world, imagining the cosmos and so on'. If one pushes Harvey's claims very far, it soon becomes apparent that what he means by Indigenous Religions needs careful consideration if the term is to be useful and not subject to multiple misunderstandings and misinterpretations. It is for this reason that scholars need to be quite precise about how they employ both parts of the classification, 'religions' and 'indigenous'. In this chapter, I begin by restating briefly my own precise definitions of religion and indigenous as I have presented them in previous publications (Cox 2007a: 53–93; Cox 2009: 99–116; Cox 2010: 1–23). I then summarize some of the chief criticisms that have been levelled against my definition of Indigenous Religions, and conclude by offering a robust defence of my interpretation of the category.

Danièle Hervieu-Léger and a restricted definition of Indigenous Religions

In several publications, I have developed a theory of religion based in part on the work of the French sociologist, Danièle Hervieu-Léger. I devoted a section in my book, *From Primitive to Indigenous: The Academic Study of Indigenous Religions* (2007a: 75–93), to applying Hervieu-Léger's theory towards developing a restricted definition of religion. Initially, I analysed an article Hervieu-Léger (1999: 73–92) wrote under the title 'Religion as Memory' that appeared in a book edited by Jan Platvoet and Arie Molendijk called *The Pragmatics of Defining Religion* (1999) and then I drew out themes from her book first published in English in 2000 under the title *Religion as a Chain of Memory*. Most recently, I proposed a reductive definition of religion, a position in which, following the work of Walter Capps

(1995: 1), I identified the sine qua non of religion (that without which religion is not religion) as the transmission of an authoritative tradition that is passed on from generation to generation and thereby enshrined in the collective memory of identifiable communities (Cox 2013a: 308–23).

In this section, I review my use of Hervieu-Léger and explicitly apply her analysis to what I argue is the necessary and essential component within a definition of religion. In her article appearing in the Platvoet-Molendijk volume, Hervieu-Léger (1999: 77) introduces her section on defining religion by quoting from Durkheim's opening statement in his *Elementary Forms of Religious Life*:

> It is necessary to begin by defining what is meant by a religion: for without this, we would run the risk of giving the name to a system of ideas and practices which has nothing at all religious about it, or else of leaving to one side many religious facts, without perceiving their true nature. (Durkheim 1915: 23)

Hervieu-Léger (1999: 77) is aware that many social scientists have avoided all definitions of religion, preferring, as she says, 'to leave the "theorizing" to the philosophers'. Sociologists of religion, in particular, simply studied as religion precisely those activities 'which the society itself designated as "religious"' (Hervieu-Léger 1999: 78). This position, she argues, can no longer be maintained in light of 'the modern proliferation of belief' (as witnessed by the upsurge of religious activity internationally) and 'the de-regulation of the domain of institutionalized religion' (as evidenced by the emphasis on individual choice in the quest for private religious or spiritual meaning) (Hervieu-Léger 1999: 78). This does not entail a return to a search for a phenomenological 'essence' of religion, but it is necessary to be equipped with a definition of religion 'which simply allows for the classification of observable phenomena' (Hervieu-Léger 1999: 78).

It is important to understand that Hervieu-Léger's discussion of the definition of religion was developed in the context of sociological theories of secularization, particularly in light of the argument that was maintained well into the 1960s that religion had entered into the last phases of an inevitable decline as society had come increasingly under the sway of scientific rationalism. Jeffrey Hadden (1987: 588) calls this a forecast 'anchored in a broad sweeping theory of secularization, which, in turn, is nested in an even broader theory of modernization'. He adds: 'Secularization ... is ... properly described as a general orienting concept that causally links the decline of religion with the process of modernization' (Hadden 1987: 598).

Hervieu-Léger suggests that the predictions of the demise of religion have been proved wrong by the contemporary situation but in a quite ambiguous way. On the one hand, in line with the secularization thesis, society in the West has for many years been experiencing the 'evaporation of the socio-religious link which once constituted long-term support for the construction of a religious culture encompassing aspects of social life', but, on the other hand, we are witnessing the unexpected or at least unanticipated wide dissemination of religious belief (Hervieu-Léger 1999: 76). This latter phenomenon suggests that 'religion still speaks. But it doesn't speak in those areas where one might expect', that is, within institutions like churches or mosques or through official channels of the historical religions (Hervieu-Léger 1999: 76). Rather, 'one discovers its presence, diffuse, implicit or invisible, in economics, politics, aesthetics, in the scientific, in the ethical and in the symbolic' (Hervieu-Léger 1999: 76). This wide dissemination of religion in modern life makes defining religion at once extremely difficult, but necessary. The scholar needs to know what to investigate as 'religion' when describing and analysing what Hervieu-Léger (1999: 76) calls 'the diverse surreptitious manifestations of religion in all profane and reputedly non-religious zones of human activity'.

One resolution to the problem of defining religion in modernity is to opt for a quite restricted or substantive definition, one that limits religion to beliefs in supernatural agents or even a belief in God. This confines religion in ways that would exclude what are sometimes called 'religion-like' activities as displayed in nationalism, Marxism or even in great sporting events. I discovered in my research undertaken in 2013 on non-religion among Australian Aboriginal peoples (Cox and Possamai 2016) that this restricted or limited definition was precisely the approach taken by the Australian Bureau of Statistics (ABS) when it formulated the 2011 census question on religion. The ABS (2011: 1266.0) defined religion as 'belief in a Supernatural Being, Thing or Principle'. For this reason, the ABS refused to classify Marxism as a religion because it lacked 'any supernatural or spiritual component' (ABS 2011: 1266.0).

The other main way of defining religion is unrestricted or open, when, for example, calling any belief that provides meaning for a person a religious belief. This could include almost anything, including families, jobs, hobbies or allegiance to ideological causes. The important aspect within this functional approach to defining religion is its diffuse and imprecise character. Hervieu-Léger cites Thomas Luckmann's (1967) discussion of 'invisible religion' as an example of this approach in which, she says, Luckmann defined religion in a way that encompasses 'the entirety of the imaginary constructs whereby society, groups within this society, and individuals within these groups, try to give meaning to their everyday experience' (Hervieu-Léger 1999: 78).

Hervieu-Léger argues that substantive definitions tend to restrict the study of religions to the 'historical' religions. This has the perhaps unintended effect of turning students of religion into the protectors and guardians of 'authentic religion' (Hervieu-Léger 1999: 83). This criticism could be levelled at the interpretation of religion provided by the ABS which coded, for example, Jedism as 'not defined', despite the fact that over 64,000 people wrote in Jedism as their religion on the 2011 Australian national census (ABS 2011: 1266.0; see also, ABS: https://www.abs. gov.au/census/find-census-data/historical). By contrast, functional or expanded definitions are so broad, according to Hervieu-Léger (1999: 83), that they 'turn out to be incapable of mastering the unlimited expansion of the phenomena they try to account for'. In other words, they become so broad that they are tantamount to saying anything can be religion, or, as Graham Harvey (2013b) argues in his provocative book, *Food, Sex and Strangers*, for religious people 'everything is religious'. Harvey provides a particularly good example of a scholar who advocates a broad, even vague, approach to defining religion, as exemplified in the conclusion to his book where he asserts that religion is about relationality (2013b: 210), and not just or primarily among humans, but includes the relation of human persons to 'other than human persons' (Harvey 2013b: 202–3).

Hervieu-Léger contends that the problem of defining religion cannot be resolved by siding either with a substantive or functional approach, but by analysing the dynamic transformations that are occurring within society. In this sense, she would agree with Harvey that religion is relational, but in contrast to Harvey, Hervieu-Léger approaches her definition from an entirely sociological perspective. For Hervieu-Léger, religion is not defined ontologically or theologically, or, as one might argue in the case of Harvey, in terms of a particular ideology derived from environmental paganism or a new animism (Cox 2007a: 161–3), but practically, as a tool to aid researchers in their attempts 'to think socio-religious change as well as to think the modern mutation of religion' (Hervieu-Léger 1999: 84). What we call religion must be understood in changing and dynamic social contexts. Although Hervieu-Léger regards belief as central to what actually is changing and dynamic in social contexts, she prefers the term the 'act of believing' to 'belief' to indicate that to believe is 'belief in motion' (Hervieu-Léger 1999: 84). She explains that 'belief in motion' incorporates 'the practices, languages, gestures and spontaneous automatism' in which beliefs are inscribed, which means that the student of religion must study '*the mutating structures of believing*' (Hervieu-Léger 1999: 84) (emphasis in original). This leads to the conclusion that the content of religion can no longer be thought of as restricted to a certain way of believing, either excluding or including political, social and economic factors, as required both by substantive and functional definitions. 'Religious believing', she asserts, must be understood as '*a particular modality of the organization and function of the act of believing*' (Hervieu-Léger 1999: 87) (emphasis in original).

If we follow Hervieu-Léger's train of thought to this point, we will see that the question confronting scholars is not, for example, could a modern spectator sport like football be considered a religion any more than it asks if modern expressions of Christianity, Judaism or Islam can be considered a religion. If I am correct, Hervieu-Léger would not want to fall into the trap of substantive definitions as displayed by the ABS, which restricted the number of recognized religions to 154 and coded those outside the recognized religions as 'Other' or 'No Religion' (ABS 2011). According to Hervieu-Léger, the important issue for a socially embedded modern definition of religion depends not on the now-dated debate between substantivists and functionalists, but it pivots on the question of legitimization. How is the act of believing legitimized? And here Hervieu-Léger arrives at the essential and necessary condition for religion to exist in any human community: 'There is no religion without the explicit, semi-explicit, or entirely implicit invocation of *the authority of a tradition*; an invocation which serves as support for the act of believing' (Hervieu-Léger 1999: 87–8) (emphasis in original). These considerations lead to Hervieu-Léger's definition of religion 'as an ideological, practical and symbolic framework which constitutes, maintains, develops and controls the consciousness (individual or collective) of membership to a particular heritage of belief' (Hervieu-Léger 1999: 88). And here we reach her important conclusion with relevance to the first part of my definition of Indigenous Religions: religious groups define themselves 'objectively and subjectively as *a chain of memory*, the continuity of which transcends history' (Hervieu-Léger 1999: 89) (emphasis in original). By relating to a chain of memory, religious communities collectively share in acts of remembrance of the past which give meaning to the present and anticipate the future. Hervieu-Léger concludes:

> Insofar as transmission [of the tradition] is bound up within the processes of elaboration of this chain of memory whereby a group of believers becomes a religious group, transmission is the very movement itself whereby the religion constitutes itself as a religion: it is the continuing foundation of the religious institution itself. (Hervieu-Léger 1999: 90)

Based on Hervieu-Léger's sociologically inspired definition of religion, I contend that the necessary or indispensable condition for religion to be present in any human activity, *its fundamental defining characteristic*, requires the existence of an identifiable community (either explicitly visible or implicitly acknowledged), which is constituted by its being bound by and subservient to an overpowering authoritative tradition that is passed on from generation to generation. This restricted definition is sociological and culturally based rather than theological or quasi-theological (as in most substantive definitions). It does not depend on belief in supernatural entities or refer to a postulated transcendental object towards which the community directs its attention. This definition is limited entirely to the socially sanctioned authority of a tradition that exercises overwhelming power over communities that accept its authority. It is not restricted substantively to a particular belief in supernatural agents nor is it so broad as to include nearly everything, as in functional definitions. My definition is determined by sociological factors that circumscribe and delimit specific and identifiable communities.

A narrow, restricted definition of Indigenous Religions

Having offered a narrow definition of religion that is neither tied to supernatural entities nor vague and all-encompassing, but based on social analysis, I now turn to advocate an equally restricted definition of indigenous. The first characteristic I have identified as an essential component of Indigenous societies accentuates the fact that Indigenous belief systems and social structures revolve around ancestors. Myths of origin often relate in quasi-legendary language tales about how the people were established in the land in the first place, either by autochthonous ancestors who brought the people into being, often by miraculous exploits, or by founding ancestors who led the people to the land they now occupy. Contemporary beliefs, which are derived ultimately from the foundational myths, are centred on how ancestors relate actively to living communities by maintaining a reciprocal relationship with them. The descendants must regularly honour their ancestors ritually and follow the social regulations they originally established. In exchange, the ancestors protect their descendants from misfortunes and the potentially malign interference of alien spirits or witches. Ancestral traditions stretch back beyond the memory of living communities, but even those who are long forgotten are remembered in rituals, since the more recently deceased are honoured by name and are able to convey the respect of the people in a chain stretching all the way back to the original ancestors (Cox 2007a: 125–9).

Indigenous societies are restricted by kinship relations. One is born into an extended family or one marries into it. Marriage regulations are carefully controlled to ensure that kinship ties are preserved and that traditional relationships between different kinship groups are observed. The particular social role ancestors occupy in the tradition varies according to the way the Indigenous society is organized, some being hierarchical, others more egalitarian, some patrilineal, others matrilineal, but the one factor they share in common is that they are all defined by and limited to patterns of kinship. If one applies this interpretation of 'indigenous' to the religions of Indigenous peoples, this means that, unlike religions with universal cosmologies, one can never be converted into an Indigenous society, since ancestors belong only to precise kinship groups (Platvoet 1992: 21–2; Cox 2007a: 61–71).

The second primary characteristic I have identified as unique to Indigenous societies stresses that they are restricted not only by kinship ties, but relate exclusively to a particular geographical place or location fixed in the tradition by their quasi-legendary myths. Foundational stories are relayed to the young and passed on from generation to generation. These local myths form the background on which rituals performed regularly in honour of the ancestors are conducted. When misfortunes occur, explanations are sought to explain why the ancestors have withheld their protection. The reasons given usually point to the failure of the descendants to remember and honour the ancestors in rituals or they refer to some serious social infraction committed within the community that offends the ancestors. The resulting series of catastrophic events can only be rectified when the ancestors are reconciled to the community, almost always by performing rituals aimed at restoring relations with the ancestors and by making compensation to injured parties for infringing traditional social mores. The problems encountered by communities, including divining the causes and prescribing proper treatments, occur exclusively within specific geographical regions over which the ancestors are responsible and do not extend beyond the boundaries of their traditional authority.

If we combine my definition of religion with my narrow interpretation of indigenous, we arrive at a clear, scientific definition of Indigenous Religions. For any identifiable community to qualify as religious, it must submit to an authoritative tradition that is transmitted from generation to generation with an overwhelming force or power. For the community that adheres to this authoritative tradition to be Indigenous, the tradition must operate within a society that is restricted by kinship ties and it must relate to a specific place or location, and, in each instance, it must apply to no other lineage group or geographical region.

Indigenous Religions have been defined in scholarly literature in terms other than kinship and location, but these are always secondary to these two primary characteristics. It often is stressed that Indigenous peoples do not have a word in their languages corresponding to 'religion' since almost everything in their traditional cultures can be regarded as religious, including such things as work, eating and sexual activity (Baylis 1988: 3). It is also pointed out that Indigenous societies transmit their traditions orally through story and ritual, which has consequences for the way their religious beliefs and practices are understood by participants (Schmidt 1988: 45–8). In addition, Indigenous Religions have been described as pragmatic rather than dogmatic or doctrinal, meaning that their religious explanations are flexible and can even appear to outsiders as contradictory (Platvoet 1992: 23–4). Each of these characteristics is secondary because any one of them can apply in particular cases to non-Indigenous religious traditions. For example, it could be argued that all religions, in their pure form, urge their adherents to integrate every activity of life with the central tenets of faith. Or, all religious traditions, even those traditions of the 'book', like Judaism, Christianity and Islam, originally were oral in nature. And certainly, not every religion with a universal cosmology, such as non-dualistic philosophical Hinduism, is dogmatic in nature by insisting that a particular belief is exclusively true and necessary for salvation.

On my narrow and restricted definition of the term 'Indigenous Religions', kinship and location, as irreducible, defining qualities, provide students of religion with clear, testable and scientific criteria for denoting what is and what is not an Indigenous Religion. If an identifiable community seeks converts, aims at expanding its followers or members beyond a specific geographical location through missionary efforts (as opposed to migrations or warfare) and defines adherents in terms of beliefs and practices that are not limited by kinship ties, they cannot be considered an Indigenous Religion. In accordance with a scientific method that depends on empirical verification to test the data, the transmission of tradition within any community can be designated Indigenous only if the overwhelming authority of the tradition derives from ancestors and the primary identity of the community is confined to a specific geographical location.

A critique of a narrow definition of Indigenous Religions: Bjørn Ola Tafjord

An incisive critique of my restricted definition of Indigenous Religions has been written by Bjørn Ola Tafjord, of the University of Tromsø – The Arctic University of Norway, in an article published in 2013 under the title, 'Indigenous Religion(s) as an Analytical Category' (2013: 221–43). Tafjord lists five basic objections to my use of Indigenous Religions: (1) I have uncritically taken for granted that 'indigenous religions' are the religions of 'indigenous peoples'; (2) I have assumed similarities among Indigenous Religions globally when in fact they are not similar at all, or at least the differences are as significant as any alleged similarities; (3) by stereotypically depicting Indigenous Religions as being tied to ancient traditions, my definition ignores the globalizing forces that have transformed Indigenous Religions in the contemporary world; (4) by restricting 'indigenous' to ancestors and location, I have reverted to a nineteenth-century taxonomy that placed 'primitive religions' at the most basic, elemental stage in religious development; (5) kinship and location are not unique characteristics of Indigenous Religions, since almost all religions relate to local situations and revere their forebears. These objections are penetrating and serious, and need to be explored in some detail.

In the first instance, Tafjord wants scholars of Indigenous Religions to challenge the naïve assumption that Indigenous Religions and Indigenous peoples are interchangeable. This unreflective position takes for granted that "'indigenous peoples" are the ones who have "indigenous religions"' (Tafjord 2013: 223). He argues that this simply is not the case. He contends that 'peoples and communities do not necessarily stop considering themselves indigenous just because they take up a foreign religion' even if 'they have quit completely the religion of their ancestors' (Tafjord 2013: 234–5). In fact, some Indigenous people may regard their newly adopted religion, despite its universal ambitions, as 'indigenous' by viewing it as a continuation of the older traditions or a better expression of the original without actually contradicting it (Tafjord 2013: 235). To imply that Indigenous Religions and Indigenous peoples are identical overlooks the dynamic interaction between foreign, proselytizing religions and the traditions that were dominant before the missionary religions came on the scene. To convert to the universal religion does not mean that the Indigenous people who belong to the new religion are no longer Indigenous.

Tafjord's second point criticizes any attempt to create a universal classification for Indigenous Religions. In particular, by reducing the term 'indigenous' to the two principal characteristics, kinship and location, Tafjord accuses me of making gross generalizations that cannot be tested scientifically. In most cases, he contends, Indigenous societies are not related to one another, since their histories and geographical locations are widely dispersed and are totally disconnected: 'The vast majority have had nothing to do with each other' (Tafjord 2013: 226). It is Europeans who have placed Indigenous Religions into one category based on Western scholarly assumptions about the need to find a classification for religious groups that do not fit nicely within the construction known as the 'world religions'. In actual fact, what the religions that have been called Indigenous (or previously, primitive, primordial or primal) share in common 'is close to nothing' (Tafjord 2013: 226). The only thing they actually hold in common 'is the way they have been looked upon, and acted towards, from the outside, by Europeans' (Tafjord 2013: 226).

A third criticism levelled by Tafjord against my construction of Indigenous Religions contends that I have ignored the dynamic character of Indigenous Religions by restricting them to ancient traditions that, in accordance with my definition of religion, are passed on authoritatively from generation to generation. He suggests that the reality is quite the opposite from how I have described it. Indigenous peoples have been affected in the modern era by a plethora of outside forces: educational, economic, political, social and religious. These have produced inevitable changes, witnessed in the religious sphere by the fact that 'a great number of those who identify themselves and/or are identified by others as indigenous people, are Baha'is, Buddhists, Christians, Muslims, or members of any other religion or variety of a religion' (Tafjord 2013: 231). Tafjord admits that the homogeneous use of the category 'indigenous' has been adopted by diverse groups advocating for political, economic and land rights, but, he argues, to confuse an international political agenda with an academic category distorts legitimate scholarly attempts to understand 'complex social and historical processes' (Tafjord 2013: 231). Contemporary movements to reclaim Indigenous rights by Indigenous peoples are responses to recent historical developments, a fact which further underscores the dangers of oversimplifying a definition of Indigenous Religions in terms of 'rare, age old, and unchanged religious customs' (Tafjord 2013: 231)

This point leads to a fourth, related, contention advanced by Tafjord. By defining Indigenous Religions as limited to kinship and location, Tafjord accuses me of classifying Indigenous Religions in ways similar to nineteenth-century scholars who contrasted small-scale societies, with their limited world-views, to religions with universal cosmologies. This classificatory scheme inevitably lends itself to ideas of higher and lower forms of religion, and to the adjunct notion that the lower forms of religion ultimately will disappear as they are absorbed into the higher, universal religions, precisely because the latter are capable of coping better with the demands of a global society. This, of course, is not what I have argued, a fact admitted by Tafjord, but he insists that this conclusion follows necessarily from my 'emphasis on place-bound, small-scale, and – adding the focus on ancestors – traditional societies' (Tafjord 2013: 233). Although I have tried to dissociate my own analysis from what Tafjord calls 'pioneer models' for classifying religions, he suggests that, perhaps unwittingly, I have adopted the same methods. As a result, rather than advancing the study of Indigenous Religions, as I have claimed, Tafjord (2013: 233) concludes that I have actually re-introduced approaches to the study of religions that even at the time they were first proposed 'were seen as problematic and unsatisfying'.

Tafjord's final point attacks what I have called the defining characteristics of Indigenous Religions. Against my contention, following J. G. Platvoet, that 'kinship rules religion' (Cox 2007a: 53), Tafjord (2013: 233) counters that 'kinship rules religion in most cases and almost everywhere'. The notion that adherents of the world's religions somehow transcend local kinship ties is to create an idealized picture of these religions divorced from what actually happens on the ground. Tafjord cites the example of Christianity, which would be regarded as a universal religion and certainly not an Indigenous Religion on my definition. Tafjord (2013: 233) argues that 'most become and are Christians because their family is Christian'. Moreover, Christians speak about being in a family of believers, by which they often are referring to fellow members of their local church. He asserts that some Christians 'even claim that they belong to a particular Christian lineage', an idea that is so strong that the deceased 'can play prominent parts in Christian communities, as role models, as saints, and even as gods!' (Tafjord 2013: 234). The fact that lineage plays an important part in Christian communities further corroborates that such communities relate to a specific place or location. If Christianity can be defined in terms of kinship and location, this renders my defining characteristics of Indigenous Religions absurd, since the religion with perhaps the highest claim to being a universal religion fits perfectly into my classification.

Although Tafjord is dealing specifically with my limited definition of Indigenous Religions, his critique can be applied more generally to wider discussions of the category. For example, Graham Harvey (2013a: 1) has argued that strict definitions of Indigenous Religions tend to 'box in' the practices of Indigenous peoples and thereby distort the reality that Indigenous religious practices are highly diverse and multifaceted. Or Ulrich Berner (2013: 53–60) of the University of Bayreuth has suggested, by examining the case of the nineteenth-century Anglican bishop in South Africa, John William Colenso, that the term 'indigenous' can be applied to both a kinship-based *and* a universal religion. Or in a paper delivered at a one-day conference at the University of Sydney on 18 October 2013, Jack Tsonis (2016: 59) argued that simply substituting the term 'indigenous' for earlier terms such as 'primitive' and 'primal' does not address the more fundamental problem caused by attempts to amalgamate diverse cultures under 'single-word' classifications. In general, these further discussions of the category Indigenous Religions largely fall under the five objections raised by Tafjord, to which I now turn to consider in detail.

In defence of a restricted use of Indigenous Religions

Can we separate Indigenous peoples from Indigenous Religions, as Tafjord suggests? If he means that we need to dissociate the category 'Indigenous Religions' from the people who fit into this classification, then, of course, the answer is 'no'. This would be like saying 'Christianity' is a religion devoid of Christians. Of course, this is not what Tafjord means. He is not suggesting that we divorce a religion from its adherents, but that for historical, and even political, reasons we should not imply that Indigenous peoples cannot be Indigenous if they adhere to Christianity, Hinduism, Buddhism or other religions with cosmologies that are universal and not restricted to a specific location. Tafjord is correct on this point. In most places today, Indigenous peoples are Christians or Muslims or adherents of other invading religions, but they still claim to be Indigenous. In many cases, such as in Zimbabwe, people practise Indigenous rituals, honour ancestors and tell traditional stories while still following Christian teachings and attending church worship services. They are both/and rather than either/or. In my book, *The Invention of God in Indigenous Societies*, I describe how Aboriginal Elders in Northern Queensland in Australia have adapted the traditional symbol of the rainbow-serpent into an Indigenous Christian theology by depicting Jesus Christ as the incarnation of the rainbow-serpent (Cox 2014a: 105).

If Indigenous peoples, defined as bound to ancestors and restricted by location, become part of a religion that is universal, both cosmologically and spatially, does that mean, following Tafjord, that they remain fully Indigenous while at the same time no longer belonging to an Indigenous Religion? This is what is implied by the notion that we must separate Indigenous peoples from Indigenous Religions. This assertion begs the question as to what is meant by Indigenous peoples, as opposed to Indigenous Religions. What are the defining qualities of Indigenous peoples? Here we are thrown back to trying to isolate some characteristics that distinguish 'Indigenous' from 'non-Indigenous'. Do we mean autochthonous, or original, peoples? Are we referring to the people who resided in an area when they were subjected to the forces of colonialism? Do we settle for the idea that Indigenous people are Indigenous if they define themselves as Indigenous and are accepted as such by Indigenous communities? Or do we even fall back onto extremely vague and romantic ideas of indigeneity as being somehow associated with identifying with nature and promoting environmentalism? (Cox 2003: 13–16). I maintain that if we intend to employ a term with any specificity, we must state with absolute precision what we mean when we use it. None of the solutions above actually clarify the term 'Indigenous'; rather, they complicate it. If we mean original or autochthonous people, most of the populations we now regard as Indigenous would not fall into this category. If we are speaking strictly of victims of colonialism, the boundaries of the category become extremely fuzzy. The same is true when using 'self-defining' as the primary criterion of who is Indigenous. And the assumption that Indigenous communities are innately friendly to nature and respectful of the environment, even if true, would not help establish the boundaries separating Indigenous people from those we would classify as non-Indigenous.

I agree with Tafjord that it is possible to belong to a society that is kinship-bound and restricted to a location and still adhere to a religion that is universal. But belonging to a society that is defined by ancestral traditions, which are respected as holding an overwhelming power over the society, is, on my definition, the same as belonging to an Indigenous Religion. The issue then becomes not whether we can separate an Indigenous society from an Indigenous Religion – they are the same – but how Indigenous populations reconcile competing authoritative traditions. Universal religions, like Christianity or Islam, become indigenized when they are absorbed into traditional, ancestral and local lines of authority, as is evident in the Rainbow Spirit Theology in Australia (Cox 2014a: 89–111), or in the manner Indigenous Catholics in Zimbabwe have incorporated the teaching about the communion of saints into the traditional 'bringing home' (*Kurova Guva*) ceremony, the aim of which is to establish ancestral authority over the living community (Cox 2014a: 83–7). In this sense, Indigenous peoples can be Christians and Indigenous, but they also adhere to Indigenous Religions, precisely because they have made the universal religion subservient to traditional authority. If the Indigenous authoritative tradition is undermined, replaced or destroyed, then the people are no longer Indigenous and, logically, no longer adhere to an Indigenous Religion. When considered alongside my definition of religion, kinship and location remain identifying characteristics of Indigenous Religions, even when those who constitute an Indigenous society become Christians, Muslims, Buddhist, Baha'is or members of other religions that are not bound by kinship and location.

A second problem with my definition of Indigenous Religions, as posed by Tafjord, does not follow directly from my definition, but would apply to any attempt to create a general classification into which Indigenous Religions can be fitted. Because Indigenous peoples are so widespread, diverse culturally and historically, and have had little or no influence over one another, any common characteristics suggested among them must certainly be developed for reasons entirely disconnected from the concerns of the Indigenous peoples themselves. This means primarily that academics have created the classification to satisfy predetermined aims about how to classify religions in general. The notion that religions can be categorized as being universal or local has developed from the distinction between the 'world religions' and the 'rest', the latter of which must have something in common in order to fit them into a taxonomic scheme. Suggestions as to how these other religions can be classified generally have been determined in contradistinction to the characteristics assumed to be held in common by world religions, such as literate opposed to oral, missionary rather than non-proselytizing, doctrinal as opposed to practical, containing an idea of a universal salvation rather than being concerned with immediate problems affecting the community. These characteristics, both of world religions and the other religions, as Tafjord correctly notes, have been developed to uphold the teaching of religion in universities. This implies that Indigenous Religions do not share in common the many characteristics that academics have assigned to them, but they all have been subject to the European gaze and made to fit into a general classification on the basis of what Western scholars have deemed necessary to establish the proper relations among the religions of the world.

This critique is largely accurate, and I have made it myself in my own attempts to challenge the assumptions beneath what I have called 'the world religions paradigm' (Cox 2007a: 33–52). Nonetheless, when Tafjord applies this critique to my definition of Indigenous Religions, it is a bit like employing the ad hominem fallacy, which attacks the person rather than the argument. In this case, the charge is made against those who try to define, rather than the definition itself. My response is simply this: if societies that have nothing in common with one another are bound by kinship ties and are restricted to a place, I do not need to justify classifying them within a common category by trying to establish any connections at all. They simply fit or they do not fit into a class of societies that centre on ancestral authority and relate to the location where the ancestors reside. I do not need to explain why ancestors are dominant in such disparate societies, but at the same time, I have not naively contended that ancestors are always understood in the same manner among Indigenous peoples. In fact, in my case studies contrasting ancestors among the Yupiit of Alaska and the Shona of Zimbabwe (2007a: 96–139), I have demonstrated that the lines of authority operate quite differently. Despite this, both are bound by kinship and are linked to a specific location. The fundamental issue is scientific, irrespective of Tafjord's assertions to the contrary. If a society is organized around kinship ties through which authority is passed on according to lineage (even though authority may be understood quite differently) and the society is bound to a location (even though some Indigenous peoples may no longer reside in the place of their ancestors), then the society is Indigenous. This test can be applied empirically to determine which societies can be regarded as Indigenous and which cannot be so regarded. Of course, there will be blurred boundaries, particularly in an ever-increasing globalized world with mass communication and travel, but the boundaries are much more distinct on my definition and more amenable to scientific verification than alternative, non-specific and vague definitions. That this is a concern to Western academics from an analytical perspective (as opposed to political concerns) is obvious, but this is the case with all subjects considered along disciplinary lines within scholarly research, including politics, economics, sociology, health studies and cognitive science. In the end, we need to know what we mean by the terms we use, or we better not use them at all.

A one-day conference held at the University of Edinburgh on 29 May 2014 explored the theme, 'Indigeneity Goes Global'. It focused squarely on the issue posed by Tafjord that to define Indigenous as kinship-bound and local is to operate on nineteenth-century assumptions about the limited world-views maintained within Indigenous societies. Nowadays, people living in remote regions have mobile phones, computers with access to the internet, televisions with satellite connections and they travel by air to various parts of the world. To refer to Indigenous peoples in the modern world as restricted to a location appears anomalous and anachronistic, or it applies only to very isolated communities in extremely remote locations. In addition, some societies, like the Yoruba of Nigeria, are expanding outreach programmes globally and even training non-Yoruba to become Ifa diviners in various countries, chiefly the United States (see the website of the Ifa Foundation International, http://www.ifafoundation.org). This situation suggests that Indigenous Religions indeed are going global. My definition seemingly ignores this fact and retains an outdated image of Indigenous populations as backward, cosmologically restricted and concerned only with the immediate welfare of their kin. The corollary of this description is that Indigenous Religions inevitably will be superseded by religions with global aspirations.

Just like the argument made by Tafjord that Indigenous peoples cannot be equated with Indigenous Religions because many Indigenous people have converted to one of the world religions, this critique misses the point. Societies that are identified according to lineage and restricted to location do not as a result isolate themselves from the outside world. Just as many are both Indigenous and Christian, so too do Indigenous peoples live both according to their traditions and engage with global forces. The fundamental issue concerning my definition again relates to how authority is exercised and transmitted within such societies. Competing authorities will be present, of course, and different authoritative structures will hold sway in different situations. Nonetheless, in so far as the tradition of ancestors is maintained and continues to operate with an overwhelming authority for the community, Indigenous Religion is present, even if members of the community also acknowledge other authorities, such as the church or the national government. Nor is it necessary that members of the community reside in the location to which they owe allegiance. They can still be bound to the authority of the ancestors while living in cities or in far-off countries, and identify with the place from which they originate. If, by contrast, a religion seeks converts by acting with missionary intent, as in the case of non-Yoruba practitioners performing as Yoruba diviners, this no longer can be called an Indigenous Religion. American Ifa diviners using computers to advise clients on personal problems in their American homes is not an expression of an Indigenous Religion, no matter how the practitioners have been trained, what traditional clothes they wear or even what language they speak (see http://www.ifafoundation.org/divination-training/).

It follows from this that I am not suggesting that Indigenous Religions eventually will die away as they become increasingly influenced by globalization. I am convinced that Indigenous Religions are highly adaptive and, although they often adopt practices from outside cultures, they can still maintain their allegiance to their ancestral traditions. Such allegiance is dynamic, rather than static, as is evidenced by various movements in such societies that have taken aspects of other religions and made them their own, as I have shown in the Australian case of the rainbow-serpent (Cox 2014a: 147–8). My argument is not that Indigenous Religions should be compared with other, universal (higher), religions, but that they should be studied in their own right rather than, as in previous times, as a preparation for one of the world religions (usually Christianity) or as some basic, primal foundation on which all religions are constructed (as advocated by framers of the 'primal religions' theory) (Cox 2007a: 9–31). As scholars of religion, we should study each religion in its own context, historically, socially and culturally, and allow the practitioners to speak for themselves before we apply academic interpretations in response to our research agendas. In so far as we treat every other religion as worthy of study on its own terms, so too should we regard the many expressions of Indigenous Religions with respect and scientific accuracy. My definition aims at doing just that and does not project categories derived from predetermined concepts of 'higher' or 'lower', 'advanced' or 'primitive', or any other criteria based on judgements of value. In response to Tafjord's third and fourth objections, I am convinced that my definition is thoroughly scientific, testable and usable as a heuristic device, and thus is neither a reversion to older, now-inadequate and outdated, methods, nor one that ignores the impact of globalization on Indigenous societies.

In a rather odd twist, Tafjord concludes by arguing that all religions are bound by kinship and location, even Christianity. Here, I think he misinterprets the way I am using kinship and location. Of course, all religions are local in that practitioners live in specific places and perform their rituals and observances in space and time. It is also true that in many instances, Christians, for example, pass on their traditions to their kin and expect them to pass them on to their descendants. This occurs particularly in Christian denominations that practise infant baptism, where the parents make pledges on behalf of their children. It is also common to speak of the church as a family that honours the deceased and remembers them in prayer, or in some Christian groups, appeals to them for assistance. Nonetheless, the Christian 'family' is not limited by lineage or kinship, nor does it focus on a specific location. The Christian family, like the Islamic Ummah, is universal, is not bound by place and welcomes any person who professes the faith into its community. This is not the case among Indigenous societies, and it cannot be the case. My ancestors are not your ancestors; my ancestors relate to me and to my kin, not to yours. There is a fundamental difference between religions dominated by kinship and those that use kinship symbolically to represent a universal family. This is not a value judgement, but a statement of fact, on the basis of which we can distinguish Indigenous Religions from other types of religions that clearly seek converts and whose outreach is global.

Indigenous Religions and the 'Mutating Structures of Believing'

This then brings me back to my own definition, which I have always insisted provides a starting point for discussion and is not intended to occur at the end as a conclusion or operate as the final word on the problem of identifying who is Indigenous and what is meant by the term Indigenous Religions (Cox 2007a: 73). For this reason, I welcome the intervention of Bjørn Ola Tafjord and others in this debate. I have argued from the outset that we need to begin any discussion of Indigenous Religions by stating explicitly what we mean by the language we employ, not as a final or definitive claim to have circumscribed a category, but as a pragmatic way of engaging in dialogue. Rather than 'boxing in' the category 'Indigenous Religions', as Graham Harvey contends, this opens it up by encouraging scholars to clarify their denotative and connotative uses of terms and thereby make it possible to examine their varying interpretations analytically and critically.

I want to add just one last word on the notion of belief, as I discussed it in the context of my definition of religion as derived from Hervieu-Léger, which, if left unstated, would allow the unrelenting barrage against the category or typology 'belief' in religion to remain unchallenged, as, for example, in Graham Harvey's recent work in which he states that the primary aim in his book is to 'turn the tables on ... learning about belief systems' (Harvey 2013b: 202). In my book, *An Introduction to the Phenomenology of Religion*, I have argued that belief constitutes a 'special case' among phenomenological classifications (Cox 2010: 132–45). The current reaction against the role belief plays in religion is built somewhat naively on the assumption that scholars of religion continue to depict, describe and teach religion as if it were obtained from a textbook on systematic Christian theology. This, of course, could be said to characterize flawed earlier books written about the religions of the world, but this does not mean that the cognitive side of religion should be dismissed as irrelevant or unimportant. For example, it would be impossible for a spirit medium to go into a trance and for the assembled community to speak to the spirit directly if an underlying belief in the power of spirits to influence human circumstances were not present. It simply would not happen. What we believe affects how we experience the world and how we behave in it. Of course, this is not just a one-directional dynamic: experiences influence beliefs and behaviours, just as behaviours have an impact on our experiences and beliefs. The current tendency to debunk beliefs as a Protestant left-over, nevertheless, is too obvious and does not consider the complex relationships between cognitions, experiences and actions, as is being shown increasingly within the cognitive science of religion and has been evident in cognitive-behavioural psychology for a very long time (Cox 1998a: 119–28; Marks 2012: 1–24; International Association for the Cognitive and Evolutionary Sciences of Religion: www.iacesr.com).

The concept of belief I am defending in this case is consistent with Hervieu-Léger's (1999: 84) 'mutating structures of believing', which are dynamic constructions that transform over time and under the influences of numerous social forces. This concept applies perfectly to how I have interpreted Indigenous Religions as adapting to contemporary circumstances, not by reverting to static, age-old unchanging traditions, but by reformulating the authoritative tradition, re-configuring it in new terms, and at the same time relating it in ways that allow it to maintain an enduring hold over particular kinship groups in specific locations. This interpretation of belief, Hervieu-Léger's 'belief in motion' (1999: 84), when applied to Indigenous Religions, suggests that the term 'indigenous' needs to be understood equally as a verb as a noun: dynamic, adaptive, adoptive and persistent.

Part IV

INDIGENOUS RELIGIONS IN GLOBAL CONTEXTS

Chapter 10

SECULARIZING THE LAND: THE IMPACT OF THE ALASKA NATIVE CLAIMS SETTLEMENT ACT ON INDIGENOUS UNDERSTANDINGS OF LAND

The Annual Report for 2002 of the Cook Inlet Region, Inc. (CIRI), a Native Alaskan Regional Corporation created by the Alaska Native Claims Settlement Act of 1971, lists among its investments: The Westin Kierland Resort and Spa in Scottsdale Arizona, partnership in VoiceStream Wireless Corporation and BellSouth Corporation (a communications system operating in major US cities), ownership of multi-tenant business parks in Anchorage and other locations in the lower forty-eight states (including Miami, Florida and Kent, Washington), venture interests in Peak Oilfield Service Company, partnership in the Ritz-Carlton, Lake Las Vegas luxury resort hotel and full ownership of the Casino MonteLago, which is attached to the Ritz-Carlton Hotel (Cook Inlet Region, Inc. 2003: 11–15). These capital ventures run and operated by a major Native Alaskan Regional Corporation paint a far different picture of the Indigenous peoples of the Arctic and sub-Arctic regions of Alaska than are depicted in popularly held stereotypical images, such as those outlined by the Alaskan anthropologist, Wendell Oswalt (1999: 1):

> Eskimos are for many reasons the most exotic people in the world. After all, what is more demanding than living in a land where it is nearly always cold? What is more unprecedented than a diet of meat or a house built from snow? What could be kinder than never punishing children or more pacific than being ignorant of war? What is more bizarre than killing one's children or aged parents without showing emotion? What is more daring than hunting great whales from frail skin-covered boats or facing a polar bear when protected by nothing more than a spear backed by bravery?

Of course, these characterizations of Indigenous life in the Arctic regions are presented by Oswalt to underscore what he calls the 'overstated qualities' found in customary images of Native peoples (Oswalt 1999: 1). Another Alaskan anthropologist, Ann Fienup-Riordan (1990: xii), suggests that the Indigenous populations of Alaska have been depicted quite misleadingly 'as conservationists practicing waste-free management and consumption of scarce and limited resources; as being peaceful and nonaggressive; as living free from law in a state of "contained anarchy"; and as lacking the concepts of leadership, territory, and landownership'. She calls these 'half truths', which have resulted in part from the tendency of Arctic scholars to lose themselves in the 'minutiae of their own field' and thus leave such popular characterizations of Eskimos 'to the generalists' (Fienup-Riordan 1990: xiii).

It would be easy, following conventional notions, to suggest that the changes that occurred in 1971 following approval by the United States Congress of the Alaskan Native Claims Settlement Act (referred to throughout Alaska simply as ANCSA) created a sudden change of direction among Alaskan Natives away from traditional life towards an American, free market, capitalist culture. In fact, the history is much more complex than this. It would be more correct to see the enshrinement of Indigenous land in corporate shares as an innovative attempt finally to achieve the long-standing aim of the US government to assimilate Native peoples into the lifestyle and culture of mainstream America. Initial efforts at Native assimilation were undertaken by Sheldon Jackson, the architect of the Protestant mission in Alaska and the US Government's General Agent for Education in Alaska from 1885 to 1907. Under Jackson's leadership, schools and mission stations were established throughout Alaska with the aim of changing the Indigenous way of life in virtually every aspect, including replacing subsistence and communal living with an individualized cash economy by teaching Indigenous people how to work, live in single family units and, in Jackson's words, 'how to make more money in order to live better, and how to utilize the resources of the country in order to make more money' (cited in Cox 1991: 27).

The Alaska Native Claims Settlement Act of 1971, therefore, must be seen as the culmination of over a century of concerted, but at times sporadic and uneven, US government efforts to assimilate Alaskan Indigenous populations into the dominant American culture. ANCSA implemented a policy that affected every Native (born by the date the law was enacted) by providing each with shares in village and regional corporations in exchange for any future Indigenous claims to the land. I argue in this chapter that ANCSA had the effect of secularizing the land, which in traditional society was understood in terms of a 'religious' relationship (as I define it below) to the animals, sea mammals and fish that lived on the land and within the adjacent seas. By reformulating land as ownership of corporate shares, the US government sought to ensure that any sense of a spiritual connection to the land held by the Native population at last was eliminated in favour of making profits and increasing personal wealth.

Distinguishing religion from the secular

The distinction between the religious and the secular is pivotal for understanding the progressive colonization of Alaskan Native lands from the time the United States 'purchased' the territory from Russia in 1867 until ANCSA was enacted in 1971. It is important, therefore, at the outset to clarify in what ways I am using the terms 'religion' and 'secular'. I am helped in this by the French sociologist, Danièle Hervieu-Léger, in a book first published in French in 1993, with the English version appearing in 2000 under the title *Religion as a Chain of Memory*.

According to Hervieu-Léger (2000: 48–9), sociologists in the tradition of Durkheim have defined religion by referring to spiritual entities or to a 'sacred' understood as 'a tangible reality, a subject which can be identified by its properties and that is generally to be found in every religion'. Properties of the sacred include 'mysterious power, total separation between a sacred and profane world and an ambivalence which renders the sacred an object at once of fascination and revulsion' (Hervieu-Léger 2000: 49). Hervieu-Léger contends that this way of thinking transforms the concept of sacredness from an adjective into a noun, and thereby renders the sacred the unique subject matter of all religions. In support of this, Hervieu-Léger cites François-André Isambert, the nineteenth-century French lawyer, historian and politician, who contended that the sacred 'in a rather confused way' denotes 'the relationship in subject matter between all religions, indeed between all beliefs and between all religious feelings' (cited by Hervieu-Léger 2000: 49).

Hervieu-Léger (2000: 53) argues that the French sociologist Henri Desroche demonstrated conclusively that Durkheim defined religion in terms of a primary experience of the sacred, which is then transposed into institutional forms or a social order. This makes religion, in the words of the Durkheimian sociologist, Henri Hubert, 'the administration of the sacred' (cited by Hervieu-Léger 2000: 52). On this reading of Durkheim, at a primary level, religion is constituted by an experience of what Hervieu-Léger (2000: 53) calls 'emotional contact with the divine principle', but at a secondary level, this experience is 'socialized and rationalized, by being differentiated into beliefs and into offices and rites'. This has the effect of distinguishing between what might be called an experience of the sacred – 'a pure religious core' – and its institutional expressions (Hervieu-Léger 2000: 53). The sacred becomes in this way the unique social reality behind 'the multiplicity of religious expression in humanity' (Hervieu-Léger 2000: 49). Religious practices are understood as converging into the concept of a singular sacred (a homogeneous social entity rather than an ontological reality), characterized in modernity 'by the individualization and the subjectivization of systems of meaning' (Hervieu-Léger 2000: 49).

Because in modern, secular societies, religion is expressed widely in intensely individualistic and non-institutional ways, the term 'sacred' has been substituted for religion and used to identify the uniquely religious elements hidden within the symbolic expressions of modernity. This approach, according to Hervieu-Léger, has produced just the opposite effect: 'The notion of the sacred is bound to reintroduce surreptitiously the very thing it was supposed to eliminate, namely the preponderance of the Christian model in thinking about religion' (Hervieu-Léger 2000: 51). Hervieu-Léger thus challenges us to re-think the usefulness of Durkheimian interpretations of the religion-secular dichotomy, which outline a primary experience of the sacred and a secondary institutionalization of the experience. She asks if religion really can be understood best in contemporary society as referring to 'this first intense experience of the sacred', rather than the way it is administered through institutions (Hervieu-Léger 2000: 52).

In order to answer this, she employs the example of sport, initially by drawing attention to the primary emotional experience of individual athletic achievements, such as those attained in mountaineering, surfing or canyoning, so-called high-risk sports. These all share a sense of danger that pushes participants towards an experience that can be likened to religious mysticism (Hervieu-Léger 2000: 54). By contrast, the institutionalization of individual achievement is best exemplified in spectator sports that draw huge crowds often into a state of high excitement during which they collectively create a 'shared sacred' (Hervieu-Léger 2000: 55). It is here that the Durkheimian analysis becomes most evident: 'Across the emotive intensity which makes the crowd one, society affirms itself' (Hervieu-Léger 2000: 56). Sport thus contains the primary and secondary elements, which in Durkheim's analysis, constitute religion by combining its experiential and social components. In Hervieu-Léger's (2000: 56) words: 'It would appear that, in modern societies, sport fulfils the social function of self-affirmation which in traditional societies belonged to religion.' The analysis of sport can be expanded to apply to other collective activities that bind people together in modern society on the basis of an elementary emotional experience, such as rock concerts or political rallies. On this account, it would appear that, since the primary experience of the sacred can be expressed in numerous institutional forms, it provides an effective analytical model for understanding religion in secular terms.

Although she finds this argument intellectually compelling, Hervieu-Léger ultimately rejects it, suggesting that the emotional experience of the sacred, rather than confirming the persistence of religion in modern society, actually signals its demise. This is because 'sacredness' and 'religion' cannot be equated; they 'refer to two types of distinct experience' (Hervieu-Léger 2000: 58). Although the two types usually run in tandem one to the other, they can and do at times stand in firm opposition to one another. For example, the growth of charismatic movements around the world, with their overwhelming emphasis on emotion, reflects a modern rebellion against the institutionalization and bureaucratization of religion. Hervieu-Léger theorizes that Pentecostalism, on one level, because it insists on speaking in 'unknown tongues' (glossolalia), represents a new language for those most deprived of a voice in society. On another level, the phenomenon of glossolalia demonstrates that in modern society belief has been so eroded that the only avenue for expression for many is found in that which is inexpressible, quite literally. Rather than providing evidence that religion is being renewed in contemporary society by what Hervieu-Léger (2000: 60) calls 'the definitive fantastication of religious utterance', emotional experiences as fostered within the charismatic movements expose a thorough alienation in modernity from rational belief. For Hervieu-Léger, the bond between the experience of the sacred and religion must be disconnected so we can identify 'what is specific to the experience of both the one and the other' (Hervieu-Léger 2000: 60).

It is important to note that Hervieu-Léger's analysis thus far has in part served the purpose of exposing the essentialist and Christian assumptions beneath many prior attempts to analyse the relationships between the sacred and religion in modernity. She explicitly rejects the idea that the sociologist should employ ontological definitions of religion by arguing that the aim of the sociologist is 'to comprehend changes in the sphere of religion, considered by way of its tangible socio-historical manifestations' (Hervieu-Léger 2000: 69). For this reason, any definition of religion must be operational or instrumental, aimed at assisting the scholar to describe and understand socio-religious change. Moreover, if traditional or historical religions and so-called secular religions share certain characteristics, these should not be assumed to reflect identical beliefs. There are many differences, for example, between a Marxist eschatology and an Islamic one. Religion must be understood in its own sociocultural and historical contexts.

For Hervieu-Léger, the meaning conveyed to individuals by religion is connected inextricably with institutions that transmit authority. This leads her to identify religion as existing whenever 'the authority of tradition' has been invoked '(either explicitly, half-explicitly or implicitly) in support of the act of believing' (Hervieu-Léger 2000: 76). She explains: 'Seen thus, one would describe any form of believing as religious which sees its commitment to a chain of belief it adopts as all-absorbing ... *As our fathers believed, and because they believed, we too believe*' (Hervieu-Léger 2000: 81) (emphasis in original).

The stress on believing is central to understanding Hervieu-Léger's reconstruction of religion in the modern world. For her, changes in the context of believing define fundamentally the transformations that are occurring in contemporary society. She deliberately refers to believing as opposed to beliefs because she wants to underscore the dynamic process that is occurring. By believing, she means 'the body of convictions – both individual and collective – which are not susceptible to verification, to experimentation and, more broadly, to the modes of recognition and control that characterize knowledge, but owe their validity to the meaning and coherence they give to the subjective experience of those who hold them' (Hervieu-Léger 2000: 72). Acts of believing play a major role in social processes in modernity because they construct meanings for individuals and for society. Although scientific rationality has in some sense eroded traditional meanings, this does not lead us to conclude that the human need for meaning is thereby diminished. On the contrary, what it indicates is that meaning is 'no longer fixed and stable ... but unpredictable and unprotected, where change and innovation have become the norm' (Hervieu-Léger 2000: 73). It is precisely through the operation of meaning making that believing interacts with social processes. As a result, scholars of religion need to develop methods that investigate the key elements of religion, which, for Hervieu-Léger, include expressions of believing, memory of continuity and the legitimating reference to an authorized version of such memory (Hervieu-Léger 2000: 97).

For Hervieu-Léger, religion is best defined as 'an ideological, practical and symbolic system through which consciousness, both individual and collective, of belonging to a particular chain of belief is constituted, maintained, developed and controlled' (Hervieu-Léger 2000: 82). This definition implies that religion cannot be equated with the 'sacred', which is experienced in multiform ways and in numerous manners of intensity. Religion denotes institutions of society, which bind adherents together through a shared allegiance to an overwhelming, authoritative tradition that provides meaning for individual adherents. Many people in contemporary society, of course, testify to profound 'religious' experiences, even though these are not connected to an authoritative tradition. Hervieu-Léger calls such testimonies evidence of experiences of sacredness, understood as emotional responses to particular sociocultural contexts, including sporting events, political rallies, rock concerts and gatherings dominated by speaking in tongues.

The process of secularization

Hervieu-Léger's definition of religion in modernity leads us naturally to consider how this relates to theories of secularization. In particular, her perspective forces us to ask if the individualistic and atomized experiences of sacredness, so common in contemporary society, foster the decline of religion, understood, in Hervieu-Léger's terms, as an authoritative 'chain of memory'. Hervieu-Léger answers by classifying the 'religious' as those who maintain allegiance to a unitary tradition that is passed on authoritatively, and often dogmatically, from generation to generation. Secularism, on the other hand, is marked by a 'disaffiliation' from organized religion, which results in widespread indifference to the authoritative tradition. Hervieu-Léger (2000: 127) refers to this as 'the crumbling memory of modern societies'.

The process of secularization involves more than people in modern Western societies rejecting the authority of a tradition that had for previous generations been all-consuming. It includes processes at work which, under the influence of increasing globalizing forces, create an overarching homogeneity of power, resulting, according to Hervieu-Léger (2000: 128), 'from the eclipse of the idiosyncrasies rooted in the collective memory of differentiated concrete groups'. For example, as Jan Platvoet (2002: 83) notes, despite the overall domination of Christianity in Holland up until the middle of the twentieth century, what he calls a 'monochromatic Christian scene', the distinctive expressions of Christianity in The Netherlands 'were heavily polarised and segmented'. Dutch religion, although derived from the authority of an allegedly single revelatory tradition, found its allegiances devolved into quite distinct and historically defined religious groupings. The homogeneity of modern society, by contrast, differs because secularization aligns all social life, in Hervieu-Léger's (2000: 128) words, with 'the sphere of production'. This, accompanied by mass and almost instant communication, has produced a collective memory that is far different from the religious memory; secularized memory is 'surface memory, dull memory, whose normative, creative capacity' has been dissolved (Hervieu-Léger 2000: 128). This process is embodied today in the dominating and total power of world capitalism, which coerces all differentiated societies with their various collective memories into one mould, defined and exploited by market forces.

The very factors that create a homogeneous economic system lead at the same time to a radical fragmentation of what Hervieu-Léger (2000: 129) calls the 'individual and group memory'. In modern societies, individuals belong to numerous, specialized and atomized groups. Although each operates within a general framework dictated by market forces, none is able to sustain a singular commitment to an all-consuming authority. In other words, individuals in modern societies are unable to coalesce around a unified memory. Because modern institutions are fragmented in space and time, individuals relate to them in a piecemeal fashion. No real central, organizing tradition can be sustained. As soon as a bit of memory is established, it is nearly always immediately destroyed. For Hervieu-Léger (2000: 129), 'the collective memory of modern societies is composed of bits and pieces'. The secular, as opposed to religion, therefore, is best defined as the homogenization in the contemporary global society of a surface memory, promulgated under the guise of the world economic system, which in turn is accompanied by a radical fragmentation of all collective memories.

Religion, tradition and secularization in Alaska

I am suggesting in this chapter that 'religion' in the Alaskan context corresponds to traditional ways of relating to the land and the life that the land and surrounding seas and waterways sustain. The tradition, moreover, depends on an authority that the people acknowledge by respecting socially constructed boundaries and rules, and which they experience through the oral transmission of stories, ritual performances and particularly through the mediation of the shaman, who acts as a boundary-crosser between the seen and the unseen worlds (Fienup-Riordan 1994: 305–10). I acknowledge that no equivalent word for the Western term 'religion' existed among Indigenous Alaskan groups, but they nevertheless passed on their traditions and customs authoritatively from generation to generation and adhered to them closely in order to ensure communal well-being and to avoid calamities and misfortunes. This is why they referred to themselves through variations of the term 'Inuit', meaning the 'real' or 'authentic' people, which I interpret as referring to the ways in which their authoritative traditions were preserved in the collective memory.

The 'Inuit way of life' defines the best term in this context to indicate what I mean by the Western category 'religion', since for such a way of life to persist depended on the authoritative transmission of tradition. This 'way of life' can be contrasted sharply with what I am calling the secularizing forces of Americanization, which not only challenged traditional authority, but systematically sought to displace it with a different kind of authority, rooted in a postulated and invented homogeneous American cultural model. When Sheldon Jackson began his mission to Alaska as US General Agent for Education in 1885, he and his missionary teachers emphasized values that included Western concepts of hygiene, a cash economy, wooden-framed houses, classroom education, marriage according to American law, nuclear and patrilineal families, permanent settlements, a church building at the centre of the permanent settlement, a Protestant clergyman with responsibility for the permanent settlement and the exclusive use of the English language. By calling the Americanization of Alaskan Natives a process of secularization, I am suggesting that the authority on which the imposition of American values was based was alien to the tradition that for Alaskan Natives was all-consuming and which demanded full and total allegiance. The Americanization perpetrated on Indigenous Alaskans was based on an ideology of power aimed at subduing and controlling Alaskan Natives by making them subservient to the new American political and social systems.

It is true that Sheldon Jackson postulated an 'American way of life', which he and his selected missionary teachers enforced in Alaska. This, however, did not conform to a unified 'American' system of beliefs, since no such singular way of life ever existed. Americans, even at the end of the nineteenth century, did not all reside in permanent settlements; they did not all participate in classroom education; they did not all live in wooden houses; they certainly were not all Protestants; family life was never free from strife and divorce; they did not even all speak English. The authority demanded of the Native Alaskan by the US government after 1867 was rooted in political expediency, not the authoritative transmission of a tradition, and thus, can rightly be called 'secular' (void of a collective memory) as opposed to 'religious' (where the collective memory is passed on authoritatively from generation to generation).

The Americanization of Alaska, which began in the late nineteenth century, can be understood as the gradual unfolding of a strategy of assimilation. The American missionary teachers, who began arriving in increasing numbers after 1880, could not have envisaged the methods that would be employed eighty years later finally to eradicate Indigenous traditions. Nevertheless, they began a process that flowed naturally into land policies that would be controlled by the dictates of the market economy and global capitalism. Hervieu-Léger's 'dull' memory thus was already beginning to replace the traditional memory in ways that would have devastating consequences for Indigenous ways of life in Alaska. As I shall try to explain in the remainder of this chapter, by 1971, when the land was transferred to Native Corporations, a whole new class of individual shareholders was created. The homogenizing power structure of the free market had at last fragmented the collective, deeply rooted and authoritative memory of Alaskan Native traditions.

Some preliminary limitations and clarifications

Before discussing the secularizing effects of the Alaska Native Claims Settlement Act on traditional understandings of the land, I need to identify the context about which I am writing and define some basic terms. Alaska extends over 663,000 square miles (1.7 million square kilometres) crossing nearly 20 degrees of latitude. Within this wide area, numerous Indigenous peoples reside including the Aleuts, who inhabit the chain of islands extending into the Pacific Ocean in the direction of Asia, the Alutiiq or Pacific Eskimos who are found along the Gulf of Alaska, the Yupiit, who comprise the Yup'ik speakers in southwest and central Alaska (often referred to simply as the Yup'ik Eskimos), the Inupiat, whom Ernest Burch (1998: 3) calls the 'Inuit-Eskimo speaking inhabitants of the northern part of Alaska and extreme northwestern Canada', the Athabascans, an Indian group living in the interior regions, and the Southeast Coastal Indians, primarily the Haida and Tlingit. The anthropologist Steve Langdon (2002: 4) explains that 'these groupings are based on broad cultural and linguistic similarities', but in a strict sense they 'do not represent political or tribal units'. Since I am not attempting in this chapter to write an exhaustive description of Alaskan Indigenous peoples, but instead to identify some key components within the traditional patterns of life that confirm the secularizing impact of ANCSA on these patterns, I will restrict my discussion to the Yupiit, about whom Ann Fienup-Riordan (1990, 1994, 2000) has written extensively, and the Inupiat, with whom I have some limited personal experience (Cox 1991). For my purposes, sufficient similarities exist between Yupiit and Inupiat peoples to reach conclusions about the consequences of ANCSA for contemporary expressions of traditional Alaskan culture.

Since terminology in these cases can be confusing, I will use the terms Yupiit and Inupiat (both plural forms), following Langdon (2002: 48–77), but it should be noted that these often are designated, as has been done by Oswalt (1999: 5), under the broad general categories of Yuit and Inuit. Oswalt's basic classifications denote the connections between the Alaskan Yupiit and Siberian Yup'ik speakers, and the links between the Inupiat and Inuit groups stretching from northern Alaska across Canada and into Greenland, all of whom speak similar dialects of Inupiaq. The Yup'ik and Inupiaq languages have common roots, but they are likened by Langdon (2002: 11) to the differences between German and English and thus they are mutually unintelligible. The terms 'Yuit' and 'Inuit', or their derivatives, translate into English as 'the real people' or as Burch (1998: 3) suggests, 'authentic' or 'special' human beings. Scholars today persist in lumping Yupiit, Inupiat and Alutiik Alaskan Indigenous peoples under the generic term 'Eskimo', which Oswalt (1999: 5) contends originally had a derogatory meaning, since it was derived from the Algonkian-speaking Indians of Eastern Canada who referred to the Canadian Inuit as 'eaters of raw flesh'. I should also clarify that the term Native (note with an upper-case N) is used widely today by all Indigenous peoples of Alaska to designate themselves collectively, particularly in the context of land claims and Indigenous rights.

Ann Fienup-Riordan (2000: 9) explains that the Yupiit are members of the larger family of Inuit cultures that extend from Prince William Sound on the Pacific Coast of Alaska to the Siberian and Alaskan sides of the Bering Sea and from there thousands of miles north and east along Canada's Arctic coast and into Labrador and Greenland. Both Yupiit and Inupiat peoples claim a common ancestry in Eastern Siberia and Asia, probably appearing on the west coast of Alaska in relatively recent times, perhaps just over 2400 years ago. According to Oswalt (1999: 6), the Yupiit and Inupiat were characterized by the manufacture of 'harpoons, tailor-made skin clothing, oil-burning lamps, and skin-covered boats known as kayaks or *umiaks*'. They became sea-mammal hunters along the coasts of the Bering and Chukchi Seas, or in more inland regions, they hunted caribou or fished the rivers and streams.

Despite their common origins with other Inuit peoples, the Yupiit and Inupiat of Alaska varied in significant ways from related groups, particularly those living in Canada and Greenland. Oswalt (1999: 203) notes that the economies of the Alaskan Inuit were more diversified than their Canadian, Greenlandic or Polar counterparts since they 'did not base their livelihood on hunting seals at breathing holes' as those in Canada did nor did they 'concentrate on open-water sealing' as was done in East Greenland. Snowhouses were rarely constructed in Alaska, but instead semi-underground dwellings insulated with sod were built. Unlike the Inuit living in Canada or Greenland, the Yupiit and Inupiat of Alaska developed well-established centres for trading, which were accompanied by elaborate ceremonies aimed at re-enforcing relationships with neighbouring groups. Numerous complex rituals were observed at various levels in which, according to Oswalt (1999: 203), 'all the members of a village participated and great wealth might be redistributed'. Often the rituals included dramatic dancing that was enhanced by the use of masks symbolizing the spirits of animals, birds or sea mammals. These peculiar characteristics of Alaskan Yupiit and Inupiat peoples make research on both groups relevant to understanding Indigenous Alaskan patterns of subsistence and concepts of the land.

Traditional concepts of the land

Patterns of life among the Yupiit and Inupiat peoples traditionally were based around subsistence activities. A Canadian judge, Thomas Berger, who in the early 1980s conducted an extensive survey of Alaskan Native experiences of ANCSA on behalf of the Inuit Circumpolar Conference (to which I will return in detail later), quotes an old woman who testified at one of the over sixty village meetings he conducted as saying, 'Subsistence to us is … our spiritual way of life, our culture' (Berger 1985: 47–8). Berger explains this comment by referring to the tradition of whale hunting in north and northeast Alaska:

> For thousands of years, Inupiat Eskimos have lived and taken bowhead whales …. The Inupiat believe that these great whales give themselves to their hunters, if they have been hunted by Inupiat rules that govern the relationship between the people and the whales. (Berger 1985: 48)

Berger observes that throughout Alaska the traditional economy was based on similar activities to those he found amongst whaling communities. Success in hunting and fishing depended on observing rules in relation to the natural environment. Berger (1985: 51) calls these 'cultural values', which include 'mutual respect, sharing, resourcefulness, and an understanding that is both conscious and mystical of the intricate interrelationships that link humans, animals, and the environment'.

Further south along the coast of the Bering Sea, where the Yupiit live, the waters are too shallow for hunting bowhead whale. Instead, the people hunt seals, beluga whales and sea lions. The region stretching inland from the sea is crossed by numerous streams and rivers that yield abundant supplies of salmon, trout, northern pike, several species of whitefish, burbot, blackfish and stickleback. In addition to sea mammals and fish, a variety of birds, including geese, ducks and swans supplement food sources (Fienup-Riordan 1990: 8–9). Among both Yupiit and Inupiat peoples, Caribou herds are hunted, as they move through the inland mountain passes to the coasts. In addition, mountain sheep, polar bears, grizzly bears and moose provide sources of food for those living in inland areas. Various types of berries, which are also abundant throughout Alaska, are harvested annually. In some regions, these are mixed with seal fat and preserved.

Despite the abundance of natural resources available to the Yupiit and Inupiat, in pre-colonial times, due to the extreme climate and, in many places, the barrenness of the land, a certain fragile relationship with nature existed. The people had little control over the environment and depended on their own skill and ingenuity in hunting and fishing to ensure adequate supplies of food and materials needed for survival. This tenuous relationship to the land explains why, in the traditional world-view, life, spirit or soul (*inua* or personhood) was attributed to the animals and fish, which provided the primary sources for sustenance (Dupre 1975: 207). Spirits were thought also to inhabit the instruments used in hunting and fishing, and to be connected to the weather, particularly the winds blowing from the cardinal directions that brought quite distinct climatic conditions (Fienup-Riordan 1994: 317). The spirits, which were necessary for survival, could be influenced in rituals, or even controlled by shamans, but mostly they could be counted on to respond favourably to the needs of the people if the rules of the society were followed.

An example of the spiritual sense in which animals were regarded is demonstrated by the customary bladder festival in which, before missionaries arrived, annually the bladders of the seals killed in the seasonal hunt were inflated and hung in the traditional men's house (*Qasgiq* in Yup'ik) (Fienup-Riordan 1994: 283–92). The bladders, representing the *inua* of the seals, were 'entertained' for five days before being released through holes in the ice ready to return for the next cycle of hunting. The seals would not offer themselves to be killed if they were not respected in this way. Fienup-Riordan suggests that seals had the ability to ascertain both the merits and intentions of the hunter. If the hunter is 'awake to the rules of the proper relationship between humans and animals, and between humans and humans, then the seal will allow the hunter's harpoon or bullet to kill it' (Fienup-Riordan 1990: 45).

Subsistence and tradition were closely intertwined throughout Alaska, since survival depended on adhering strictly to a way of life that had been passed on authoritatively from generation to generation. Fienup-Riordan (1990: 47) asserts that the people 'are not simply surviving off the resources of their environment but are living in a highly structured relationship to them. This relationship is important to comprehend, not as an exercise in Eskimo esoterica, but as a key to why they act and feel the way they do'. Subsistence is also related directly to the land, since it is on the land and adjacent seas and waterways that the animals and fish live in their cycles of birth, death and rebirth. As has been implied in Fienup-Riordan's research, traditional concepts of the land defined how resources were shared, dictated trading practices and constituted the proper rules governing social relationships.

In his report developed for the Inuit Circumpolar Conference on ANCSA, Thomas Berger argued that the issue of land stands at the centre of the cultural divide between Alaskan Native peoples and Western society. He calls land 'inalienable' for Alaskan Natives and asserts that 'every member of the community in succeeding generations acquires an interest in the land as a birthright' (Berger 1985: 173). He cites Paul Ongtooguk from Kotzebue, an Inupiat town located on the northeast coast, as saying in a village meeting: 'I believe that if people, if the vast majority of Alaska Natives, were given the opportunity to either kill or die for their land, that most of them would do just that – if it was that simple' (Berger 1985: 173). On the same issue, Jimmy Stotts of Barrow on the far northern coast of Alaska, testified: 'The single biggest fear that we Inupiat have ... is the fear of losing control over our own lands, which we need for subsistence purposes' (Berger 1985: 173).

That land and subsistence are connected to traditional social relations and understandings of shared ownership is demonstrated by the annual whaling festivals among the northern Inupiat which, unlike the seal bladder rituals described by Fienup-Riordan, still occur, although in modified forms. In the tradition of the coastal Inupiat, preliminary preparations for the whaling season began in early March when the whaling equipment was cleaned and the crew were given new sets of clothing. The captain of a whaling crew, called an *umelik*, was one who, according to Oswalt (1999: 213), had earned respect in the community, had acquired wealth and commanded the loyalty of his men. During the early spring preparations, the *umelik*'s wife supervised making a new cover for the boat and, just before the hunt began, prepared a special meal for those about to embark. During the time of preparations, prohibitions against sexual intercourse were observed. The sea was watched carefully to ensure that the exact timing for beginning the hunt coincided with the break-up of the ice. For this reason, a shaman, acting as a clairvoyant, was consulted to 'see' into the precise moment when the whale hunt should commence (Oswalt 1999: 213).

The whaling season lasted from two to six weeks, beginning usually in late April, depending on weather conditions. The *umelik* and his crew observed food taboos during the hunt, while those remaining in the village followed ritual prohibitions. The *umelik* carried with him in a wooden box a small carved figure of a whale, which represented the life, spirit or *inua* of the whale being hunted. Capturing a bowhead whale required exact skill and close cooperation among the crew since the animal usually extends to around 33 feet (10 metres) and weighs over 30 US tons (27,215 kilograms). It also required the cooperation of the spirit of the whale that was being hunted. The harvest was shared equally among the members of the crew. Following the hunting season, the residents of the village held what Oswalt (1999: 217) calls a 'victory celebration', *nulukatuk*, "'to let the whale know we are happy'". Games and feasting occurred, including demonstrations of strength or endurance. Members of the various fishing teams shared *muktuk*, the black skin of the whale that is considered a delicacy, amongst the entire community. This sharing was a sign of generosity and thanksgiving for the successful whaling season and helped to bind the community together (Oswalt 1999: 217–18).

Ann Fienup-Riordan (1990: 39–43) describes a similar village event among the Yupiit called a 'seal party', which was held when 'the men and boys of the village brought home the first seals of the season.' During her early research trips in the 1970s to Nelson Island, just off the west coast of central Alaska, Fienup-Riordan describes how she was sitting in her room having a cup of tea, when she heard noise from the neighbouring house, which indicated the beginning of a series of events associated with seal parties. She went out to witness 'a woman standing on her porch throwing Pampers and packs of gum into the waiting hands of a large group of women'. She followed the group to the next house where the same sharing of goods occurred, although the group was not comprised of the same women. Fienup-Riordan records: 'By this time I was extremely excited. Here was a distribution of goods through which social relations were articulated', since sisters, mothers, mothers-in-law and parallel cousins were excluded from a particular seal party. During any seal party, the hostess allowed an older woman, usually the mother of the hostess's cousin, to select a special person from the group to receive a gift of raw meat. The next day after these series of seal parties had been completed, dances occurred in the community hall (the modern replacement for the *Qasgiq*) in which the women carried in, literally 'danced in', gifts for the men of the village. That evening the men 'danced in' gifts to the women in a similar way the women had done for them. Fienup-Riordan observes: 'The entire sequence of dances and gift-giving takes hours and hours, as everyone in the community has a turn on the dance floor'. Through this elaborate arrangement of dances and gifts, the Yupiit 'world view, their whole cultural mode of being, has … been put on stage along with the dancers, acted out, and so re-established and reaffirmed.' It begins with the harvesting of the first seals of the season and culminates with rituals of sharing, confirming that, in Fienup-Riordan's view, 'living off the land is still the preferred pattern' (Fienup-Riordan 1990: 43).

These examples, taken largely from ethnographic accounts and anthropological studies from the early to late twentieth century, suggest that the Yupiit and Inupiat traditions for centuries had been connected closely to the land and the subsistence patterns they had spawned. The concept of spirits, the communal and social relations that were welded together by the spirits, the rules of respect which were strictly adhered to and the elaborate rituals and festivals were all associated with subsistence activities and were legitimated by reference to ancient authoritative traditions. Justice Berger's hearings on ANCSA, conducted during the early 1980s, revealed that the land and its related subsistence way of life were referred to repeatedly by rural Native Alaskans as being under threat, thereby confirming that the traditional understanding of the land persisted widely amongst Alaska Natives late into the twentieth century and well over ten years after the Alaska Native Claims Settlement Act had been ratified. It is to ANCSA and its implications for the Indigenous way of life that I now turn.

The provisions of the Alaska Native Claims Settlement Act

The Alaska Native Claims Settlement Act of 1971 extinguished all Indigenous claims to the land in exchange for 44 million acres (nearly 18 million hectares) of land, which is approximately 10 per cent of the state's territory, plus $962.5 million in compensation for the 321 million acres of land, or 90 per cent of the state's territory, that was appropriated by the State of Alaska and the US federal government. All US citizens with one-fourth or more Alaskan Indian, Eskimo or Aleut blood, who were living when the settlement bill was enacted, were qualified to participate. Natives would receive their settlement through twelve regional corporations and more than 200 village corporations created by ANCSA (Berger 1985: 24). This process was explained in a volume authorized by the Alaska Native Foundation and written for use in schools as a basic guide to the law:

> Benefits under the settlement act would accrue to Natives not through clans, families or other traditional groupings, but, instead, through the modern form of business organization, called a corporation. All eligible Natives were to become stockholders – part owners – of such corporations (Arnold 1976: 146).

To take advantage of the settlement, the first step for an Alaskan Native was to register as a permanent resident in a particular village and region. The new stockholder would then be given 100 shares of stock in one of the twelve regional corporations and in most cases 100 shares of stock in a village corporation. Natives who did not live in a village were given shares in regional corporations and became known as at-large stockholders. Those who did not reside permanently in Alaska were not excluded from receiving benefits, but were permitted to register in one of the regional corporations or a thirteenth corporation, which was created for non-resident Natives and based in Seattle, Washington. The thirteenth corporation was not granted land, but received a portion of the $962.5 compensation package on a pro rata basis. Since there was only one issue of shares, no one born after 18 December 1971, the day President Nixon signed the bill into law, received shares (Berger 1985: 24–5; Mitchell 2001: 492–3).

The village corporations, which were granted 22 million of the 44 million acres of land, received only surface rights to the land, meaning that their ownership would not extend to minerals below the ground. The rights to the minerals would belong to the regional corporations so that 'the subsurface estate of lands selected by village corporations would go to regional corporations' (Arnold 1976: 151). Village corporations were given the option of registering as non-profit entities, but all chose to become profit-making organizations. Each regional corporation was required to distribute 70 per cent of the income it earned from the sale of timber and mineral rights among the other regional corporations 'to balance regional disparities in natural resources' (Berger 1985: 25). To protect the land, the law instituted a time restriction that forbade any Native corporate shares to be sold to non-Natives for twenty years, until 1991, when all such restrictions would be removed. In addition, the corporations would be exempt from state taxation until 1991.

These main provisions of ANCSA indicate that the law was extremely complex, but one outcome is indisputable, in the words of Norman Chance (1990: 165), it 'forever transformed the relationship between the Native peoples of Alaska and the land.' The words of the Act itself are explicit in this regard:

> All claims against the United States, the State, and all other persons that are based on claims of aboriginal right, title, use or occupancy of land or water areas in Alaska, or that are based on any statute or treaty of the United States relating to Native use and occupancy, or that are based on the laws of any other nation, including any such claims that are pending before any Federal or State court or the Indian Claims Commission are hereby extinguished. (Case and Voluck 2002: 58)

ANCSA and the land

As 1991 was approaching, it became apparent that village and regional corporations could be taken over by large non-Native interests, such as multinational corporations and oil companies. In response to this threat, the Inuit Circumpolar Conference, an international organization of Inuit peoples from Alaska, Canada and Greenland, appointed British Columbia Supreme Court Justice Thomas Berger to head the Alaska Native Review Commission to ascertain Native attitudes towards ANCSA. The study was co-sponsored by the World Council of Indigenous Peoples. Berger was selected because he had made a significant contribution to Canadian Indigenous land rights when he had been appointed in the mid-1970s by the Canadian government to conduct the Mackenzie Valley Pipeline Inquiry. Berger's new assignment for the Inuit Circumpolar Conference took him, in his own words, 'to Native villages all over Alaska to hear the evidence of Alaska Natives' (Berger 1985: vii). His findings are reported in the 1985 publication *Village Journey: The Report of the Alaska Native Review Commission*. In the sections above, in which I outlined traditional subsistence patterns among the Yupiit and Inupiat peoples, I have already made extensive use of this book, but I have not yet explored the most influential result of Berger's report, that which underscored the risk ANCSA posed to Indigenous land rights.

According to the original provisions of ANCSA, precisely twenty years after the law came into effect, on 18 December 1991, all Native corporations, both village and regional, were required to call in their shares and issue new shares which would be entirely unrestricted. Berger (1985: 96) explains: 'After 1991, shareholders will be free to sell all or any portion of their shares, to pledge them as collateral, or to use or dispose of them in any other way.' Individual shareholders could sell their shares in any way that they chose, even if such choices were opposed by other shareholders or by the majority of those who held stock in the relevant corporation. The threat was clear: 'The Native corporations can then become targets for takeover' (Berger 1985: 96). The possibility of government confiscation of the land also loomed in 1991, since state and local authorities could then levy taxes on the land, whether it was developed or undeveloped. This second threat meant that if a village or regional corporation could not afford to pay the taxes, the land could be claimed by government authorities. In his extensive hearings conducted throughout Alaska, Berger (1985: 96) found the same fear repeated: 'Alaska Natives expressed fear that their ancestral lands will be lost after 1991.' The importance of this concern cannot be minimized, primarily because it demonstrates that for Native peoples, in rural regions at least, the law linking corporations to the land had not transformed the traditional subsistence culture. The success or failure of the village and regional corporations was not the crucial issue; retaining the land and the tradition of subsistence were paramount.

Berger found just this concern voiced over and over again. For example, Dean George from Angoon in southeast Alaska is reported by Berger (1985: 96–7) as testifying:

> The biggest issue that I see before me now is 1991, and I don't believe it is a stock issue. For me, it is the land issue because the people who do hold stock hold title to the land, when that stock is sold, traded, or revested back to the corporation, so does their right to the land.

A similar concern was voiced by Alice Tucker, a Yup'ik woman from the village of Emmonak: 'After 1991, when we are able to sell our shares … and perhaps have our land taxed, what little we have left, we may never have anymore' (Berger 1985: 97–8). At a hearing conducted by Berger in the city of Fairbanks, Sam Demientieff underscored the connection between land and Native culture: 'One hundred shares represents the past life of the Native people, it represents the culture, the land, lifestyle, village living. And this portion, this hundred shares, is something that's going to become available for sale to the public in 1991' (Berger 1985: 98).

Another threat to community life that resulted from ANCSA is not quite so obvious. This relates to excluded Natives who were born after 18 December 1971. The Act granted shares only to those who were alive on that date. Thus, a child born on 18 December 1971 was a shareholder, but one born on 19 December 1971 was not. As the children of the same generation grew older, this created wide disparities in the community, when some of almost the exact age owned 200 shares in village and regional corporations and others owned none. Of course, inheritance laws applied, meaning that when shareholders died, they could leave their shares to their children. Yet, this also created the possibility of increasing inequity, disharmony and competitiveness. For example, if one shareholder had two children, these might receive 100 shares each in inheritance, but if another had four children, these would receive fifty shares each. As the generations succeeded, the inequities would increase. What began as an absolutely equitable distribution among Alaska Natives would become over time highly disparate with the long-term effect, in Berger's (1985: 106) words, that 'increasingly smaller divisions of the shares will reduce dividends, already trivial, to insignificance'. The subsistence culture of sharing and community involvement, as demonstrated in the whaling festivals and the seal parties I described earlier, would be eroded into an individualistic and competitive system in which shareholders sought ways to overcome the problems of diminishing return, often at the expense of one's fellow shareholder.

Berger's findings demonstrated that at the time he conducted his hearings, despite having lived under the village and regional corporate structure for over ten years, for rural Alaskans, subsistence remained the fundamental way of life. The land may have been connected legally to market performance, but for day-to-day living, fishing, hunting and whaling continued as normal. However, if the corporations could be taken over by non-Native commercial interests, the land could also be taken away from the people and could thereby divest them of their ancestral heritage and radically change their traditional patterns of life. The potential effects of ANCSA were shown by the Berger Commission to undermine and eventually destroy the Native Alaskan subsistence culture by transforming the concept of land into a system of shareholding within a corporate structure. Alaska Natives, who had relinquished all rights to the land, eventually would have no recourse but to assimilate into the patterns of life imposed by the dominant Western society.

Those who conceived this solution to Alaska Native claims were not unaware of the social consequences entailed in the legislation. In their review of the history of Alaska Natives and American laws, David Case and David Voluck (2002: 176) assert that 'the intent of ANCSA, as initially enacted, was pretty clearly to incorporate the Alaska Natives into the mainstream of the American free-market economy and its values'. They cite the testimony of Douglas Jones at a roundtable discussion organized in 1984 in Anchorage (Alaska's largest city) by Berger's Alaska Native Review Commission. Jones had been a member of Alaska's US Senate staff at the time ANCSA was first considered and participated in the various stages leading up to its enactment into law by the US Congress. Jones (cited by Case and Voluck 2002: 176-7) testified at the Anchorage roundtable that the concerns voiced by Alaska Natives to Berger throughout rural Alaska about the possibility of corporate takeovers 'was exactly the possibility that we had in mind'. Jones explained that the intention of ANCSA was to instil 'normalcy' within Alaskan Natives, which he defined as 'normal commercial behaviour, a movement toward business as usual'. He added: 'It's got nothing to do with … cultural traditions … but in part of one's life, it's important to be like everyone else.' Jones (cited by Case and Voluck 2002: 176) concluded his testimony by admitting that the 'mechanisms' of ANCSA, 'how the land was allotted and the money provided', were chosen 'to accomplish … *social engineering*' (cited by Case and Voluck 2002: 176) (emphasis in original).

In the report of the Alaska Native Review Commission, Berger (1985: 155–72) sought to reverse the assimilating impact of ANCSA on Native people, as articulated by Jones, primarily by recommending that ANCSA's provisions relating to land be revoked in favour of laws recognizing tribal sovereignty. These included retribalization of the land, Native self-government and Native jurisdiction over fish and wildlife. Berger was aware that the land could not simply be transferred to tribal governments, since ANCSA had made the land the private property of Native corporations. However, he suggested that this could be accomplished by shareholders themselves: 'I recommend that the shareholders of village corporations who are concerned that their land may be lost should transfer their land to tribal governments to keep the land in Native ownership' (Berger 1985: 167). In order to achieve this, Berger (1985: 167) argued that the US Congress should pass legislation that would enable tribal governments to 'claim sovereignty with respect to the land' by facilitating 'the transfer of land by the village corporations to tribal governments without regard for dissenter's rights'. Village and regional corporations could still exist, since Berger's recommendations related only to the land, and primarily to village life. The corporations could retain their business assets, but without the land, he conceded, it would be most likely that village corporations would dissolve (Berger 1985: 168). Berger (1985: 168) argued that the regional corporations, which own the subsurface of village lands, should transfer these rights to the village tribal governments. In this way, tribal governments would obtain full legal jurisdiction over the original functions of village corporations and maintain ownership of both surface and subsurface land. Moreover, under Berger's recommendations, no Natives would be excluded, since each Native resident within particular villages would be members of the tribe, regardless of his or her date of birth. Berger (1985: 161) concluded his recommendations by insisting that Congress 'must fully acknowledge that ... Native governments are legitimate political institutions, and that they have a right to retain ancestral lands in perpetuity'.

ANCSA in the post-1991 situation

There can be little doubt that the Alaska Native Review Commission exercised a powerful effect by raising consciousness about the threats posed by ANCSA to traditional Native culture and subsistence patterns. Berger's recommendations that effectively would have destroyed village corporations by transferring them to tribal governments, however, were not implemented. Rather, in 1987 the US Congress passed several crucial amendments to the law. The most vital was to alter the conditions of the automatic termination of restrictions on the sale of Native shares scheduled for 18 December 1991. The prohibition against selling individual shares was extended indefinitely, or until 'a majority of all the outstanding shares in any particular corporation voted to eliminate them' (Case and Voluck 2002: 177). The result was that after 1991 individuals could sell their shares only by collective, or at least by majority, consent.

A second critical amendment allowed the shareholders of Native corporations to issue stock to those born after 18 December 1971. In the opinion of Case and

Voluck (2002: 177), this appeared to give priority to kinship relationships of the shareholders over 'ANCSA's original goal of fostering "normal commercial behaviour"'. This did not materialize, however, since between 1988 and 1998, only six Native corporations, three regional and three villages, voted to issue shares to the children of the original shareholders, and these on different conditions. Unlike the original shareholders, the children received 'life estate' stock that lasted only for the lifetime of the particular shareholder. Because life estate stock could not be inherited, it reverted back to the corporation at the death of the shareholder. Two corporations set no limits on the issuing of life estate shares to children of shareholders, whereas some issued shares only for those born between 19 December 1971 and 31 December 1992. This meant that throughout Alaska, disparity increased among shareholders in village and regional corporations with some experiencing increasingly diluted value of their shares as more children were issued stock, as had been predicted by Berger.

A third amendment to the original act altered the law regarding taxation, allowing taxes to be levied only on developed land. Native corporations were further protected against claims from creditors, court judgements and bankruptcy (Case and Voluck 2002: 184–5). These provisions clearly were responses to fears that, as business ventures, the failure of Native corporations would dispossess the people of their land. By protecting against the consequences of serious financial losses, Congress eased concerns that unsuccessful commercial ventures by Native corporations would lead to corporate takeovers. Case and Voluck (2002: 185) observe that these provisions make Native corporations 'unique', since they are protected from loss and are exempt from many regulations that affect 'normal' corporations. They conclude: 'The Alaska Native Claims Settlement Act is an experiment that is still evolving' (Case and Voluck 2002: 185).

The issue of tribal sovereignty in Alaska that was raised by the Berger Commission has been addressed in part by the US Congress. Although this is a complicated issue, it is clear that at the time Berger wrote his report, Alaskan Natives were being treated differently from other Indigenous groups in the lower forty-eight states, which had been recognized as tribes with sovereignty over reservation areas. Since there were no reservations in Alaska, this had not been applied to Indigenous groups there. In their detailed discussion of this issue, Case and Voluck observe that Native sovereignty in Alaska was confused for many years. Now, however, they argue, 'the federal government recognizes Alaska Native tribes with the same status as tribes in the lower forty-eight states' (Case and Voluck 2002: 427–8). This means that Alaska Native villages must 'be treated as sovereign tribes with the same rights, responsibilities, and immunities as tribes in the rest of the nation' (Case and Voluck 2002: 428). Alaska Natives, however, operate under different conditions with respect to the land. Because of ANCSA, the US Supreme Court has ruled that ANCSA lands, the precise land that was offered to the Natives of Alaska in the 1971 settlement, do not qualify as so-called Indian country. Case and Voluck (2002: 428) maintain that this leaves 'Alaska Native tribal governments as sovereigns without territorial reach'.

Conclusions

Despite changes in the law since its original enactment, the Alaska Native Claims Settlement Act persists as a tool of social engineering aimed at assimilating the Native peoples of Alaska into the mainstream American free market, competitive culture and, as such, operates as an instrument of power. As I noted at the beginning of this chapter, the aim of assimilation has been demonstrated by business ventures that in many cases are very far removed from the culture of subsistence and its connection to the land. A regional corporation, such as Cook Inlet Region, Inc., can invest widely in projects that have no relevance to Indigenous ways of life, including, as we have seen, a major hotel and casino in Las Vegas. Although in rural Alaska, subsistence lifestyles endure and progress has been made towards Native sovereignty, the land, which I have argued is crucial to self-identity and cultural awareness, has been severed from its concrete relation to the people and its role in the collective memory and placed into the abstract notion of shares in stocks. Property owners and shareholders now are identical. This has not been altered by the protections set in place by the government against financial failure.

This leads to my conclusion that the land in traditional Alaska, which was viewed as the locus of customary ways of life, has been secularized by the Alaska Native Claims Settlement Act. I have argued that traditionally the land was linked with the forms of life that provided the means of subsistence for the people who lived on it (the 'real people'). These forms of life were perceived by the people as possessing souls or spirits (*inua*), which in turn fostered a reciprocal relationship between humans and the natural environment. All life, both natural and human, was understood as enveloped by cycles of birth, death and rebirth. Although, again as I noted at the outset, it would be easy to romanticize the Indigenous world-view and to present Alaskan Natives in quite exotic terms or, as Fienup-Riordan calls it, in 'half-truths', it is clear that the Indigenous people traditionally maintained a religious relationship with the land, in the sense that I have defined it following Hervieu-Léger. The rules governing their relationship to the land, particularly the animals, fish and sea mammals, which dwelt on or near it, were translated into well-defined social regulations aimed at ensuring survival and well-being in an oftentimes harsh environment.

These dimensions of Indigenous Alaskan culture, which had been passed on authoritatively for generations, can be contrasted starkly with the atomization of life in Western capitalist society, which is based on maximizing profits in a competitive economic market. The transformation of the traditional concept of land pinpoints decisively the secularizing effect of ANCSA, precisely because it disrupts the authoritative transmission of tradition in Native Alaskan communities by fragmenting communal life through private shareholding. Indeed, after nearly 150 years, it could be said that the Americans have largely secularized Native Alaska according to Sheldon Jackson's original formula: 'to make more money in order to live better ... and to utilize the resources of the country in order to make more money.'

Thomas Berger (1985: 182) concluded his landmark report for the Alaska Native Review Commission by commenting that when ANCSA was adopted by the US Congress, it 'shone as a beacon of hope' for Indigenous peoples in other parts of the world. Ironically, he added, it was rejected as a model for Indigenous land rights. Instead, Indigenous peoples in other parts of the world 'have reaffirmed their conviction that Native lands should be passed intact from one generation to the next' (Berger 1985: 182). Although Berger's recommendations were not implemented in the form he envisaged, his call for Native control over the land can be understood fully only in the light of a traditional way of life and its opposition to what I am calling the secularizing impact of ANCSA. Berger's penultimate words in *Village Journey* sound very much like a rallying cry to return to an authoritative transmission of tradition: 'Indian country must remain Indian Country, Eskimo Country must remain Eskimo country, Aleut country must remain Aleut Country' (Berger 1985: 187). Whether Berger's vision is fulfilled or not very much depends on widespread acceptance of the argument that a fundamental contradiction exists between the core of traditional Alaskan culture and the secularizing intentions of the Alaska Native Claims Settlement Act.

Chapter 11

THE STUDY OF RELIGION AND NON-RELIGION IN THE EMERGING FIELD OF 'NON-RELIGION STUDIES': ITS SIGNIFICANCE FOR INTERPRETING AUSTRALIAN ABORIGINAL RELIGIONS

The category 'non-religion' is frequently associated with debates over the secularization process in the West and it has been linked to controversies surrounding the 'new atheism' and cognitive approaches within the sciences of religion. Often overlooked in this field of study are Indigenous populations. This is partly because it is commonly assumed that traditional, small-scale societies make no distinction between religion and non-religion in the sense that every activity of life possesses some spiritual significance. It is also pointed out that Indigenous populations almost never have a word in their vocabulary which equates to the Western idea of religion. For example, the African theologian and scholar of African religions, John S. Mbiti (1969: 1), famously claimed that 'Africans are notoriously religious'. Or, the Methodist leader and scholar of Yoruba religion, E. B. Idowu (1962: 5), in his important study, *Olodumare: God in Yoruba Belief*, wrote: 'The real keynote of the life of the Yoruba ... is their religion. In all things, they are religious. Religion forms the foundation and the all-governing principle of life for them.' E. G. Parrinder, who originally studied West African religion and became a leading scholar in the comparative study of religions during the latter part of the twentieth century, in his important and widely read book, *African Traditional Religion*, noted that in Africa 'religion is not just the province of one particular class, though there are specialists in ritual. Nor is it only for those who feel piously inclined, though there are differences of temperament. But religion enters into the life of every individual' (Parrinder 1974: 27). Such claims are not limited to scholars of African religions. In his book, *An Introduction to Maori Religion*, James Irwin (1984: 5–6) observed: 'Maori people do not see the sacred and secular as separated but as parts of the whole. Theirs is a holistic view of life.' And in her *Introduction to Primal Religions*, Philippa Baylis (1988: 3) argued that everything in primal societies, including work, family relationships, eating and sexual activity are all 'religious'.

These commentators on Indigenous Religions all agree that religion is embedded in the social milieu within Indigenous societies. What is less clear is exactly what it is that is embedded. The leading scholar in the methodology of religions, Jan G. Platvoet (1992: 22), when writing about African religions, rightly observed that 'African Traditional Religions ... are co-extensive with their societies; religion is an undifferentiated part of social life'. Platvoet, who clearly writes from a non-theological perspective, by arguing that religion is co-extensive with society, implies that, although the two are interconnected, each has a separate identity. Religion and society can be disentangled, at least for theoretical and analytical purposes. But in this context, for Platvoet, as for Mbiti, Idowu, Irwin, Baylis, Parrinder and a host of others, religion remains ill-defined; its meaning is simply presumed beneath the claims that religion permeates all aspects of life in Indigenous societies. A central problem then, following the theme of this chapter, as it applies to Australian Aboriginal peoples, is precisely to identify and clarify the meaning of the terms, 'religion' and 'non-religion'.

Religion and non-religion in the emerging field of 'non-religion studies'

In order to make this identification, in this chapter, I begin by analysing the way 'religion' and 'non-religion' are being used by Lois Lee and Johannes Quack, two leading scholars within the newly emerging field in the academic study of religion called 'non-religion studies'. I then offer a critique of the ambiguous and at times confusing use of the concept 'non-religion' as it has been explained by these advocates of the term. I follow this by presenting my own definition of religion, which I contend is necessary if we are to clarify what it is that 'non-religion' actually negates. I then examine two seminal works dealing with non-religion: one by the British sociologist Colin Campbell whose book, *Toward a Sociology of Irreligion*, first published in 1971, has been introduced into the contemporary discussions by Lee and Quack, and the other, the largely unnoticed contribution to the discussion of 'non-religion', or 'irreligion', by the French agnostic philosopher, Jean-Marie Guyau, who was writing towards the end of the nineteenth century. By contrasting the views of these earlier writers on non-religion in the light of my own definition of religion, I show how it is possible to make space for the category 'non-religion' as a useful and positive tool for analysing contemporary social and cultural movements.

The new field within the academic study of religion called 'non-religion studies' finds its most organized and ambitious expression through the Nonreligion and Secularity Research Network (NSRN). On its website the NSRN, which was founded in 2008, describes itself as 'an international and interdisciplinary network of researchers', the aim of which is 'to centralise existing research on the topic of nonreligion and secularity and to facilitate discussion in this area' (NSRN: https://thensrn.org). Other examples of the growing interest in 'non-religion' can be witnessed in the recent establishment of academic centres or research projects, such as the Institute for the Study of Secularism in Society and Culture (ISSSC) at Trinity College, Hartford, Connecticut, the creation in 2011 of a programme in 'Secular Studies' at Pitzer College in Claremont, California, the Programme for the Study of Religion and Non-Religion in the Anthropology Department at the London School of Economics, and the Research Project on the Diversity of Nonreligion at the University of Zurich in Switzerland.

In an article appearing in a special edition of the *Journal of Contemporary Religion* devoted to exploring the theme 'non-religion and secularity', Lois Lee offered a preliminary definition of the term by arguing that 'non-religion' is 'anything which is *primarily* defined by a relationship of difference to religion' (Lee 2012: 131; see also, Bullivant 2010: 109–24; Bullivant and Lee 2012: 19–27). In her introduction to a reprint of Colin Campbell's *Toward a Sociology of Irreligion*, Lee clarified that non-religion as a category conveys a positive meaning and does not operate simply as a negation of religion. She explained that non-religion is 'etymologically relative but ontologically autonomous', arguing that non-religion 'exists in and impacts upon the world, and it can in turn be shaped by forces acting upon it, including but not limited to religion' (Lee 2013: xiv). This same point has been made by Johannes Quack, Principal Investigator of The Diversity of Nonreligion Research Project in the University of Zurich, who refers to 'the tension between understanding the independence of nonreligious phenomena as well as their dependency on religion' (Quack 2014: 443). The notion that non-religion is discrete from religion and yet in some way related to it requires some clarification as to what is actually meant by this claim.

In her article appearing in the *Journal of Contemporary Religion*, Lee (2012: 130) identifies what she calls 'three essential terms ... that make up the core terminology for non-religion studies'. The first takes religion as its root, including such notions as 'non-religion, irreligion, a-religion, anti-religion'. The second focuses on theism, primarily 'atheism' and 'non-theism'. The third makes 'the secular' its root as is found in numerous sociological theories of secularism or secularity. Among these three areas, Lee (2012: 130) argues that 'non-religion' should be defined in such a way that 'qualifies it as the master ... concept in the field'. This is because terms related to theism are restricted to god beliefs and secularism is defined by the marginalization of religion in society. Following the lead of Colin Campbell, Lee (2013: xxii) maintains that the secular refers to 'the space that is left after religion has withdrawn' and hence, as a term, can be described as 'a subtractive or absentive condition'. By contrast, non-religion, or using Campbell's term 'irreligion', is 'a concrete phenomenon, identifiable by its presence in the empirical world' (Lee 2013: xxii).

Quack (2014: 443) makes a similar point when he argues that 'studies of nonreligion' must be distinguished from traditional approaches associated with '"secularization theory" and its resulting problems'. In the first place, he contends, theories of secularization are closely associated with nineteenth-century assumptions rooted in outdated evolutionary concepts. Second, secularization theory has become entangled with what Quack (2014: 443) calls 'problematic political connotations and implications' as evidenced by commonly maintained oppositions such as 'modern–backward, rational–irrational, liberal–dogmatic, and democratic–theocratic'. Third, secularization theory oversimplifies the actual changes affecting religion in contemporary society by reducing religion to an essentialist category that describes it (religion as a singular entity) either as being in decline or in a process of transformation. This, Quack (2014: 443) complains, makes nuanced interpretations of religion in society impossible since religious phenomena are subjected to a 'superficial either-or logic'.

So, thus far, we are told by Lee and Quack that 'non-religion', as a field of study in its own right, should not be understood simply as a negation of religion, nor should it be bound by traditional theories of secularization. But what then, precisely, is 'non-religion'? How can 'non' religion be understood apart from what it negates? How is it possible to speak about the impact of non-religion on society without, by definition, limiting it, in Lee's words, to what it ontologically excludes? In her introduction to the reprint of Colin Campbell's book, Lee tries to answer these questions by situating non-religion as a contextually determined word, just like religion, and thus one that defies a fixed definition. She asserts that non-religion 'is a response to religion and is therefore as amorphous and shifting an object as religion is' (Lee 2013: xxi). This means that 'there is no fixed nature of irreligion; rather, irreligion responds to the religion of the day' (Lee 2013: xxi). In line with this somewhat obtuse interpretation of religion and non-religion, in her article appearing in the *Journal of Contemporary Religion*, Lee (2012: 131) includes, as examples of non-religion, belief systems such as atheism and agnosticism, some forms of secularism, contemporary humanism, anti-religious movements, irreligious experiences and indifference towards religion, but she excludes rationalism, 'New Age' or alternative spiritualities (for a discussion of 'irreligious experiences', see Bullivant 2008: 7). These latter movements, according to Lee (2012: 131), 'are usually defined by their own core principles and practices', which means that for them 'differentiation from religion' is a 'secondary' rather than a 'primary' consideration.

The reader can be forgiven for having difficulty following this line of thinking, precisely because the terms 'religion' and 'non-religion' are used by Lee without stating explicitly how she is employing them as conceptual categories. Non-religion is supposed to operate as a social force in its own right, in relation to religion, but not restricted to it. What this entire discussion calls for is clarity of meaning in the use of terms. Perhaps this is what Lee (2012: 134) intends when she urges scholars to develop a 'robust theory concerning the ontology of non-religion' and to explore 'how this relates to the ontology of religion'. But she does little towards achieving this goal and even confounds the distinction between religion and non-religion when she argues that non-religion should be understood in a similar way as 'gender', which, of course, applies to all: 'everyone is understood to have a gender'. This, she says, cannot be said of religion: 'not everyone has a religion' (Lee 2012: 134).

Quack (2014: 445) attempts to overcome the confusion into which Lee has fallen by introducing a distinction between different kinds of 'contrast'. He asserts that what is important conceptually is to distinguish between describing the relationship between religion and non-religion as contrary or contradictory. As an example, he notes that the terms 'alive' and 'lifeless' are contradictory because 'everything either has life (is alive) or lacks life (is lifeless)' (Quack 2014: 445).

So, we are correct if we conclude that 'nothing is both alive and lifeless'; they are contradictory. But where would we place the concept 'dead'? Certainly, something that is dead is lifeless, but the notion 'dead' implies that what is being referred to as dead must once have been alive, which cannot apply, for example, to a stone which has never been alive. Therefore, something that is dead, rather than acting as a contradiction to life, must be regarded as a subcategory of lifeless, operating in a contrary relation rather than being in a contradictory relation to the state of being alive. Quack (2014: 445–6) applies this to the relation between religion and non-religion by calling 'religious' and 'not religious' 'contradictory terms': 'something is either religious or it is not religious, any third possibility is excluded'. He follows this assertion immediately by claiming that 'both "nonreligious" and "areligious" are contrary to religion' (Quack 2014: 446). He explains that 'nonreligious' and 'areligious' 'are both mutually exclusive sub-fields of all things not religious', adding that 'nonreligious phenomena require a relation to "religion", while areligious phenomena are generally described and analysed without reference to religious phenomena' (Quack 2014: 446). In terms of his analogy, 'non-religion' is in a similar relation to 'religion' as 'dead' is to 'being alive'.

In my view, both Lee and Quack are employing language in an obscure and at times convoluted manner, which only serves to mystify the reader and promote misunderstanding. It would be much easier and clearer simply to define what is meant by religion and non-religion quite explicitly. For this reason, I contend that, even at the risk of being accused of promoting outdated, essentialist, decontextualized and, what Quack calls 'anachronistic' ideas (2014: 449, fn 10), I maintain that we must first define what we mean by 'religion' before social phenomena associated with 'non-religion' can be described, studied, tested empirically and subjected to critical analysis. I agree with both Lee and Quack that we need to treat the category 'non-religion' as a field of study in its own right, and that this must be seen in relation to religion, though not limited strictly to religion, but I contend that this cannot be done unless we begin by defining religion.

Demarcating religion

In my book, *An Introduction to the Phenomenology of Religion* (Cox 2010: 15–8), I proposed what I called a 'working definition' of religion or what I referred to in another publication as a 'preliminary' definition derived from an intuitive sense of the meaning of the term (Cox 1999: 267–84). I devoted a section in my book, *From Primitive to Indigenous: The Academic Study of Indigenous Religions* (2007a: 75–93), to using the French sociologist Danièle Hervieu-Léger's theory of religion towards developing my own restricted definition of religion. Initially, I analysed an article Hervieu-Léger (1999: 73–92) had written, entitled 'Religion as Memory', that appeared in a book edited by Jan Platvoet and Arie Molendijk called *The Pragmatics of Defining Religion* (1999) and then I drew out themes from her book first published in English in 2000 under the title *Religion as a Chain of Memory*. Most recently, I have attempted to isolate the sine qua non of religion –

that without which religion is not religion. I called this the necessary condition for religion to be identified in any phenomenon we are describing. I separated the basic elements of religion into three components: identifiable communities, a tradition and authority. I contend that, put together, these three components comprise what is necessary for religion to be religion. Other conditions may exist in religions, but without these three elemental components, religion is absent (Cox 2013a: 308–23).

By use of the term 'identifiable communities', I am arguing that the scholar of religion cannot study individual experiences as religion, unless the experiences are embedded in shared social constructs that are codified, symbolized and institutionalized in communities. The qualifying term 'identifiable' refers to the requirement that a scholar place limits around communities under study, sometimes using historical methods, at other times defining them geographically or in contemporary contexts as they may be expressed in virtual or online communities. In every case, the identifiable communities must accord to commonly understood and shared cultural criteria, even if these criteria are dictated by the new forms found in social media (see, for example, Rice 2009). Within these identifiable communities, the thoughts and experiences of those who identify within them, although not identical, can be regarded as similar, since they are shared among members of the group.

The two further fundamental defining characteristics of religion are found in the concepts, 'tradition' and 'authority'. Identifiable communities, to be constituted as a religion, always are subject to a structure of authority that has been developed and instituted by appeals to tradition, even if the tradition is invented or merely postulated. Thus, the way a community legitimizes its authority is closely bound to its identity. The key question confronting scholars is not, for example, could an online community be considered a religion. What is important is the authoritative source for the tradition that has been, or allegedly has been, transmitted from generation to generation. The key indicators of a religious, as opposed to a non-religious, legitimization of a tradition are consolidated in the singular term 'authoritative transmission'. The transmission of a tradition must be accomplished with an overwhelming authority, which establishes a community and makes it entirely distinct from any other community. These elements clearly apply to the historic religions, which have a long tradition that is passed on from generation to generation (usually by appeals to revelation or claims that their institutions have been divinely established), but they can also be fitted into an interpretation of new religious movements, which develop prophets or charismatic leaders so as to provide fresh interpretations of the authoritative tradition and thus affect the way it is transmitted. Further work needs to be done on how powerfully a tradition can be transmitted in online contexts, but this does not alter the fundamental requirement that for religion to be present in any cultural context, the community must legitimize its tradition by appeals to the transmission of an overwhelming authority (Johnson 2010).

These considerations lead me to conclude that the necessary or indispensable condition for religion to be present in any human activity, its irreducible defining components, requires the existence of an identifiable community, which is constituted by its being bound by and subservient to an overpowering authoritative tradition that is passed on from generation to generation. This restricted definition is sociological and culturally based rather than theological or quasi-theological. It does not depend on belief in supernatural entities or refer to a postulated transcendental object towards which the community directs its attention. This closely demarcated definition of religion can be tested empirically; it is embedded in sociocultural contexts and it avoids the error of many definitions which seek to isolate an ontological 'essence' of religion. The components of this definition are entirely objective and therefore in the context of this book can be applied to distinguishing religion from non-religion among Indigenous peoples, but, within the broader study of religion, they shed new light on the somewhat convoluted interpretations of what constitutes the subject matter of the emerging field of 'non-religion' studies.

Campbell and Guyau on non-religion

I now want to take a brief historical detour to set the context for the argument that my definition of religion paves the way for constructing the positive content of 'non-religion studies'. As I have indicated, Lois Lee credits the 1971 publication by Colin Campbell, entitled *Toward a Sociology of Irreligion*, as anticipating the development of non-religion studies. She claims that Campbell, who is now Emeritus Professor of Sociology in the University of York, was ahead of his time, and that it took over thirty years after his ground-breaking study for non-religion to emerge as a distinct field for academic research (Lee 2013: xiv–xv). In his publication, Campbell made it clear that he was urging scholars to treat irreligion seriously as a phenomenon in and of itself, a point reiterated and emphasized by Lee. Campbell (2013 [1971]: 7) wrote: 'Irreligion as a social and cultural phenomenon is worthy of serious investigation, independent of any light which such investigations may shed on the future of religion.' Yet, as one reads further into his book, we find irreligion clearly being defined in terms of a rejection of religion (Campbell 2013 [1971]: 26). He explains that this avoids the problems associated with conflating irreligion with secularism, which is marked by 'the absence of religion' (Campbell 2013 [1971]: 27). By defining irreligion as the rejection of religious traditions, Campbell suggests that he has introduced a potentially interesting feature of contemporary life that calls for thorough sociological analysis.

According to Campbell, in sociological terms, irreligion must be understood as the rejection of, or at least indifference towards, religious institutions, or what he calls 'available religious traditions'. By defining irreligion 'as a relationship of hostility or indifference to religion' (Campbell 2013 [1971]: 28), he is vulnerable to the charge that he has made the study of irreligion an entirely negative affair. He attempts to overcome this complaint by introducing the academic method he calls 'contextual specification', by which he means that descriptions and instances of irreligiousness must be analysed by placing them within social and cultural contexts

(Campbell 2013 [1971]: 280). Where, for example, a single religious tradition dominates a society, irreligion can be identified rather easily as a rejection of the tenets of the dominant tradition. In societies characterized by religious pluralism, such rejections become more complex and can be confused with unorthodox beliefs and practices. For Campbell, this is not an overwhelming obstacle to his definition of irreligion, since it is possible to 'have an established orthodoxy within a diverse and pluralistic religious structure, as is the case with Anglicanism in Britain, or, in a rather different way, with Protestantism, Catholicism and Judaism in America' (Campbell 2013 [1971]: 29). The bottom line for Campbell is that irreligion or non-religion must be understood as a rejection of contextually determined religious traditions. The remainder of his book is devoted to spelling out in detail the contexts he thinks clarify his position, by focusing on irreligious movements in Britain and America during the nineteenth and twentieth centuries, including, for example, humanist, positivist, ethical and rationalist movements.

If we were to follow Campbell, I do not think we would achieve Lois Lee's and Johannes Quack's goal of establishing a field of study that, although it is described as being in relation to religion, does not depend on religion to demarcate precisely what constitutes its subject matter. The cases cited by Campbell indeed all identify themselves by their common rejection of religion, but if non-religion is to be treated as a field in relation to religion, but not defined exclusively by it, we need to identify subjects for study that clearly are non-religious, but which can be defined in ways that do more than reject religion. And here I want to draw the reader's attention to an overlooked and seldom cited scholar who wrote a book on non-religion in the late nineteenth century, over seventy years before Campbell's volume appeared. I refer to Jean-Marie Guyau (1854–88), whose book on the study of non-religion first appeared posthumously in English in 1897 as *The Non-Religion of the Future: A Sociological Study*, following its initial publication in French in 1887 under the title *L'Irreligion de l'avenir*.

Guyau was writing at a time that was dominated by Darwinism and in particular by Herbert Spencer's form of social evolution and therefore, of course, he needs to be interpreted in the context of the intellectual climate of his era (Cox 2014a: 11–34). Nonetheless, in many ways, he transcended the trends of his day by defining non-religion as containing content in its own right and not discussing it strictly in terms of the rejection of religion. Guyau began his analysis by defining clearly what he meant by religion. He argued that religions consist of three fundamental defining characteristics: (1) myths, (2) systems of dogmas and beliefs that are not verifiable scientifically or philosophically and (3) a fixed system of ritual practices (Glatzer 1962: 14). He added that the manner whereby these three categories are displayed in religions is conditioned by historical and social contexts, but that these fundamental features can be found in all religions.

As a result of this scheme for classifying the characteristics of religion, Guyau was able to define what he meant by non-religion: the diminution of the force or power of myths, the breaking up of dogmatic forms of religion and the dissolution of communal rituals by the rise of individualism. N. N. Glatzer, the Jewish philosopher and theologian, who wrote the introduction to the 1962 reprint of

Guyau's book, summarized Guyau's interpretation of non-religion: 'Ultimately, with the rise of science, industry, independent ethics, and individualism, religious forces fail; decline of ritual sets in, dissolution of dogma: a religion has ceased to exist' (Glatzer 1962: 14). Following Guyau, the study of the non-religion of the future, or to put it in contemporary terms, 'non-religion studies', would focus on the social conditions that reflect the decline of religion: a fundamental trust in the scientific method; acceptance of the premise that all we can know depends on testing assertions by recourse to empirical means of verification (or falsification); an emphasis on prioritizing individual actions and personal choices over communal decision-making.

Towards the conclusion of his book, Guyau makes explicit what he believed to be the positive content of non-religion. He recounts a conversation he had with Ernest Renan, the nineteenth-century French philosopher and author of the classic book, *The Life of Jesus*, in which Guyau (1962 [1897]: 373) declared to Renan: 'It is the word of nature and humanity, of free-thought and free sentiment, which is taking the place of oracles and of supernatural revelation, of dogmatic religion.' He then cites Renan's response: 'We are all marching toward non-religion. After all, why should not humanity do without religious dogmas? ... Even at the present day, among advanced peoples, dogmas are disintegrating, the incrustations of human thought are breaking up.' Guyau (1962 [1897]: 373) adds his own interpretation: 'Science offers a field for disinterestedness and research, but does not tolerate vagaries of the imagination. It encourages enthusiasm but not delirium, and possesses a beauty of its own, the beauty of truth.' We can infer that Guyau, although clearly a writer of his time, anticipated that the study of non-religion would include the impact of the scientific method on human societies, how it has affected religious dogma and how, as a result of the decline of religion, individualism has become the ideal form of what previously was maintained by religious institutions. Guyau (1962 [1897]: 375) concludes: 'Instead of accepting ready-made dogmas, we should each of us be the makers of our own creed.'

The positive content of non-religion studies

Following Guyau's insightful discussion at the end of the nineteenth century of the positive content of non-religion, and taking the lead from what I think is Campbell's and Lee's failure to clearly demarcate religion from non-religion, I want to return to my definition of religion as a way of demonstrating how non-religion can become a field of study in its own right. Since, on my analysis, religion is never an individual experience exclusively, but requires a community that is bound by an authoritative tradition, non-religion logically is defined by the following three components: (1) lack of a community, (2) having no tradition or a very weak tradition and (3) having no authority or a very weak authority. On this accounting, 'non-religion studies' would employ social scientific principles to analyse trends in contemporary society that are characterized by an emphasis on individual autonomy, governed by self-interest and whose values are thoroughly relativistic.

As Campbell and Lee correctly note, the term 'secularization' has often been associated with 'irreligion' or, more recently on Lee's analysis, secularizing movements have been cited as part of the larger discussion of 'non-religion'. This is the way, for example, Jan Platvoet (2002: 83) explains secularization in the Dutch context, which he argues has over the past fifty or sixty years witnessed a rapid change away from 'a fairly monochromatic ... Christian scene ... to one of dazzling diversity, tolerance and religious indifference'. This occurred, according to Platvoet (2002: 83), as a result of the 'disaffiliation from the Dutch mainline churches ... which turned Dutch society from the "most Christian" nation of Europe in 1950, to probably, the most secularised and irreligious one in 2000'. If we follow Platvoet's line of thinking, which is very similar to Campbell's analysis, we would cite as evidence of 'non-religion' all instances of 'disaffiliation' from organized religion and indifference towards or even rebellion against authoritative traditions (Cox 2007b: 76). Although I think this goes some way towards defining 'non-religion' as a field of study, I find Campbell's and Platvoet's descriptions too limiting; they tend to relegate non-religion studies to the role of analysing the negation of religion in contemporary social and historical contexts.

Like Guyau, I want to describe non-religion as a positive field of study with its own content in relation to religion but not circumscribed by religion. Lee wants this too, but I think her attempts to identify the field of non-religion studies are unclear and confusing. On my analysis, non-religion studies as a positive area for scholarly research, with its own substantive content, could include, for example, research on the impact of capitalism and the world market economy as forces promoting individualism, disintegration of communities and consumerism. Although we could equally study world capitalism as a religion, since today it represents a dominating force that exercises almost total power over the way individuals act in society, the very factors that create a homogeneous economic system lead towards a radical fragmentation of communal cohesion by encouraging individual autonomy and personal self-interest. On this analysis, religion could be identified by the homogenization in contemporary global societies of values and practices dictated by the hegemonic force of world capitalism, whereas non-religion would refer to the radical fragmentation and acute individualism fostered by the almost total dominance of the same capitalistic system. Or, to cite another example, research on 'non-religion' in modern societies could focus on individuals who belong to numerous specialized but atomized groups, to whom they owe only faint allegiance and over which such groups exercise little authority. Although each group might operate within a general framework dictated by market forces (Jakobsen 1999: 167–76), in so far as they do not foster a singular commitment to an all-consuming authority, they would constitute examples of what is meant by 'non-religion'.

In terms of my clarification of the relative relationship between religion and non-religion, non-religion would be characterized by forces in society where no real, central organizing and authoritative tradition can be sustained. Following Hervieu-Léger, non-religion would be present wherever 'the collective memory of modern societies is composed of bits and pieces' (2000: 128) or what she calls in the same context, 'the crumbling memory of modern societies' (2000: 127). This entirely non-theological definition of religion and non-religion clarifies, exemplifies and demystifies Lois Lee's (2012: 131) statement that 'non-religion is any position, perspective or practice which is *primarily* defined by, or in relation to, religion, but which is nevertheless considered to be other than religious'. By clearly demarcating religion from non-religion and by stating explicitly what the terms mean, I have shown how the relationship between them can be a source for promoting in-depth analysis and understanding of wide and diverse contemporary social movements, rather than one that is obscured by enigmatic language.

Application of the distinction between religion and non-religion to Aboriginal peoples

The last issue to consider in this chapter is how the distinction between religion and non-religion can be applied to the study of social movements among Aboriginal peoples. In numerous publications I have described Indigenous Religions generally as bound by an authoritative tradition dictated by kinship relations and restricted to specific locations or places (Cox 2007a: 53–74; Cox 2013a: 308–23; Cox 2013b: 3–18). I have argued that ancestral traditions dominate in such societies and that living representatives of the ancestors perpetuate their authority by appeals to a line of authority stretching back in time, appeals that are confirmed in contemporary situations through rituals that re-enforce existing social structures. I have also argued that Indigenous societies are restricted not only by kinship ties, but that they relate exclusively to a particular geographical place or location fixed in the tradition by their quasi-legendary myths. Foundational stories are relayed to the young and passed on from generation to generation. These local myths form the background on which rituals performed regularly in honour of the ancestors are conducted. In traditional Aboriginal Australian contexts, these conditions apply to the manner that totemic ancestors relate to a particular place in the landscape, how individuals at conception become identified with a specific totemic ancestor and how these fit into a complex structure, referred to by T. G. H. Strehlow (1978a) in reference to the peoples of Central Australia as 'polytotemic' communities.

My general description of Indigenous societies has been criticized for denying that Indigenous peoples have responded dynamically to the impact of modernity and the influences of invading, proselytizing religions (Tafjord 2013: 231). I am aware that Indigenous populations around the globe have been exposed to forces that create conflicts between tradition and modernity, and that they have responded in ways that include combining the old with the new without denying either. I have demonstrated how this has functioned in Northern Queensland in the case of the Rainbow Spirit Theology, where the traditional image of the rainbow-serpent, called by A. R. Radcliffe-Brown (1926: 24) a ubiquitous symbol throughout Australia, has been converted into the figure of a Creator God, so much so that Jesus Christ has been described as the incarnation of the rainbow-serpent (Cox 2014a: 105). In this way, my restricted definition aims at achieving clarity of terms. In Indigenous

Australia, wherever ancestral traditions dominate, religion is restricted to a place where ancient myths are passed on from generation to generation, where rituals are performed that instruct the young in the tradition and which, when taken together, support the authority of the Indigenous social system.

Simply because religion in Aboriginal societies is restricted to lineage and location does not mean that non-religion among such societies necessarily is characterized by the transformation of ancestral traditions into regional, national or global allegiances. These changes could represent the impact of authoritative traditions that do not focus on totemic ancestors or are not limited to specific places. This has occurred clearly when Aboriginal peoples have been converted to Christianity or Islam, or when forces of modernization and globalization have so disrupted traditional myths, rituals and lines of authority that ancestors no longer maintain an overwhelming power over the society. In other words, the breaking down of Indigenous traditions does not necessarily imply that this has resulted in the population becoming non-religious.

Evidence of non-religion among Aboriginal peoples would be signalled by the disintegration of traditional communities and the failure to replace these with alternative communities. It would also be reflected by those in the population who no longer adhere to the authority of age-old customs and by members of the society maintaining only a minimal sense of subservience to the demands of elders, who, according to tradition, prescribe and monitor the performance of strictly regulated ceremonies to ensure the welfare of specific Aboriginal communities. If these traditions are replaced by other communities, such as Christian congregations that are subject to the authority of a particular leader, denomination or text, although Indigenous Religion would no longer be present, at least some members of the society would still be considered religious. If, on the other hand, individuals, regardless of whether they are living in urban or rural contexts, affirm their personal autonomy by not identifying with any community, or if they move from one group to another for reasons of satisfying their individual search for meaning, or if they regard the values, myths and traditions of their society as non-binding and relative, or if they seek to meet their own and their immediate family's needs exclusively, then these actions would provide evidence that not only had the Indigenous Religion been abandoned, but that non-religion had been pursued vigorously. The study of non-religion among Aboriginal communities, whether they are located primarily in urban or rural settings, thus is no different in substance from the study of non-religion among other societies. What differs is the social context out of which non-religion has emerged and how that plays out in relation to traditional loyalties that are defined by kinship and locality.

Back to the start

I began this chapter by referring to the popular notion that Indigenous people everywhere make no distinction between religion and non-religion because for them everything is religious. In the sense that this is meant sociologically, where religion, society and culture are described as being inextricably bound together, this description is correct. When this non-differentiation of religion from non-religion is used theologically, as it was by Mbiti and Idowu in African contexts, my argument to the contrary is that Indigenous people view the world similarly to members of other societies, where distinct ritual performances take place in a space and time that participants recognize as being set apart from activities occurring in everyday space and time. Despite this ability to separate ordinary from non-ordinary experiences, I contend that devout religious people everywhere affirm that their religion influences every aspect of their living, as was expressed by the Apostle Paul when he urged Christians to 'pray without ceasing' (I Thessalonians 5: 17, Authorized King James Version). So, Mbiti and Idowu and others writing with a theological agenda, such as James Irwin in New Zealand and arguably E. G. Parrinder in West Africa, are wrong on both counts. Indigenous people are able to distinguish religion from non-religion, but like religious people everywhere, due to their devotion to the tradition that defines their community, submit the whole of their lives, including eating, work, play and sexual activity, to the authority of that same tradition. The notable change that has been introduced into Indigenous societies by the forces of globalization, Westernization and modernity, just as it has in other contexts (as Platvoet has shown with respect to The Netherlands), has resulted precisely in the weakening of inherited authority, or even the rejection of it, by people who traditionally would have been bound by an authority that had been passed on from generation to generation. When individualism, self-autonomy and relativistic values break down traditional ways of life, non-religion has replaced religion, and Platvoet's correct description of Indigenous religion as 'an undifferentiated part of social life' no longer applies.

Throughout this analysis, I have been careful not to define religion in terms of primary attention being directed towards sacred or transcendental entities such as spirits, gods or God. I have defined religion in terms of communal authority and tradition in order to avoid conflating religion with theological interests or non-falsifiable claims. This makes the definition of religion broad, of course, but it is not so general as to include everything. It applies only to communities that subject themselves to the overpowering authority of a tradition that is passed on from generation to generation. In this sense, for all religious communities, everything can be called religion in that their lives are dictated by the power of the tradition that controls and monitors every aspect of their living. Non-religion can be identified when individuals do not relinquish their personal autonomy to the authority of a tradition. Non-religion then has nothing intrinsically to do with atheism or agnosticism any more than religion centres on theism or beliefs in supernatural agents. In this sense, religion and non-religion among Aboriginal peoples can be separated, not on grounds of how they relate to a postulated transcendental focus, but by how intensely they conform to the authority of traditions that operate and define the identifiable communities of which they are a part.

Chapter 12

GLOBAL INTENTIONS AND LOCAL CONFLICTS: THE RISE AND FALL OF AMBUYA JULIANA IN ZIMBABWE

During the discussion period following a paper I presented in June 2015 on my definition of Indigenous Religions as localized and kinship-dominated, the anthropologist Walter van Beek suggested that I replace the term 'indigenous' with 'local' and speak of 'localized' as opposed to 'globalized' religions. After contemplating this suggestion, I have rejected it because it disqualifies Indigenous Religions from fitting into a collective category, reduces them to a position of insignificance and thereby perpetuates their marginalization in light of the dominance of the world religions paradigm in the academic study of religions. Despite their limitation to specific geographical locations and their restricted outreach due to membership in their communities being constrained by kinship rules, Indigenous Religions are not passive recipients of global and modernizing forces but continue to influence religions that are transnational and missionary, oftentimes demonstrating the greater power the local maintains over outside interference.

In this chapter, I demonstrate the power the local can exert on global forces by considering the case of the Ambuya Juliana movement in Zimbabwe, which at its peak in the early to mid-1990s had extended its influence beyond its origin in southern Zimbabwe into neighbouring Botswana and Mozambique. The importance of the Ambuya Juliana movement was emphasized by some notable scholars of Africa, such as the historian Terence Ranger (1995: 237), who referred to it as having 'swept across southern Zimbabwe', while Hezekiel Mafu (1995: 293) described 'the intensity of its influence' as 'phenomenal'. At the height of its impact, it would not have been an exaggeration to predict that the teachings of Ambuya Juliana might inspire one of the most significant new religious movements to develop in Africa towards the conclusion of the twentieth century. This did not occur. The demise of Juliana developed almost as quickly as her accession to a position of regional religious and political influence so that by the end of the 1990s her movement had virtually disappeared. This chapter suggests that both the rise and fall of the short-lived Ambuya Juliana movement can be explained in terms of the conflict between local interests and global ambitions.

The case of Ambuya Juliana: Background

The early 1990s saw a series of devastating droughts affecting wide areas of southern Africa. Zimbabwe was hit particularly hard by a lack of rainfall during the 1991–92 season causing crops to fail and cattle to die. Hezekiel Mafu (1995: 288) referred to the effects of the drought as 'profound and unprecedented' causing 'devastation and immense human suffering'. It was in the wake of the ruinous drought of 1992 that Ambuya Juliana, who claimed to be a rainmaker, quickly rose to fame and exerted wide influence throughout southern Zimbabwe. Researchers Abraham Mawere and Ken Wilson (1995: 253) report that Juliana 'emerged in late 1992 and quickly became a major force across south central Zimbabwe over an area nearly 300 kms across and at least 100 kms deep'. Juliana was variously described as being in her late twenties, early thirties or as being 'about forty-two years old' (Mafu 1995: 294). The title 'Ambuya' usually is translated as 'grandmother', but in this case denoted not her age but served as a title of respect. The Swedish researcher, Gurli Hansson, who befriended Juliana, described her 'as a rather young woman', who normally 'dressed in black' and went around 'barefoot' (cited by Ranger 1995: 238).

The Ambuya Juliana movement had gained so much attention outside Zimbabwe among African scholars that the Britain-Zimbabwe Society Research Day held at St Antony's College, Oxford on 23 April 1994 devoted numerous papers to considering its likely social, political and religious significance. Mawere and Wilson sent a paper from Zimbabwe, which was read at the Research Day, dealing with what they called the 'Ambuya Juliana cult'. This was subsequently published as a substantial article in the *Journal of Religion in Africa* (1995: 252–87). Gurli Hansson also delivered a paper at the Research Day in which she described the Juliana movement as a religious innovation and as providing evidence of the revival of traditional religion in Zimbabwe (1995: 91–114). In their article, Mawere and Wilson (1995: 253) argued that the rise of Juliana can be attributed to the fact that her movement 'challenged state, business, church and traditional power' while at the same time it 'elaborated new conjunctions of ecological and political ideas, and significantly restructured local social relations and land-use practice'.

In July 1995, I visited the region of Chief Chingoma in south-central Zimbabwe near the town of Mberengwa, where I had conducted research during the drought of 1992, with the aim of determining how the persistent droughts were being interpreted by those I had interviewed previously. To my surprise, I encountered a great deal of enthusiasm and some controversy surrounding Ambuya Juliana, who throughout the sixteen chieftaincies of the Mberengwa District was introducing substantial variations in the way traditional rain rituals were being carried out and was delivering a message that contained elements of long-standing Indigenous practices combined with clear Christian teachings. Although I did not meet Juliana personally, I interviewed five people who had attended her large gatherings held in November 1994 in Chief Chingoma's region and I visited Juliana's extensive sacred enclosures where she performed rain rituals and preached to the people explaining her message to them (Cox 1998a: 141–6).

According to those I interviewed, Juliana, who is from the Karanga ethnic group, testified that at the age of seven she was taken underwater by an *njuzu*, often translated as mermaid, but actually refers to a water spirit with great powers. Frequently, stories are told about people, who after approaching the edge of a dark, deep pool or river, disappear for long periods of time. The concerned family members consult a traditional diviner or healer (*n'anga*), who tells them that the person has been taken underwater by an *njuzu*. The family members are advised to show no remorse and to brew beer in honour of the water spirit. They also are not to speak about the disappearance or to show undue concern. Eventually, the missing person returns and usually reports having learned many things while in the company of the *njuzu* and is ready to assume a role in society as a newly initiated *n'anga*. Quite frequently, those who go missing are young girls, who in some cases have offended nature spirits. One widespread story I discovered in my research relates how several girls went to the forest to pick wild fruits. One girl comments that one of the trees has humanlike breasts and expresses great surprise. This offends the spirits of the forest and the girl disappears. Later, the family learns that she has been taken by an *njuzu* through one of the many underground water passages that flow into rivers and pools. Another common story I discovered describes an exceptionally beautiful girl whose immense attractiveness creates feelings of intense jealousy in the other girls. The story relates that some of the jealous girls capture the lovely girl and fling her into a river hoping she will be eaten by crocodiles. Instead, she is taken by an *njuzu*, taught many things and after a period of time reappears carrying a bag of traditional medicine. She now is accepted by the community as a healer (Cox 1998a: 169–70).

During my research trip in 1995, my informants told me that Juliana spent ten years under the water with an *njuzu*, who taught her, at the same time, traditional African customs and teachings from the Bible. She also learned church songs from the *njuzu*. In an interview with Gurli Hansson, Juliana described her experiences:

> We lived like crocodiles, ate soil and mud. I was very skinny and pale when I returned from her. When you stay with the *Njuzu* you learn to be humble and well behaved. I was also taught about the Bible there. There is everything down there. When I left, I had a *Shanga* – reed, growing on my head. (cited by Cox 1998a: 143; see also Hansson 1995: 98)

After she emerged from her long period of initiation and instruction by the *njuzu*, Juliana went almost immediately to the Mwari or High-God shrine in the Matopos Hills in south-west Zimbabwe.

A word of explanation about the Mwari shrines is needed at this point. Today throughout southern Zimbabwe, chiefs from a wide region (up to 400 kilometres around) pay tribute at the Mwari shrines. The most notable shrine of the regional cult devoted to Mwari is located at a hill called Matonjeni. It consists of hereditary officials and various messengers. The Zimbabwean anthropologist Michael Bourdillon (1987: 279) reports that the principal officials are a high priest and priestess (a brother and sister who inherit their positions), a keeper of the shrine and the 'voice' (an elderly woman married into the high priest's family). Bourdillon explains further that the shrine is located in a cave from which the voice of Mwari speaks its oracles. Representatives from wide-ranging chieftaincies consult the voice about various matters such as the appointment of a new chief, the acceptance of a new spirit medium, drought or some other communal disaster. The representatives will have collected money, organized by each chief through his headmen and will deliver this to the keeper of the shrine. The 'voice' of Mwari speaks, but in an ancient dialect that must be translated into the language of the clients.

The relationship between the Mwari Cult and local chieftaincies represents a delicate balance between regional and local authority, which is maintained by the chief and his headman through their exercising power to raise money (*rusengwe* payments) for the Mwari shrines, by appointing the messengers (*vanyusa*) that represent them at Matonjeni and by their taking responsibility for organizing *mitoro* or rain rituals. Mawere and Wilson (1995: 274) explain:

> In south-central Zimbabwe, the Mwari cult has long been organised at the local level by chiefs, ward heads and village elders. Previous work in the area has demonstrated that these traditional leaders utilise the organisation of *rusengwe* payments for the cult, the sending of the *vanyusa* messengers, and the mentioning of Mwari during the holding of *mitoro* rain making ceremonies to complement their legitimacy, and this generates something of an alliance of convenience between local "traditional authorities" and the cult centre and its messengers.

Juliana reported that on arriving at the Mwari shrine at Matonjeni, she became an *mbonga* or virgin attendant in the Mwari cult. This corresponds to what Mawere and Wilson (1995: 286) refer to as one who is 'based out of the shrines, who in the case of women must be virgins', and to what Leslie Nthoi (1998: 70) calls the '*wosana*', whose main duty at the shrine is 'to dance and sing to the High-God during rain ceremonies'.

Hezekiel Mafu, who interviewed Juliana in July 1994, adds a further dimension to Juliana's assertions of authority. According to Mafu (1995: 294), Juliana claimed to have been authorized to undertake her mission by six spiritual forces: Musikavanhu, Mapa, Nehanda, Chaminuka, the Ancestors and Jesus Christ. Musikavanhu means creator of people, and although it is often used as an equivalent to Mwari and as another name for God, it refers frequently in oral traditions to an autochthonous ancestor or the first human from whom all people originated. It is most likely in this sense that Juliana was using Musikavanhu, since as a representative of the Mwari shrines, she would not have conflated the two names for God. Chaminuka, again according to oral traditions, is an ancient, perhaps founding, ancestor of the Shona people. Nehanda follows in the lineage from the original Chaminuka. The spirit of Nehanda, which is most associated with the first Chimurenga or war of liberation in 1896, is believed to have possessed mediums and urged the people to rise up against the colonial government. The Nehanda spirit was also alleged to have inspired the second, successful Chimurenga. Through an old woman named Charwe, who served as the medium of Nehanda, important information was communicated to the freedom fighters that contributed to their eventual victory. Ancestors operate at various levels from chiefs to extended families and provide the most frequent source of protection and guidance for communities. The addition of Jesus Christ as a source of her authority shows how Juliana was drawing from a global religious tradition to legitimize her mission. Mafu (1995: 294) suggests that only Mapa is unusual and unexpected among the six deities mentioned. He calls the Mapa 'a new and unknown element in the traditional religious structure', explaining that in Shona the word 'is associated with giving' (Mafu 1995: 294). Juliana seems to have invented this type of deity by inserting it into the traditional hierarchical spiritual scheme. She explained to Mafu that Mapa are 'Divine Beings ranked second to Musikavanhu' (Mafu 1995: 294). Mafu (1995: 295–6) adds that 'they also seem to be the agents of communication for the divine sextet'.

By the time Juliana began her mission across southern Zimbabwe in 1992, she had carefully established her authority as a religious leader by having been initiated in a traditional manner by an *njuzu* into the role of a *n'anga* with a specialization in producing rain, by her close association with the principal Mwari shrine in south-west Zimbabwe, by her knowledge of the Bible, which she had learned from the *njuzu* and by claiming to have been sent by a pantheon drawn largely from traditional religious figures, but which also included Jesus Christ and new deities that she had invented for the purposes of endorsing her commission to the nation. She was ideally placed to launch her new religious movement containing elements of local religious traditions combined with an intimate knowledge of the regional High-God rain rituals, both of which she integrated with her interpretation of Christian teachings.

Sometime in mid-1992, after the consistent failure of the rains, Juliana felt ready to begin her mission to the people of Zimbabwe by going out from Matonjeni to various regions, largely across the south-central area as an *nyusa*, defined by Mawere and Wilson (1995: 254) as a 'sacred messenger' for the 'Mwari cult'. She announced her mission as informing the people of 'their wrongdoings' and explaining 'why rainfall is not experienced' (Mawere and Wilson 1995: 254). She was received enthusiastically and by 1993 had constructed a number of enclosures she called rainmaking villages (*Majacha Emapa*), generally at the base of sacred mountains. She also had developed an organization in cooperation with the chiefs and headmen, through which money was collected for the Mwari shrine and delivered by Juliana accompanied by representatives of the chiefs whom she had selected personally. At the beginning of the 1993 rainy season, around October, Juliana began conducting rituals in her sacred enclosures, which attracted huge crowds. Similar rainmaking villages had been constructed across south-central Zimbabwe and reports indicate that Juliana was developing plans to expand her mission into Botswana to the west and as far as Mozambique to the east. Evidence of Juliana's popularity at the height of her influence can be found in the description of one of her rain rituals as provided by Mawere and Wilson. The specific ritual they witnessed occurred on 18 September 1993.

Each village had been ordered to supply five huge clay pots (*makate*) for holding beer, so hundreds of pots of beer were produced. On the assigned day of the 18th people came in large numbers, and in a state of some excitement. They were convinced that the rains would start the very same day ... During the ceremony Ambuya Juliana danced and sang in a really inspiring fashion, and people really enjoyed it. The slaughtering of cattle and goats proved astonishing. The beasts simply lay down to be slaughtered when she blew her horn. Even cattle could be killed with just knives, and goats were silent as they died. (Mawere and Wilson 1995: 261)

The content of Juliana's message

Juliana's message began with Mwari, whom she taught is the Creator of all things and hence more powerful than ancestor spirits, living humans or nature spirits. As the Creator, Mwari is responsible for providing rain on which the people depend for their well-being. Nonetheless, Mwari has devolved some responsibilities for providing adequate rainfall to lesser spirits such as *njuzu* and to spirit leopards and spirit lions that, in the words of Mawere and Wilson (1995: 255), 'live on top of hills and bring rain'. A direct connection between the failure of sufficient rainfall and human moral behaviour was made by Juliana. She demanded that the killing of wild animals must stop, since such animals attract rain. In addition, people were offending God by pretending to go into the mountains or hills to pray, but in fact they committed adultery there. The result is that God is punishing the people for such immoral acts by causing persistent droughts. All forms of promiscuity must cease if the people hope for the rains to return. Two holy days, Wednesday, which is a traditional day reserved to honour ancestors, and Sunday, the Christian Sabbath, must be observed by the people. No work is to be performed on these days. Mawere and Wilson (1995: 257) note that for Juliana this meant that 'a complete ban was instituted on normal work', including 'fetching firewood, sweeping yards, making hoe handles and yokes, drawing water and washing clothes'. She claimed further that many messengers chosen by the chiefs and sent to Matonjeni with money collected from the people were embezzling the funds and not turning the full amount over to the shrine. These misdeeds, she announced, incur the wrath of God.

Juliana's message extended also to political issues. She contended that Mwari should be honoured and thanked directly at the shrines by Government Ministers for giving the people independence in 1980. The fact that Government Ministers all the way up to President Mugabe have failed to travel to Matonjeni to thank God in a traditional way provides another explanation for the recurrent droughts. The lack of rain provides evidence to Ministers and the President himself that any power they possess comes ultimately from God. She maintained further that the Government's policies of blocking streams to make dams have interfered with the movement of the *njuzu* and should stop. Wells and boreholes that are made by using explosives should also cease since this frightens the water spirits away. Later, Juliana expanded this rule and forbade the use of boreholes altogether. Instead, people should extract water from sand in riverbeds.

Rituals were to be conducted in strict conformity to Juliana's dictates. The common practice of mediums becoming possessed during rain rituals by territorial spirits or ancestors of chiefs must stop. It is likely that Juliana regarded mediums who became possessed during her rituals as a threat to her authority. Mawere and Wilson (1995: 275) claim that Juliana 'wanted to monopolise the ritual power generated by the rain-making ritual for herself'. In a clear criticism of the practices of African Independent Churches, Juliana demanded that all drum-beating, jingling of bells and rattles during worship services be forbidden. She claimed that the people who use such methods of prayer have no idea why they employ these instruments. They should instead pray to God. In rain rituals only traditional gourds should be used in distributing the beer. No metal instruments should be employed (Cox 1998a: 144–5).

We can see from these basic teachings that, according to Juliana, beliefs about God, moral injunctions and ritual behaviour were all inter-related and acted as causal explanations for the persistent droughts. Her message emphasized that so long as God is unhappy about moral behaviour or about ritual infringements (including the failure of government officials to give thanks to God), rainfall will never be sufficient to supply the needs of the people. For this reason, she instituted strict rules regulating social and ritual behaviour that combined traditional beliefs about how spiritual forces influence material well-being with Christian ideas of the Creator God. She also elevated her own role beyond that of being a messenger to the various chieftaincies for the Mwari shrine at Matonjeni to one approaching messianic status, as confirmed by her assertion that one of her commissioning deities was Jesus Christ. She is even reported to have had a vision for extending her mission beyond southern Africa as far as the UK, which she believed stood in need of a reawakening of traditional values. At the height of her popularity in 1993, it appeared that the Juliana movement would become one of southern Africa's most important and influential new religious movements.

Explanations for the demise of the Juliana movement

Despite her apparent popular appeal and her global intentions, Juliana's influence began to fade rapidly beginning as early as 1994. In their article appearing in the *Journal of Religion in Africa*, Mawere and Wilson (1995: 253) described the Ambuya Juliana movement as being in 'terminal decline'. When I visited south-central Zimbabwe in July 1995, I learned from Chief Chingoma that many chiefs in the Mberengwa region were no longer planning to support Juliana's rain rituals, which normally would begin in late September or early October. I also detected a distinct lack of enthusiasm for Juliana's teachings about not doing work on Wednesdays and Sundays and encountered strong resistance to her restrictions against drilling and using boreholes (Cox 2014b: 206). My observations were confirmed by the research conducted by Mawere and Wilson (1995: 264), who in August 1994 interviewed a member of Juliana's assistants in Mazvihwa, near the town of Zvishavane, who told them that 'the Chief and some of the sub-chiefs are still interested in Juliana, but the majority are not'.

As we have seen, numerous explanations are offered for Juliana's rapid rise to power, the most compelling of which relates to her alliance with the chiefs, who had experienced a diminution of influence under the Mugabe regime. This alliance represented her efforts to reassert tradition in the face of modernity and confirms how she mobilized local support for her movement. This same partnership with chiefs paradoxically contributed to her rapid loss of popularity when, in the words of Mawere and Wilson (1995: 271), she challenged the chiefs' 'ritual monopolies' and usurped 'certain of their powers in the name of Matonjeni'. Mawere and Wilson (1995: 271) explain: 'Juliana banned all the small *mitoro* [rain] ceremonies used by each headman to secure his own legitimacy, and, furthermore, … she did not allow her major *mutoro* to be legitimated for the chiefs by their spirits being possessed by mediums.' They add that she wanted to claim 'the ritual power generated by the rain-making ritual for herself, by making sure it was seen purely connected to the Mwari Cult' (Mawere and Wilson: 1995: 275). By contravening the traditional authority of the chiefs' ancestors, as expressed through the chiefs' customary organization, Juliana lost the local support of the chiefs by challenging their authority and by asserting her regional, and potentially global, ambitions over each chief's identifiable and geographically restricted ancestral lineage.

In effect, Juliana set herself up in competition with the chiefs by usurping their traditional role of appointing representatives to collect money to take to the Mwari shrines. Juliana travelled with her disciples to Matonjeni and made her own representation to Mwari at the shrine. This is in line with her self-elevation to messianic status, acting within chieftaincies as Mwari's own representative and approaching Mwari on behalf of the chiefs. This brought extensive disapproval among the chiefs whom she had originally wooed successfully. With the loss of the support of the chiefs, Juliana no longer could speak as a representative of the locally entrenched authoritative tradition. Paradoxically, she also offended the officials at the Mwari shrine by claiming to represent all the chiefs collectively, thereby assuming a role inconsistent with tradition. Moreover, Juliana lost popular support because her regulations were unfeasible and unenforceable in local contexts. By prohibiting the performance of necessary activities on two days of the week, she alienated ordinary people. The eventual restriction against using boreholes was impractical and unsafe, since water from rivers often was contaminated. As a result, the people to whom her message was directed refused to follow her injunctions.

The conflict between the local and the trans-local Mwari shrines caused considerable confusion among the people in various chieftaincies, which also contributed to Juliana's eventual loss of popularity. She used local leaders, such as headmen and family elders, to gain access to their communities, but then she disregarded their positions by usurping their authority and assuming it for herself. Mawere and Wilson (1995: 275) explain: 'Although she approached the people through local leaders, her emphasis was on communicating in a direct and inspirational fashion with rural communities.'

In the end, Juliana lost her following by her refusal to adhere to long-established traditional protocols whereby the parameters of authority were rigidly enforced. Local elders, headmen and chiefs each exercised power within restricted and well-defined boundaries. Access to and the relationship with the Mwari shrines were also carefully circumscribed within lines of traditional patterns of authority. Ostensibly, Juliana observed these protocols by finding legitimization through accepted cultural beliefs, such as living for years with the *njuzu*. And, initially, she followed regulations by representing the Mwari shrines as a messenger to chieftaincies.

It was when she began to assert her own authority over the locally established traditions that her programme began to unravel. That this was her intention all along is confirmed by her interview with Hezekiel Mafu in which she disclosed that her authority derived from six deities, including Jesus Christ. This led rather quickly to her alienating chiefs by elevating her own authority above theirs. In the end, she circumvented traditional communication patterns by speaking directly and charismatically to the people while ignoring the role of headmen and elders; she contradicted the manner whereby chiefs communicate at the Mwari shrines by claiming to speak for them collectively; and her vision of establishing a transnational and potentially global movement alienated her from the localized, kinship-orientated Indigenous societies out of which she had emerged and from which she originally obtained recognition and legitimacy.

Conclusion

The Ambuya Juliana phenomenon did not develop into a major new religion in southern Africa. It was short-lived and, one could argue, as a result, was insignificant. In this chapter, I have attempted to demonstrate, on the contrary, that, perhaps quite unintentionally, the case of Ambuya Juliana confirms that local traditions exercise immense power over movements with intentions transcending local and regional limitations. If popular movements with global ambitions do not integrate local protocols into their strategies, they will alienate themselves from the base they need to succeed and ultimately lose legitimacy. This contention, which is well supported by the example of Ambuya Juliana in Zimbabwe during the 1990s, can be applied to all religions with global ambitions, including the so-called world religions, which always must adapt to and be influenced by local customs, conventions and lines of authority if they are to take root and become incorporated into the cultures they are attempting to influence.

Part V

AFFIRMING INDIGENOUS AGENCY

Chapter 13

THE DEBATE BETWEEN E. B. TYLOR AND ANDREW LANG OVER THE THEORY OF PRIMITIVE MONOTHEISM: IMPLICATIONS FOR CONTEMPORARY STUDIES OF INDIGENOUS RELIGIONS

In his seminal contribution outlining the evolutionary development of human cultures, first published as two volumes in 1871 under the title *Primitive Culture*, E. B. Tylor maintained that the origin of religion can be traced to the tendency of early humans to imagine that life forms or souls inhabit all significant objects and natural phenomena. Such primitive psychic projections were derived from dreams, visions, human imagination and experiences of death. Although it is clear that Tylor's theory of animism as the source of religion contradicted what he regarded as largely theological speculations that originally humans were all monotheistic, he did not enter directly into the debate over primitive monotheism until the publication of his influential article, 'On the Limits of Savage Religion' that appeared in 1892 in the *Journal of the Anthropological Institute*. Tylor's position, which he clearly outlined in this article, prompted the Scottish novelist, classicist, translator and latter-day anthropologist, Andrew Lang, to accuse Tylor of predetermined and largely biased views about the origin of human cultures. Lang, who initially had been a follower of Tylor, by the early twentieth century had become committed to the theory of primitive monotheism, which he argued was based on logical and empirical evidence that pointed towards an ancient, primordial and universal concept of one Supreme Being.

In this chapter, I explore the role E. B. Tylor played in the primitive monotheism debate that towards the end of the nineteenth century and well into the twentieth pitted anthropologists in the British tradition, such as J. G. Frazer in Britain and Baldwin Spencer in Australia, who were committed to the theory of the evolutionary development of religion, against advocates of primitive monotheism, such as the German missionary in Central Australia, Carl Strehlow and the German-Austrian ethnologist Wilhelm Schmidt. Strehlow believed that the languages of the Arrernte peoples of Central Australia, and thus their culture, had declined from a higher, more elevated stage into cruder expressions and Schmidt maintained that primitive peoples around the globe were originally monotheistic but had degenerated into lower forms of religion expressed in polytheism, ancestor worship, animism and fetishism (Cox 2014a: 11–34). This debate was brought most directly to scholarly and public attention at the beginning of the twentieth century through the interventions of Andrew Lang against E. B. Tylor.

I begin my discussion in this chapter by outlining Tylor's position with respect to this pivotal academic controversy, and then focus specifically on Tylor's attempt to disprove the widespread belief in a primordial High God called Baiame that allegedly had been discovered by missionaries and explorers in Australia. I follow this by presenting the contrary arguments advanced by Lang. In my concluding analysis, I suggest that both Tylor and Lang followed predetermined ideas about the origin of religion that made their respective conclusions inevitable. What was lacking in each case was a concern for the actual believing communities that comprised the subject matter on which their debate proceeded. In the process of attempting to establish convincing arguments in support of their opposing conclusions, they ignored Indigenous agency. By considering the case of the Rainbow Spirit Theology in Australia, I demonstrate how a local group of Indigenous Christians employed an oblique strategy of resistance, a strategy, following the Russian literary critic Mikhail Bakhtin, I call 'intentional hybridity'.

Tylor on primitive monotheism

Tylor's evolutionary theory must be seen in the context of his doctrine of survivals. He described animism as characteristic of 'tribes very low in the scale of humanity', which then ascend, 'deeply modified in its transition, but from first to last preserving an unbroken continuity, into the midst of high modern culture' (Tylor 1903 [1871], 1: 426). In other words, although cultures develop over time, ancient remnants of primitive beliefs and practices can be found in the most advanced societies as cultural survivals. Tylor (1903 [1871], 1: 426) explains: 'Animism is in fact, the groundwork of the Philosophy of Religion, from that of savages up to that of civilized men.'

Although Tylor drew a line of continuity between early human religious experience typified by animistic beliefs and higher monotheistic faiths with their focus on one Supreme Being, he consistently argued against the idea that monotheism preceded animism. Rather, he insisted that over time humans generated more sophisticated belief systems which evolved through such practices as tree worship, reverence for a sky or rain god, belief in divine ancestors, the ideas of multiple deities, some of which were considered good and others evil, and eventually culminating in worship of a Supreme Deity. Even the belief in a Supreme Deity, however, was not in its earliest phases monotheistic. The idea of a High God implied the existence of lower deities with restricted power over certain affairs of life. The survival of inferior spiritual beings among the monotheistic religions, such as Christianity and Islam, can be seen in beliefs in angels and demons, in Christian devotion to saints and through the devout Muslim's struggle between the opposing influences of good and evil *jinn* (spirits).

In *Primitive Culture*, Tylor argued that no peoples in the early stages of cultural development were monotheistic, although in some cases they constructed hierarchical orderings of the spiritual world, frequently as mirror images of the social hierarchy where the King was considered divine. True monotheism, he explained, must be defined by 'assigning the distinctive attributes of deity to none save the Almighty Creator' (Tylor 1903 [1871], 2: 332). In the course of the evolution of religious ideas, he admitted, 'there are to be discerned in barbaric theology shadowings, quaint or majestic, of the conception of a Supreme Deity, henceforth to be traced onward in expanding power and brightening glory along the history of religion' (Tylor 1903 [1871], 2: 332). Among contemporary primitive peoples, which have come under the influence of Christian missionaries or Islamic governance, ideas of a Supreme Being have emerged not as evidence of an original concept of one God, but as a result of primitive peoples adopting the ideas of the outside religion. He explains that under 'this foreign influence, dim, uncouth ideas of divine supremacy have been developed into more cultured forms' (Tylor 1903 [1871], 2: 333). Tylor (1903 [1871], 2: 333) cites numerous examples of this including the 'native Canadians' who, under the influence of the Jesuit missionaries, conceived of 'the Great Manitu', or how in Brazil, again in response to the Jesuits, the Indigenous deity of thunder, Tupan, was adapted 'to convey in Christian teaching the idea of God'. Among African groups that have been 'Islamized or semi-Islamized ... the name of Allah is in all men's mouths' (Tylor 1903 [1871], 2: 333). These circumstances force the critical ethnographer to 'be ever on the look-out for traces of such foreign influence in the definition of the Supreme Deity acknowledged by any uncultured race, a divinity whose nature and even whose name may betray his adoption from abroad' (Tylor 1903 [1871], 2: 333).

Tylor expanded these ideas in depth in his 1892 article 'On the Limits of Savage Religion'. His methodological starting point was explicitly outlined from the outset: 'In defining the religious systems of the lower races, so as to place them correctly in the history of culture, careful examination is necessary to separate the genuine developments of native theology from the effects of intercourse with civilized foreigners' (Tylor 1892: 283). In order to discern what is genuine from what is imported, the anthropologist must be able to identify in the accounts provided of Indigenous Religions three types of material: (1) that which clearly is adopted directly from foreign teachers, such as missionaries; (2) signs that 'genuine native deities of a lower order' have been exaggerated by elevating them into 'a god or a devil' (Tylor 1892: 284) and (3) the application of Indigenous words in ways they were never intended by transforming names for 'minor spiritual beings' into the name 'of a supreme good or a rival evil deity' (Tylor 1892: 284).

Tylor then proceeds to provide examples from around the world of precisely where these three categories have been applied and how they have led to the false conclusion that primitive peoples originally possessed monotheistic beliefs. He begins with North America, where in more detail than he had done in *Primitive Culture*, he shows how the Jesuits in Canada between 1611 and 1684 had converted the animistic beliefs of the Ojibwas and the Algonquins into 'a kind of savage version of the philosophic deism of which the European mind was at that time full' (Tylor 1892: 285). He outlines in particular how the Jesuit missionary

Father Le Jeune transcribed the Indigenous term *manitu* in upper case as Manitu, referring either to good Manitu or bad Manitu. This, Tylor claims, is the first mention of Manitu as possessing either the attributes of the Christian God or the Christian Satan. Later, this developed into the widespread notion, which has been disseminated widely across North America, that the native peoples believe universally in the Great Spirit (Kitch Manitu). This erroneous idea can be attributed directly to the teaching of the missionaries, to linguistic misunderstandings and to the magnification of animistic spirits into Christian concepts, all of which have led to a 'misrepresentation' of Indigenous beliefs resulting in 'a transformation of the native religions' (Tylor 1892: 286). Tylor then discusses similar occurrences in other parts of North America and South America, but devotes considerable attention to the alleged primordial belief in a Supreme Being in Australia promoted by advocates of the theory of primitive monotheism.

The special case of Baiame

From about 1840 onwards, accounts began to surface from early settlers and missionaries that many Aboriginal peoples in south-east Australia had believed in a male Supreme Being, called an 'All Father', prior to contact with Christianity. The name most associated with the 'All Father' was Baiame from the Wiradjuri peoples near Wellington, approximately 350 kilometres west of Sydney. Numerous other names were assigned to this Being from other peoples in New South Wales, Victoria and South Australia, including Nurrundere, Nurelli, Mar tumnere, Biamban, Bunjil, Daramulun, Mami-nga ta, Mungan-ngaua, each of which, according to Erich Kolig and Gisela Petri-Odermann (1992: 9), translates as 'father', 'our father' or simply as 'elder'. Kolig and Petri-Odermann (1992: 9) go on to explain that these names became synonymous in subsequent anthropological literature with a Sky God, High God or Supreme Being and were regularly invested with qualities 'of (almost) monotheistic proportions'.

One of the earliest references to an All-Father figure in south-east Australia was reported in the writings of the Rev. James Günther, who worked under assignment of the Anglican Church Missionary Society in the Wellington Valley from 1837 until 1843, when the Mission was abandoned. Günther clearly applied the notion of primitive monotheism to beliefs he discovered among the Wiradjuri. He wrote that the name Baiame designated the Supreme Being and that 'the ideas held concerning Him by some of the more thoughtful Aborigines are a remnant of original traditions prevalent among the ancient of days' (cited by Swain 1993: 127). In his book, *The Native Tribes of South-East Australia*, the anthropologist A. W. Howitt (1904: 501) refers to notes compiled in 1844–5 by James Manning who reported conversations he had with Aboriginal informants at his home in the bush in New South Wales.[1] Howitt observes that Manning was convinced that the Aboriginals of his area held a firm belief in a Supreme Being before the missionaries ever arrived in the area. He quotes Manning (Howitt 1904: 501–02): 'They believe in a supreme Being called *Boyma* [Baiame] who dwells in the north-east, in a heaven of beautiful appearance. He is represented as seated on a throne of transparent crystal, with beautiful pillars of crystal on each side.' Manning further refers to the son of *Boyma* as a figure called Grogorogally, who acts as a mediator between heaven and earth (Howitt 1904: 502; see also, Swain 1993: 127). Howitt (1904: 502) observes that 'in these statements I easily recognize, although in a distorted form, the familiar features of *Baiame* and his son *Daramulun*'. These beliefs preceded Christian influences, according to Manning, because 'for the first four or five years or more of that earliest time there was no church south of the little one at Bong-bong at Mittagong [approximately 150 kilometres southwest of Sydney] ... No missionaries ever came to the southern districts at any time' (cited by Howitt 1904: 501).

Howitt arrived in Australia from England in 1852 and worked as a bushman and a naturalist before turning to scientific studies of Aboriginal peoples. After some initial scepticism, he embraced the idea that the belief in Baiame had preceded Christian influence. Kolig and Petri-Odermann (1992: 12) argue that Howitt realized that if his anthropological work were to be taken seriously in the English-speaking world, he would need to relate the south-eastern Aboriginal belief in an All-Father to the dominant British academic commitment to an evolutionary interpretation of human cultures. For that reason, Howitt explained that the belief in Baiame had resulted from the generally higher and more sophisticated social structure found among the Indigenous groups of south-east Australia when compared to other Aboriginal societies. This is confirmed by Howitt's description of Baiame:

> I see, as the embodied idea, a venerable kindly Headman of a tribe, full of knowledge and tribal wisdom, and all-powerful magic, of which he is the source .... It is most difficult for one of us to divest himself of the tendency to endow such a supernatural being with a ... divine nature and character (Howitt 1904: 500–01).

Kolig and Petri-Odermann (1992: 12) conclude that for whatever reason, Howitt 'accepted the authenticity and antiquity of the concept'.

By the time Tylor published his article 'On the Limits of Savage Religion' in 1892, therefore, a consensus was developing among many scholars working in south and south-east Australia that empirical evidence pointed towards a primordial belief in a Supreme Being entirely independent of foreign influence. In addition to Howitt, other writers who advocated this view included R. H. Matthews, a surveyor and a largely self-taught anthropologist working in northern New South Wales, the Rev. George Taplin, a Congregational minister who wrote on the Narrinyeri people of South Australia, R. Brough Smyth, a civil servant and mining engineer whose book *The Aborigines of Victoria* (1878) arose from his efforts to preserve what he thought was a dying culture in Victoria and Mrs. K. L. Parker, an enthusiastic but largely untrained student of the Aboriginal people in western New South Wales, whose book *The Euahlayi Tribe* (1905) contains an introduction by Andrew Lang. Not all scholars believed that their findings based

A Phenomenology of Indigenous Religions

on Australian research confirmed that primitive peoples everywhere had some
original notion of one supreme God, but it provided support to those, like Andrew
Lang and later Wilhelm Schmidt (see Schmidt 1931: 262–3), who argued that the
Aboriginal belief in Baiame (and other 'All Father' deities) in Australia was not an
isolated case but pointed towards a much more profound conclusion that ancient
peoples everywhere were monotheistic.

Tylor's response to the alleged antiquity of the Baiame belief

In 'On the Limits of Savage Religion', Tylor devoted considerable attention to
reviewing and critiquing the case in support of the argument that an Indigenous
Australian belief in Baiame, and other terms designating an 'All-Father', such as
Bunjil, had preceded Christian influences. Tylor begins by referring to references
in the notes of Horatio Hale, the American anthropologist who joined the
surveying and charting expedition of Charles Wickes, which went around the
world from 1838 to 1842, spending time in Australia in 1840 (see Belton 2009:
138–52). Hale's notes refer in particular to the groups around Wellington where
James Günther had worked as a missionary. Tylor (1892: 292) comments that
Hale referred to the deity 'Baiami' as 'living on an island beyond the sea to the
east'. Tylor (1892: 292) adds that, according to Hale, 'some natives consider him
Creator, while others attribute the creation of the world to his son Burambin
[Daramulun]'. Tylor's documentation includes a reference in Hale's notes that
mentions a 'February dance to Baiami' that 'was brought from a distance by the
natives' (Tylor 1892: 292).

Tylor (1892: 292) then cites another early reference to a belief in a Sky God
as recorded by German Moravian missionaries, who communicated with
Aboriginal people in Victoria near Mount Franklin with the aid of 'settlers who
could interpret, and partly in the broken English of the natives'. The missionaries
describe a testimony of an Aboriginal man called Bonaparte, who pointed to the
sky and, according to Tylor (1892: 292), 'explained to the missionaries that *Pei-
a-mei* (God) dwelt up there'. Tylor (1892: 292) records that another Indigenous
name for God among the Aboriginals in Victoria was '*Mahman-mu-rok*, which
the missionaries considered to mean "father of all"'. He concludes: 'Thus it appears
that *Baiame* was already, about 1840, a being recognized among the natives, but
endowed with very native attributes in their belief' (Tylor 1892: 292).

Tylor refers to R. Brough Smyth's account in *The Aborigines of Victoria* where a
reference is made to a missionary, the Rev. W. Ridley, who is reported by Smyth to
have declared that Baiame 'is the name by which the natives in the north-west and
west of New South Wales designate the Supreme Being' (Tylor 1892: 293). Tylor
notes that when asked about Baiame, the Indigenous respondents declared 'that
he made earth, and water, and sky, animals and men' (Tylor 1892: 293). R. Brough
Smyth then cites another missionary, the Rev. C. C. Greenaway, who argues that
Baiame derives from the Indigenous word, *baia*, 'which means to make, cut out,
build' (cited by Tylor 1892: 293). Tylor quotes from the appendix in the second

volume of Smyth's book, which recounts the conclusion Greenaway reached: 'For ages unknown, this race has handed down the word signifying "Maker" as the name of the Supreme' (cited by Tylor 1892: 293).

The fact that a relatively short time had passed between the arrival of white settlers and missionaries in various parts of south-east Australia in the early part of the nineteenth century and the widespread reporting by 1840 of a belief found all across the region in a High God or 'All Father' would seem to confirm that such a belief had existed among Indigenous peoples prior to their contact with the outside world. Tylor suggests that this is just an apparent conclusion. He cites the narrative of James Backhouse, a missionary of the Society of Friends working in Victoria between 1832 and 1840, who declared that Aboriginal Australians 'have no distinct ideas of a Supreme Being' (Tylor 1892: 294). Tylor also refers to evidence given by William Buckley, the 'wild white man', who lived among Indigenous peoples for thirty years, and that of the first grammarian and lexicographer of New South Wales, the Rev. L. E. Threlkeld, both of whom testified that 'there was no being known to the natives whose name he could adopt as representing Deity' (Tylor 1892: 294). Tylor concludes that Baiame was 'unknown to well-informed observers till about 1840' but then suddenly appeared 'with markedly Biblical characteristics' (Tylor 1892: 294). The obvious conclusion from this is that belief in Baiame 'arose from the teaching of missionaries' (Tylor 1892: 294).

Tylor (1892: 294) draws attention to a primer for new Christians prepared by the Rev. W. Ridley that begins with the teaching, 'Baiame verily man made' and continues by instructing the catechists with the statement, 'Baiame verily heaven, earth, the great water, all, everything made'. This, Tylor concludes, provides evidence that the missionaries chose Baiame as their name for God and began teaching the people that Baiame was the Creator of humanity and all things in the world. This would explain why when the informant Bonaparte told the Moravian missionaries around 1850 that God dwelt in the sky and had made all things, 'he was merely repeating the very words he had been taught by other missionaries in his own part of the country' (Tylor 1892: 294).

Tylor follows this with a discussion of the Kamilaroi people who inhabited a wide area of New South Wales. On anthropological grounds, he suggests that this people, also known as the Gamilaroi, and who presently constitute the fourth largest Indigenous group in Australia, would hardly have had a belief in an 'All-Father' precisely because they 'reckon kinship on the mother's side' (Tylor 1892: 296). He adds: 'It would be remarkable and requiring explanation if the name of father were given to a native divine ancestor of all men' (Tylor 1892: 296). Citing the work of A. W. Howitt, Tylor (1892: 296) then examines linguistic evidence by looking at words that under missionary influence have developed into 'the dominant evil deity' among Kamilaroi groups. The word *murup* originally referred to 'the soul or ghost of a dead man' (Tylor 1892: 296). Tylor draws attention to Howitt's observation that it is typical for a Kamilaroi person to approach the grave of one of the deceased from the community and address the spirit (*murup*) of the dead with phrases such as, 'Hallo! There is my old 'possum rug; there are my old bones' (Tylor 1892: 296). According to Tylor (1892: 296), the word for the soul of a deceased person under missionary influence has been transformed into 'an individual name for the great bad spirit'. Now, he argues, *Murup* refers to the Devil, who lives 'surrounded by a host of devils in a place called *Ummekulleen*, … where he punishes the wicked' (Tylor 1892: 296).

The explanation for the widely reported belief in Baiame thus becomes evident: the Indigenous world-view and belief systems by 1840 had been thoroughly christianized. The original animistic beliefs which depicted 'souls departing to some island … and being re-born' have been transformed by 'imported ideas of moral judgment and retribution after death' (Tylor 1892: 296). This transformation has clearly extended to the belief in Baiame who, as the Creator, 'takes the good into heaven … but sends the bad to another place to be punished' (Tylor 1892: 296). This provides evidence that the Indigenous beliefs of the people in souls of the departed have been magnified to make singular and all-powerful forces: a Creator God, called Baiame, who is judge of all, and Satan or the Devil, who is the prince of devils assisted by a multitude of evil spirits, which under Christian influences have been modified substantially from the original belief in the souls of the dead. The contention that Baiame provides evidence for an ancient, primordial Australian monotheism thus fails on all three of Tylor's criteria: 1) it clearly has resulted from missionary teaching; 2) it cannot be supported on linguistic grounds; and 3) it obviously represents an exaggeration or magnification of original beliefs into singular and powerful forces, one good and the other evil.

Andrew Lang's critique of Tylor: Primitive monotheism and the doctrine of degeneration

The Scotsman, Andrew Lang (1844–1912), although perhaps best known as a collector of folk and fairy tales, was also a poet, novelist and literary critic. He began writing on religion in the 1880s with his books, *Custom and Myth* (1884) and *Myth, Ritual and Religion* (1887), in which, as a follower of Tylor, he was highly critical of Max Müller's idea that myths represented anthropomorphic representations that had devolved from more abstract ideas. Lang's most substantial contribution to the study of religion was *The Making of Religion* (1898), in which he had changed his perspective on the origins of religion and had become decidedly opposed to Tylor's theories of animism as explaining the source of religion in human cultural development. By 1897, he had developed his own theory that the religions of primitive societies had degenerated from original beliefs in one God into forms of polytheism and lower expressions of religious life. In 1908, Lang published *The Origins of Religion and Other Essays*, in which he included a chapter summarizing his position on the primitive monotheism debate, particularly in contrast to Tylor's theories. Specifically, Lang challenged Tylor's argument that a ubiquitous Australian belief in an All-Father called Baiame had resulted directly from missionary teachings.

In his chapter entitled 'Theories of the Origins of Religion', Lang (1908: 108) defines the 'All Father' as a 'potent being' who 'receives no gifts' and 'is asked for none'. In Australia, which he describes as a culture 'on the lowest level extant', Lang (1908: 111) asserts that some groups possess belief in the All Father but they 'do not pray to higher powers'. Lang then refers to the work of A. W. Howitt who, on Lang's interpretation, distinguished Baiame from ancestor spirits (called by Lang 'ghosts' of the dead). Baiame is conceived in anthropomorphic terms, but 'he is not ghost Headman of a tribe of ghosts' (Lang 1908: 118). No ghost 'is said to have made all things on the earth', but this is precisely how Baiame, or Bunjil among other groups, is described by Howitt (Lang 1908: 118). Lang (1908: 118) concludes: 'For these reasons, the facts being taken from Mr Howitt's own collections, we cannot regard the All Father as an idealised ghost.'

Lang was specifically alluding to how Tylor's doctrine of the soul had developed directly from his animistic theory. In *Primitive Culture*, Tylor (1903 [1871], 1: 428) had suggested that 'the ancient savage philosophers probably made their first step by the obvious inference that every man has two things belonging to him, namely, a life and a phantom'. Both are so closely connected to one another that they were conceived as 'manifestations of one and the same soul' (Tylor 1903 [1871], 1: 429). The 'ghost-soul' over time attained numerous attributes: it came to be regarded as 'the cause of life and thought in the individual it animates'; it was 'capable of leaving the body far behind, to flash swiftly from place to place'; it continued 'to exist and appear to men after the death of that body'; 'it was able to enter into, possess, and act in the bodies of other men, of animals, and even of things' (Tylor 1903 [1871], 1: 429). For Tylor, these primordial religious beliefs, although much modified over time, survive as 'heirlooms of primitive ages … in the existing psychology of the civilized world' (Tylor 1903 [1871], 1: 429).

Lang reversed the order of Tylor's evolutionary programme by arguing that the widespread Australian belief in an All Father, the primordial being, has attributes far different from a 'ghost-soul': the All Father is deathless, in, fact, he existed before death; he made the world and all things in it; he gave commandments, moral, ritual and social; he keeps his eyes on human conduct; in some cases, he rewards and punishes 'good men and evil in a future life'; he 'can go anywhere and do anything' (Lang 1908: 119). In a stinging critique, undoubtedly aimed directly at Tylor, Lang asserted that the All Father found throughout south-eastern Australia presents 'us with a being certainly not unlike the Jahveh of early Israel, and certainly not evolved by the process of raising an ancestral ghost to a very high power. That opinion can no longer be logically maintained' (Lang 1908: 120).

According to Lang, Tylor's flawed analysis became most apparent through his claim that knowledge of Baiame or other High Gods in Australia must have been learned from the missionaries. In response to this contention, Lang (1908: 120) asserted that Tylor could not answer 'two insuperable *prima facie* objections'. First, if the Indigenous peoples Howitt had discovered near Wellington had been influenced by missionaries, surely they would have prayed to him, in Lang's words, 'as the missionaries pray to their God' (1908: 120). As we have seen, following Howitt, Lang maintained that the people made no offerings nor voiced any prayers to Baiame. Second, 'only initiated men have any knowledge of the All-Father' (Lang 1908: 121). Even his name 'is concealed from women, children, and, usually, from white men, except the few who have been initiated' (Lang 1908: 121). If the idea of the All Father had been obtained from missionaries, 'it is inconceivable that ... their women and children should have been left in the dark by these evangelists' (Lang 1908: 121). Lang (1908: 121) concludes that he has seen 'no reply to these two arguments'.

In a volume commemorating E. B. Tylor's seventy-fifth birthday, Lang wrote two articles, one a summary of the contributions of Tylor to anthropology, which was entitled simply 'Edward Burnett Tylor' (1907a: 1–16) and a second entry called 'Australian Problems' (1907b: 203–18). The latter chapter deals largely with issues of totemism among the Aranda (Arrernte) with a particular focus on the problem of exogamy and the alleged ignorance of central desert peoples about the process of conception. In the opening chapter, in which he pays tribute to Tylor, Lang politely challenged Tylor's theory of animism as the source of religion by penning his now famous axiom: 'the more Animism the less "All-Fatherism"' (Lang 1907a: 11). In other words, the two extremes whereby Indigenous people express their religious sentiments, the one seeing spirits or souls in all things, the other an elevated idea of a High God, operate at opposite ends of the pole and tend to cancel one another out. Lang (1907a: 11) explains that in the Indigenous conception of the All Father, such as expressed in beliefs about Baiame, 'there is nothing animistic in the native conception of his nature'. The issue separating Lang and Tylor thus revolved around which occurred earlier, animism or belief in the All Father. Lang had already addressed this question in *The Making of Religion*, where he asserted: 'the crude idea of a "Universal Power" came *earliest*, and was superseded, in part, by a later propitiation of the dead and ghosts' (Lang 1898: 186; see also, Swain 1985: 94, emphasis in original). He reiterated this conclusion in *The Origins of Religion and Other Essays*, where he argued that evidence accrued from around the world suggests:

> Many very backward tribes believe in an All Father, not animistic, not a ghost; not prayed to, not in receipt of sacrifice, but existent from the beginning, exempt from death, and (in his highest aspects) kindly, an ethical judge of men, and either a maker of men and most things, or a father of men and a maker of many things. (Lang 1908: 121–2)

In line with his theory that the earliest forms of religion had degenerated into animism, he concluded that 'it is not at all impossible that, while they were being matured in human minds, the simpler belief in the All Father was destroyed (if it existed), and among some tribes was wholly forgotten, while in others it was partially obliterated' (Lang 1908: 123).

The Tylor–Lang debate: An analysis

Who won the argument between Tylor and Lang? This is a moot question because the conclusions of each were predetermined by the assumptions from which they began their analysis. Tylor made this perfectly clear when he asserted that where striking similarities occur between the Aboriginal belief in an All Father and the Christian teaching about 'Our Father', this can only be explained as a result of Christian influences. No other empirically based conclusion could be reached, since clearly there could have been no contact in regions as remote as Wellington with outside influences prior to the arrival of the white settlers in Sydney after 1788. The construction of a world-view, which portrayed a supreme deity living in the sky, who acted as a judge, sending some to a place of eternal reward and others to lasting punishment, could only reflect Christian teaching. That the High God was the maker of all things also can only be attributed to the biblical accounts found in the Book of Genesis. The traditional understanding of how the world came to be, as described by Spencer and Gillen and later T. G. H. Strehlow, depicted the world as we know it as having resulted from the emergence of beings living beneath the earth, who appeared as totemic ancestors, such as kangaroos, emus, lizards, plum tree men and honey ants, whose movements over the landscape created the hills, mountains, rivers, streams and forests. These beings responsible for making the world then returned to the landscape creating sacred places only to be reincarnated in their totemic descendants (see Spencer and Gillen 1899: 388–91; see also, Strehlow 1966: 8; Strehlow 1978a: 14–19). For Tylor, the contrast between what had been discovered by Spencer and Gillen about Indigenous ideas of creation confirmed the animistic roots of religious life, whereas the alleged belief in Baiame could only be accounted for by Christian missionary teaching.

Lang's position was also based on a logical argument, which in his case questioned how it would have been possible in such a short time for the missionary teaching to have been absorbed so thoroughly by the Indigenous population. He also asserted that the belief in Baiame had peculiarly non-Christian traits consistent with Indigenous culture. For example, the name 'Baiame' (or other terms for a High God) was known only to initiated males and no sacrifices or even petitions were made to the All Father, which, of course, was directly contrary to the prayer of Jesus to 'Our Father'. It also appeared to Lang as unempirical to assume on ideological grounds that primitive peoples could never have possessed an idea of a High God simply because they reflected human development at its earliest stage.

We see from this brief analysis that both Tylor and Lang started with predetermined ideas that inevitably led to their conclusions. Beginning with the assumption that animism precedes all later religious developments, Tylor sifted the evidence to support this theory and any interpretations that followed needed to be fitted into a preconceived evolutionary scheme. Lang, who declared that God had never left himself without a witness (1898: 185), believed in a form of natural theology, whereby the divine imprint could be found in every human society, no matter how crude or backward. The doctrine of degeneration also fitted nicely into the biblical teaching of the fall of humanity, which depicted an ideal creation that had collapsed through the transgressions of the prototypical figures, Adam and Eve. In light of the doctrine of the fall of humanity, the biblical view of the world dictated that the remainder of history entailed a process of redemption. For Lang, Tylor was correct in the sense that he saw humanity as involved in a process of a sometimes uneven development, but he was wrong by ruling out the possibility that the need for human progress had been determined by an initial fall from grace.

Implications for contemporary studies of Indigenous Religions

One rather simple observation derived from this discussion of the Tylor–Lang debate over primitive monotheism would be to conclude that every scholar begins with presuppositions that determine the direction of the ensuing argument. This point is reflected in a comment by Thomas Nagel (1986: 68) in his discussion of the problem of objective knowledge: 'We can never abandon our own point of view, but can only alter it.' In other words, it would be unjustified to criticize either Tylor or Lang for beginning, in Tylor's case with assumptions derived from evolutionary theories, or in Lang's case from the opposing presupposition of an original monotheism rooted in a natural theology. The best we can do is make our presuppositions transparent and try to limit any distortions that result from them. To pursue this avenue of thought would lead us into a discussion of phenomenological perspectives on the study of religion and on the value of trying to bracket out one's most distorting predispositions (performing *epoché*) (Cox 2010: 49–52).

Although I have argued for the persistent value of the phenomenological method in the study of religion, as modified by the principles of reflexivity (Cox 2006: 233–43), I want to follow another line in my conclusion to this chapter. Even if we admit that both Tylor and Lang reflected the world-view characteristic of their own period in intellectual history and that their conclusions inevitably followed from their predetermined theories, we cannot escape the fact that their arguments largely ignored the humans who comprised the actual subjects of their research. The Indigenous people themselves were incidental to the theory each was expounding and defending. The controversy was not over Baiame, as such, but centred on the relative merits of either the evolutionary theory of social development or a theology of primitive monotheism.

In this sense, the Tylor–Lang debate is instructive for contemporary students of Indigenous Religions, who often enter into discussions about how localized, small-scale societies are being affected by globalizing forces as if those living in local situations lack agency. Scholars in the study of religions, including Christian theologians, have analysed the interaction between global and Indigenous Religions by reference to such ideas as syncretism, development, contextualization, indigenization, human rights and a host of other concepts, but frequently the same error committed by Tylor and Lang that robs Indigenous people of agency has been repeated. In my book *The Invention of God in Indigenous Societies* (2014a: 144–7), I have sought to correct this by employing the concept 'intentional hybridity' as a mode of analysis that acknowledges that Indigenous peoples themselves are active players in constructing their own responses to modernity by framing subversive strategies to counter the hegemonic power of globalizing political, economic, social, cultural, educational and religious forces.

I derived the term 'intentional hybridity' from the work of the Russian literary critic, linguist and philosopher, Mikhail Bakhtin, who, when discussing the ways in which a language changes as it interacts and mixes with other languages, introduced the term 'hybridization', which he defined as a 'a mixture of two social languages' that have been separated by varying factors, such as temporal or social contexts (Bakhtin 1981: 358). He further distinguished between two types of hybridization: organic and intentional. Organic hybridity entails an 'unintentional' or 'unconscious' mixing of languages that occurs naturally. Intentional hybridity, on the other hand, is planned, deliberate and strategic (Bakhtin 1981: 358–9). The best example of intentional hybridity in literary works, according to Bakhtin (1981: 359), can be seen in the novel where the author constructs 'two individual language-intentions'. One intention resides in the mind of the author, who possesses 'consciousness and will' and the other exists in the mind of the character, who takes on another, separate, consciousness and will (Bakhtin 1981: 359). The result is a 'collision' of differing views of the world expressed in the conflicting wills of the author and the character to whom the author has given will or intention (Bakhtin 1981: 360).

Bakhtin's distinction between 'organic' and 'intentional' hybridity has been applied to the interactions between cultures. For example, Andreas Ackermann (2012: 12), Professor in the Institute of Cultural Studies in the University of Koblenz-Landau, Germany, has defined organic hybridity as 'the unintentional, unconscious everyday mixing and fusing of diverse cultural elements'. Intentional hybridity, by contrast, emphasizes deliberate acts that are constructed by various players in cultural interactions. In ways that scholars have often overlooked, local Indigenous cultures have constructed their own, deliberate and intentional responses to the perceived authoritative power of colonial invaders. Ackermann suggests that it is important to understand both organic and intentional hybridity in historical contexts, but he stresses that whereas organic hybridity 'tends towards fusion', intentional hybridity 'enables a contestatory activity' (Ackermann 2012: 13).

In *The Invention of God in Indigenous Societies*, I provide a particular example of intentional hybridity by focusing on the Rainbow Spirit Theology, which developed in Northern Queensland in Australia through a series of meetings held in 1994 and 1995 involving Aboriginal Elders from the Catholic, Lutheran, Uniting and Anglican Churches (Cox 2014a: 89). The Rainbow Spirit Elders produced a book entitled *The Rainbow Spirit Theology*, which was first published in 1997, with a revised version appearing ten years later. In this groundbreaking and at times controversial publication, the Rainbow Spirit is described as the 'life giving power of the Creator Spirit active in the world' (Rainbow Spirit Elders 2007: 31). The Elders selected the term 'Rainbow Spirit' rather than 'Rainbow Serpent' largely because of biblical associations between the serpent and Satan (Cox 2014a: 99; Rosendale 2004: 7). Nonetheless, it is clear from the context of the book and also from actual references in it that the Elders equated the Rainbow Spirit with the traditional figure of the rainbow-serpent, which numerous anthropologists writing in the early to mid-twentieth century, such as A. R. Radcliffe-Brown, regarded as a ubiquitous symbol throughout Australia (Radcliffe-Brown 1930: 342).

At one point in the book, the Elders (2007: 56) describe the Rainbow Spirit as being closely linked to the land and the sea and who 'as a powerful snake … gives life to the land and all living creatures'. Elsewhere, the Elders (2007: 13) write: 'As the Creator, the Rainbow Spirit is often portrayed by our Aboriginal artists as a powerful snake who emerged from the land, travelled the landscape leaving trails of life, and returned to the land through caves, waterholes and other sacred sites'. Further evidence that the Rainbow Spirit was co-terminus with the rainbow-serpent described in traditional myths is found in a training guide for Indigenous church leaders written by one of the Rainbow Spirit Elders, George Rosendale, who has been described by the Lutheran theologian Norman Habel (2007: viii) 'as the true elder of the group'. In the training guide, Rosendale describes the Creator as the 'Rainbow Snake', and asserts that the Rainbow Snake 'remains watching and caring for the people and the land' (Rosendale 2004: 6). He then makes the connection between the Christian God and the Indigenous belief in the rainbow-serpent unequivocal when he declares: 'The rainbow snake made the world in creation' (Rosendale 2004: 6). In these ways, the Rainbow Spirit Elders transformed the rainbow-serpent into the Rainbow Spirit, whom they equated with the Christian God or the All Father; they even refer to the Rainbow Spirit as an overarching word for the Indigenous God, of which Baiame is included as one of his names (Rainbow Spirit Elders 2007: 31).

At first glance, the Rainbow Spirit Theology appears to capitulate to Christian missionary influences by replacing an Indigenous symbol with the Christian idea of God. This could be conflated with the missionary theory of 'fulfilment' in which Jesus Christ is seen as completing the vague anticipations that people around the world possessed of a loving and powerful God. When the missionaries brought the message of Christ, according to this theory, Indigenous peoples responded because God had already planted in them the seeds of the gospel, which then came to fruition when they heard the Christian message proclaimed. The highest and best aspects of their pre-Christian religious beliefs and practices, in this case the rainbow-serpent, were fulfilled by Christ (Sharpe 1965; Sharpe 1986: 144–71; Hedges 2014: 191–218). Although it is possible to read the Rainbow Spirit Theology as a form of the fulfilment theory, on closer scrutiny, it becomes clear that this is not the case.

Aboriginal representations of the rainbow-serpent depict the snake as a symbol of fertility, as evidenced in numerous myths and as reported by A. P. Elkin's descriptions and photographs of cave and rock paintings in which the rainbow-serpent appears as a human-like figure called *wondjina* (also spelled *wandjina*) that is always drawn as a face with two eyes, a nose but no mouth (Elkin 1930: 262–3). The anthropologist L. R. Hiatt argues that this figure represents explicitly the erect penis entering the vagina, and thus symbolizes not just procreation but lineage, ancestor traditions and an authority that is passed on from generation to generation (Hiatt 1996: 114–5; Cox 2014a: 97–9). The importance of the *wondjina* and its relation to the rainbow-serpent has been acknowledged by George

Rosendale, whose training guide for Indigenous church leaders contains a drawing of the *wondjina* that exactly replicates the cave paintings described by Elkin of a face with two eyes, a nose but no mouth (Rosendale 2004: 5). In *The Rainbow Spirit Theology*, the Rainbow Spirit Elders even go so far as to insist that Jesus Christ is the incarnation of the Rainbow Spirit (read rainbow-serpent) (Rainbow Spirit Elders 2007: 58).

I am convinced that the Elders were not ignorant of what they were doing. They were exercising an oblique strategy of resistance by intentionally using the language of the invading culture (God the Creator) and transforming this central doctrine of Christian faith into the principal symbol of ancestral traditions as depicted by the *wondjina*. Rather than calling this an example of fulfilment, as if the Indigenous symbol remained somehow inauthentic outside its configuration as a Christian representation, what actually is occurring is 'intentional hybridity', in which two living organisms, each with will and intention, have been fused to create a new, vibrant entity. By inserting 'intentional' in front of 'hybridity', I contend that the Indigenous participants in the creation of this new organism were active, even subversive, agents rather than passive victims acquiescing to the influences of an outside dominating force.

If I relate the concept 'intentional hybridity' to the debate between E. B. Tylor and Andrew Lang over the origin of religion, it becomes clear that it is largely immaterial whether belief in Baiame was a pre-Christian idea or if it appeared after the interventions of missionaries. When seen in the light of the Rainbow Spirit Elders, Baiame becomes an Indigenous God, which has been constructed through many examples of local agency, and thereby has been made thoroughly Indigenous (rather than thoroughly Christian), even so far as to incorporate within it symbols of fertility, procreation, lineage and ancestral authority. This is not to say that the Rainbow Spirit Elders are not Christian; they clearly are, but the missionary form of Christian faith has been sabotaged by Indigenous cultural symbols. This analysis shifts power away from the outside, invading culture to the original culture and makes apparent what often has been kept hidden in academic analyses, partly due to the predetermined interests of members of the scholarly community itself, that Indigenous responses to globalizing processes and 'world' religions have been deliberate, intentional and at times revolutionary, but they always have involved the active participation of local agents of change.

Chapter 14

T. G. H. STREHLOW AND THE REPATRIATION OF KNOWLEDGE

Repatriation commonly is associated with returning objects, artefacts or skeletal remains that were regarded as sacred or of important cultural value to their original Indigenous owners. During colonial times, such sacred objects or remains had been taken from Indigenous populations and transported to museums or other sites, often located in major cities around the world. The return of sacred objects does not imply that knowledge of their original meanings and uses is understood by Indigenous communities. This is because the objects have been separated from their original cultural contexts for generations. T. G. H. Strehlow (whom I introduced in Chapter 3 of the present volume), contended that Indigenous knowledge among Arrernte groups in Central Australia was preserved only in his personal research collection, which was comprised of notes about secret-sacred objects, interviews with Indigenous Elders, films of ceremonies, recordings and transcripts of songs, maps and genealogies. Most of this material is now stored in the Strehlow Research Centre in Alice Springs. In this chapter, I analyse the role of Strehlow's Collection in the current repatriation project being developed at the Strehlow Research Centre in light of Strehlow's assertion that the collective memory of the Arrernte Elders had been so severely disrupted by the mid-1960s that virtually all knowledge of traditional ceremonies, songs, symbols and stories associated with secret-sacred objects (*tjurunga*), and even the location of sacred sites, had been forgotten.

The repatriation of objects, artefacts and skeletal remains in Australia

On 15 May 2012, the Department of Communications and the Arts of the Australian Government announced membership of the newly established Advisory Committee for Indigenous Repatriation. On its website, the Department explained that the Advisory Committee 'provides guidance on issues relating to Aboriginal and Torres Strait Islander repatriation from the collections of Australian and overseas cultural institutions' (http://arts.gov.au/indigenous/repatriation). The backdrop for establishing a programme of Indigenous Repatriation is explained by the Department:

For more than 150 years Aboriginal and Torres Strait Islander ancestral remains and secret sacred objects were removed from communities and placed in museums, universities and private collections in Australia and overseas. During the 19th and 20th centuries, ancestral remains were collected by medical officers, anatomists, ethnologists, anthropologists, and pastoralists, in some cases for the purposes of scientific research linked to explaining human biological differences. (http://arts.gov.au/indigenous/repatriation)

The aim of repatriating ancestral remains and secret-sacred objects to the communities from which they were taken, the Department notes, 'helps promote healing and reconciliation for Aboriginal and Torres Strait Islander peoples' (http://arts.gov.au/indigenous/repatriation).

The Advisory Committee for Indigenous Repatriation was established as a continuation of the Return of Indigenous Cultural Property (RICP) programme that the Australian Government initiated in 1999 with funding of $1.5 million, which in turn was matched by the states and territories. In the 2007–08 budget for Indigenous Affairs, the Australian Government provided another $4.5 million for four years explaining that 'the return of Indigenous cultural property to the traditional custodians and places of rest is extremely important to the Indigenous communities and to the Australian Government' (http://arts.gov.au/indigenous/repatriation). The Return of Indigenous Cultural Property programme aimed at returning all Indigenous ancestral remains and secret-sacred objects 'where possible', keeping in mind that 'repatriation can only occur where remains and objects have been adequately provenanced and where the communities are prepared to receive their ancestral remains and secret-sacred objects' (http://arts. gov.au/indigenous/repatriation). The programme acknowledged that in some cases Indigenous communities preferred museums to retain their ancestral remains and secret-sacred objects under the proviso that ownership was transferred from the museums to the community. The RICP programme involved eight major museums within Australia, which the Government estimated collectively held '7070 ancestral remains and 11,448 secret-sacred objects' (http://arts.gov.au/indigenous/repatriation). The eight museums are: The Australian Museum, the Museum and Art Gallery of the Northern Territory, Museum Victoria, the National Museum of Australia, Queensland Museum, South Australian Museum, Tasmanian Museum and Art Gallery and the Western Australian Museum.

Under its current Indigenous Repatriation project, the Australian Government has expanded its efforts to return cultural property beyond Australian museums to include international holdings, most of which are retained in museums in 'the United Kingdom, Germany, France, Poland and the United States of America' (http://arts.gov.au/indigenous/repatriation). On its web page outlining the aims of the Indigenous Repatriation project, the Ministry for the Arts explained that 'the Australian Government seeks the unconditional return of Aboriginal and Torres Strait ancestral remains' (http://arts.gov.au/indigeneous/repatriation). In pursuit of this objective, the Ministry noted that it has established relationships with the countries holding the majority of the remains and secret-sacred objects and, in addition, 'is developing relationships with a number of other countries in order to progress the repatriation of Indigenous ancestral remains' (http://arts.gov.au/indigenous/repatriation). It will be clear from these descriptions of cultural property that repatriation is interpreted by the Australian Government in material terms: ancestral remains and secret-sacred objects. The connection between material and intellectual cultural property is not discussed in any detail in these documents.

This connection was emphasized in an article written by Kenan Malik for the *Index on Censorship* in 2007 under the title, 'Who Owns Knowledge?' Malik, who is an independent researcher, writer and broadcaster, begins his article by noting that 'the debate about the repatriation of human remains has been especially fierce in America, Australia and New Zealand, where guilt about the treatment of indigenous peoples – Native Americans, Aborigines and Maoris – runs deep' (Malik 2007: 158). He adds that 'museums in these countries have thrown open their storage rooms, and returned thousands of bones to indigenous communities for burial' (Malik 2007: 158). He argues that 'many of the remains were taken from native countries in acts often little short of grave-robbing' (Malik 2007: 158). Although he contends that many Indigenous peoples have romanticized their cultural heritage, Malik acknowledges that tangible objects must be related more broadly to an intangible cultural heritage, in support of which he cites the UNESCO International Convention of the Intangible Cultural Heritage, which defines heritage as 'all of those things which international law regards as the creative production of human thought and craftsmanship, such as songs, scientific knowledge and artworks' (UNESCO: http://www.unesco.org/culture/ich/en/convention; Malik 2007: 166).

In this way, Malik has drawn attention to the fact that repatriation has more to do with a broad interpretation of cultural heritage than is implied strictly by references to material objects. Repatriation includes the meaning of the remains and secret-sacred objects associated with them, much of which is contained in the memory of communities through oral traditions, songs and ritual performances. What happens when the memory of communities has been disrupted by forces of modernity, including colonial oppression, missionary activities, Western education, global economic structures, rapidly advancing communication systems and urbanization? If contemporary events have obscured the meaning contained within the traditional cultural heritage of the tangible objects being returned, this would appear to render repatriation projects largely symbolic, and arguably, in service of an Indigenous political agenda (Krmpotich 2012: 163).

The current repatriation of knowledge project
at the Strehlow Research Centre

In order to address the issue of the disruption in the transmission of traditional knowledge, I turn now to consider the case of the repatriation of knowledge project currently being developed at the Strehlow Research Centre in Alice Springs. The last ten years of T. G. H. Strehlow's life were consumed by controversy over how he and his wife Kathleen dealt with the vast material he had collected over his years working among the Arrernte people, including the *tjurunga* that were entrusted to him for safekeeping by Aboriginal Elders. After his death in 1978, negotiations between Mrs Strehlow and the Government of the Northern Territory resulted in the opening of the Strehlow Research Centre in 1991 under terms of the Northern Territory's Strehlow Research Centre Act of 1988. John Morton (n.d.) reports that Mrs Strehlow 'was employed by the Centre as part of the agreement', which resulted in 'constant dispute, something which came to public prominence in 1992 when an Adelaide auction room offered for sale some 260 Aboriginal artefacts including secret-sacred material allegedly belonging to Carl Strehlow (Ted and Kathy's son)'. The material never became part of the public domain, since, as Morton (n.d.) notes, it 'was impounded under South Australian heritage legislation', which, after several years, saw most of Strehlow's Collection deposited at the Strehlow Research Centre. According to Morton, the material collected by Strehlow included '700 objects (largely secret-sacred), 15 kilometres of movie film, 7,000 slides, thousands of pages of genealogical records, myths, sound recordings, 42 of Strehlow's diaries outlining his ethnographic work, as well as paintings, letters, maps and a 1000 volume library' (Morton n.d.; See also, Hawley 1987: 28).

Strehlow's far-reaching Collection is now being used increasingly by Indigenous leaders to return not just secret-sacred objects to their legitimate owners in accordance with recognized genealogical data collected by Strehlow, but as a source for restoring knowledge of Indigenous cultural traditions, ceremonies, stories and social customs that have been lost or forgotten by members of the contemporary generation. In an interview in 2010 with the then Deputy Director of the Strehlow Research Centre, Michael Cawthorn, Penelope Bergen cites Cawthorn as stating, 'the bulk of the audio and film recordings are ceremonial acts', most of which 'aren't performed anymore and we try to be very active in digitally repatriating that material where we can' (Bergen 2010).

A project that documented the developing use of the Strehlow Collection began in 2010 under the direction of Hart Cohen and Juan Salazar of Western Sydney University, in conjunction with Michael Cawthorn, and later in collaboration with Wendy Cowan, a teacher at the Ntaria School in Hermannsburg. Initially, Cohen, Salazar and Cawthorn received funding from the Australia Research Council for a project entitled 'Digital Archives and Discoverability: Conceptualising the Strehlow Collection as a New Knowledge Resource for Remote Indigenous Communities'. In a seminar presented at Western Sydney University, Parramatta Campus, in August 2015, Cohen, Salazar and Cowan presented a paper that outlined the project's aims and raised important questions about digital repatriation of cultural knowledge. Cohen, Salazar and Cowan referred to how knowledge contained in the Strehlow Collection and the interest of local Indigenous communities cross, particularly how digital technology is being used 'in the re-mediating of image collections' and informing, particularly young Indigenous people, of the stories connected to their traditions. This innovative project is engaging Elders in Hermannsburg/Ntaria and young people by using T. G. H. Strehlow's vast collection, combined with modern technology, to restore knowledge that has been lost to the current generation of Elders and assisting them in passing it on to the next generation (http://www.uws.edu.au/ics/events/seminars/seminars_in_2015/seminars_2015/ics_seminar_series_2015_hart_cohen_juan_salazar_and_rachel_morley). Indigenous repatriation in this sense is consistent with the aims of UNESCO's International Convention of Intangible Cultural Heritage that seeks to repatriate knowledge in the form of stories, ceremonies and art that were replaced, at least in part, by Christian religious symbols or Western cultural expressions as a result of missionary and colonial interventions (http://www.unesco.org/culture/ich/en/convention).

In Penelope Bergen's interview, Cawthorn referred to the connection between the Strehlow Collection and the Return of Indigenous Cultural Property programme of the Australian Government. He is quoted as saying that the RICP programme 'provides us with the opportunity to be pro-active in terms of actually contacting people and making them aware that they have material housed in the centre' (Bergen 2010). In 2009, Adam Macfie was appointed as the Repatriation Anthropologist managing the Indigenous Repatriation Program for the Museum and Art Gallery of the Northern Territory (MAGNT). Based at the Strehlow Research Centre, Macfie has consulted extensively with the Arrernte community in researching the sacred objects and genealogical records held in the Strehlow Collection. In 2013, MAGNT employed two Arrernte researchers, Mark Inkamala and Shaun Angeles, to assist in the development of the Repatriation Project at the Strehlow Research Centre. The purpose of the Indigenous Repatriation Programme in Macfie's words 'is to reconnect Indigenous communities of the Northern Territory with their ancestral remains and their secret sacred objects held in the collections under the care of MAGNT' (http://www.strehlow.co.uk/conference_2014.html, see Abstracts of papers).

In 2014, Macfie, Inkamala and Angeles presented a paper at a conference held in Alice Springs, organized by John Strehlow, the son of T. G. H. Strehlow, in which they outlined the current work of the Repatriation Project. They explained how central T. G. H. Strehlow's research diaries had become in the efforts to repatriate knowledge among the Arrernte peoples:

> Over the past few years our attention has been drawn more and more to the maps found in the archive which Strehlow … annotated on published government survey map sheets for the region …. The origin of all of these maps can be found in his forty or so handwritten field diaries produced between 1935 and 1971 …. Our cultural mapping project is based on archival research and participatory engagement with the traditional owners and has become an invaluable practice for the Strehlow Research Centre and its repatriation programme. (http://www.strehlow.co.uk/conference_2014.html, see Abstracts of papers)

Indigenous agency

On 28 September 2016 an event was held at the Strehlow Research Centre to commemorate the twenty-fifth anniversary of the opening of the Centre in

1991, which was recorded by Kieran Finnane, a reporter for the *Alice Springs News,* whose account appeared in the newspaper on 30 September 2016. The ceremony honouring this important anniversary contained a welcome speech by the Chairman of the Board, Ken Lechleitner, and an address by Shaun Angeles, who as I noted above, is one of the Indigenous researchers involved in the repatriation project at the Strehlow Research Centre. In his opening remarks, Lechleitner highlighted an important concept that has often been overlooked in repatriation discussions, that of Indigenous agency, which in the case of the Strehlow material, acknowledges that T. G. H. Strehlow was not in total control of his own data collection. Rather, Indigenous Elders decided what to share with him, which *tjurunga* to entrust to him and which ceremonies he was allowed to film and record. Lechleitner suggested that the Strehlow Collection was formed in a partnership between 'the real visionaries in this story – the elders who entrusted Theodore [TGH] Strehlow with their cultural knowledge and Theodore himself who dedicated his life to collecting and preserving this knowledge' (Finnane 2016).

In his address to the assembly, Shaun Angeles pursued the theme of Indigenous agency. He explained first that he is 'a Penangke man from Ayampe country' (around 70 kilometres northeast of Alice Springs), who began working at the Strehlow Research Centre in September 2013 as an 'Indigenous Repatriation Researcher' (Finnane 2016). He added that he had

worked intimately with the collection for three years – analysing field diaries, editing the ceremonial film footage, working with individuals and families with the genealogies, digitising the ceremonial song catalogue and travelling to museums within Australia searching for artefacts that left this landscape in some instances over a hundred years ago. (Finnane 2016)

Throughout this process, Angeles observed, he had begun to feel as if he knew 'these old men, in sometimes tracking their lives through four decades of work with TGH' (Finnane 2016). After paying respect to Strehlow and the work he completed during his life, Angeles then made a telling remark: 'I want to ... elevate the story of the Aknegerrapte (senior cultural leaders) who ... possessed the greatest agency in this story' (Finnane 2016). By agency, he explained, he was referring to the fact that 'they chose what to show Strehlow' (Finnane 2016). Certainly, Strehlow had gained their trust, but the Elders freely chose to share their secret knowledge with him; they also selected which information to withhold from him. Angeles argued that it was just this choice which has preserved 'the deepest aspects of Aboriginal men's culture in Central Australia for the benefit of their future generations' (Finnane 2016).

Indigenous agency is illustrated by the complex circumstances surrounding Strehlow's descriptions of a series of important kangaroo increase ceremonies, called *utnitjia,* that he witnessed at Alice Springs in 1933 as public performances lasting sixteen days. In *Aranda Traditions,* he calls the *utnitjia* cycle 'the most secret of all the multitudinous rites performed near the Northern kangaroo centre, rites which in past times might be witnessed only by members of the inner kangaroo clan of Krantji' (Strehlow 1947: 29). According to tradition, the kangaroo increase ceremonies Strehlow observed should not have occurred in Alice Springs but at the *pmara kutata* [ceremonial centre] at Krantji, which lies approximately eighty miles west of Alice Springs. Strehlow (1947: 140) notes that it was at Krantji that 'the kangaroo chief Krantjirinja first came into being'. Strehlow (1947: 140) described the myth of Krantjirinja as it was told to him by the Elders who referred to Krantjirinja as a 'true kangaroo', who during the day 'was shaped like an animal', but at night 'assumed human shape'. At the bottom of the soak at Krantji 'was the home of the ancestor' beneath which 'lay all his tjurunga' (Strehlow 1947: 140). Strehlow (1947: 14) adds that this location literally is the source of 'all kangaroo ancestors' who 'emerged in the form of kangaroos, and then assumed human bodies'.

The fact that the sacred kangaroo increase ceremonies in 1933 were public and performed at a place other than the Krantji *pmara kutata* severely altered their significance and would have made the rituals ineffective in producing a plentiful supply of kangaroos. In his contribution to a book edited by W. E. H. Stanner and Helen Sheils, Strehlow (1963: 249) underscored just this point when he asserted that 'local earth-born supernatural beings were associated with definite local sacred centres, as were all ceremonies, sacred songs and magical practices'. The seriousness of failing to conduct the rituals at the appropriate ceremonial centre had severe consequences: 'Each centre had its own separate cycle of ceremonies which in the old days could be performed nowhere else – on pain of death – but at that particular site' (Strehlow 1963: 249).

In *Songs of Central Australia*, Strehlow explained that because the series of rituals was not held at the sacred ceremonial site at Krantji, two important changes were made by the Elder Ekuntjarinja, who was in charge of the event. First, due to its being held at Alice Springs, 'outsiders', men who were not members of the kangaroo totem and young men, who normally would have been excluded, were permitted to observe the kangaroo increase ceremonies. This condition also applied to Strehlow, who was the only white man at the event and, he assumes, the first white man allowed to view these particular kangaroo rituals (Strehlow 1971a: 307). The presence of outsiders led to a second significant change: Ekuntjarinja omitted important elements in the ceremonies including, according to Strehlow, 'the nightly utnitjia spear-singing; the night acts with their rhythmically different verses; and above all, the final magic fertilization of the ibantera by means of the ceremonial phallus' (Strehlow 1971a: 307). Ekuntjarinja made these changes because, on Strehlow's (1971a: 307) interpretation, he 'wanted to preserve the secrecy of the particular features which were believed to give this utnitjia series its special potency'.

At the beginning of the cycle, Strehlow (1971a: 308) notes, the spectators 'were called to … a hollow scratched out by kangaroos', which represented the bottom of the waterhole at Krantji where the original kangaroo ancestor was believed to have emerged. For ceremonial purposes, the hollow had been hardened with blood taken from the 'veins of the kangaroo totemites at Krantji' and it had been covered with white down, which, Strehlow explains, 'was said to represent the …

kangaroo fat from which all the remaining kangaroo ancestors had sprung into life'
(Strehlow 1971a: 308). At Krantji, the hollow measured around 30 inches across
(76 centimetres) with a deep hole in the middle of it, but at Alice Springs, the hole
was much smaller due to the rocky terrain on which the ritual was performed. At
Krantji, the hole would have been as deep as a person could have dug by hand,
meaning that a man could have extended his arm all the way to the bottom of the
hole. At Alice Springs, it was only 6 inches deep (15 centimetres). These geological
differences affecting the size of the holes were significant because the ceremonial
'*para*' or headgear, which represented the phallus, was meant to fit into the hole,
in an obvious reference to fertility. This could only have been accomplished at
Alice Springs symbolically because the *para* was two feet long (61 centimetres),
and clearly would not fit into the small hole at Alice Springs.

The fundamental and critical variations in performing the ritual, however,
cannot be explained primarily by the differing geological features present at Alice
Springs in comparison to Krantji because, as we have seen, the actual hollow
located at Krantji represented the genuine origin of the kangaroo ancestor, whereas
at Alice Springs it was merely a representation of the event where the original
kangaroo ancestor was believed to have emerged from the earth at the beginning
of time. As a result, Ekuntjarinja altered what Strehlow (1971a: 312) calls 'the vital
final scene' by refusing to reveal the most sacred part of the ritual to outsiders and
by performing it at a profane location. Strehlow (1971a: 312) says that Ekuntjarinja
felt 'too much shame at the idea of displaying the last mysteries to the vulgar gaze'
of non-totemites. As a result, Strehlow did not witness the most crucial concluding
act in the series of rituals. Instead, he claims, the younger men 'gave me a detailed
account of what would have been the correct procedure' (Strehlow 1971a: 312).
He explains that the younger men told him that had the ceremony been held at
Krantji and had it been restricted solely to members of those kangaroo totemites
from Krantji, in the central concluding act of the ritual, the *para* or head covering
would have been placed between the legs of the men. They would then approach
on their knees the arm-length hole that had been dug and, in Strehlow's words,
would have performed acts involving 'twisting and turning the para from side to
side, and finally thrusting it towards the central hole' (Strehlow 1971a: 312). This
act, simulating copulation, was intended to ensure the increase of kangaroos, and
without this act, the ritual would have been rendered ineffective. Strehlow adds in
a footnote that to change any part of the sacred ceremony or to omit any section,
particularly in the case of the most important element, was 'a very serious offence'
(Strehlow 1971a: 312: fn 142). The Elder Ekuntjarinja faced an insurmountable
dilemma at Alice Springs: either he left out the most sacred part of the ritual or
he profaned it by revealing it to those who were strictly prohibited by tradition
from witnessing it and by performing it at a site far removed from the traditional
ceremonial centre.

Two different interpretations of this same situation are presented by Strehlow,
the first in *Aranda Traditions* and the second the one I just recounted from *Songs
of Central Australia*. In *Aranda Traditions*, Strehlow maintains that if any changes
'in the slightest' were inserted into the traditional kangaroo increase ceremonies

at Krantji, or if they were 'irreverently' shown to uninitiated men, 'some terrible evil is certain to fall upon the offender as a punishment' (Strehlow 1947: 29). Strehlow notes that this infraction of strict rules caused Ekuntjarinja to experience 'acute pains in the neck' (Strehlow 1947: 29), which he and other Elders attributed 'to the anger of the offended Krantjirinja himself, who had struck Ekuntjarinja because the latter had frivolously exhibited the sacred ceremonies to people to whom he had been strictly forbidden to show them by his elders when they first instructed him' (Strehlow 1947: 30). Strehlow (1947: 30) comments that the belief that Ekuntjarinja's illness resulted from the anger of the original kangaroo ancestor remained 'unshaken, despite the fact that Krantji is over eighty miles west of Alice Springs'. By contrast, in *Songs of Central Australia,* Strehlow presents Ekuntjarinja as prohibiting the most secret of the traditional rites from being performed for quite honourable reasons. According to tradition, such scenes must not be witnessed by 'outsiders' and the complete performance of the ceremonies should only have occurred at Krantji. On this interpretation, Strehlow pits Ekuntjarinja against the younger men who considered omitting sections of the ceremonies 'sacrilegious' (Strehlow 1971a: 307).

Both accounts and their interpretations provided by Strehlow confirm Shaun Angeles's contention that the Elders were in control of what they chose to reveal to Strehlow and what they deliberately omitted. Strehlow was not permitted to witness key elements within the Krantji kangaroo increase ceremonies held in 1933 following the decision of the Elder Ekuntjarinja, but he was informed of the content of the key stages in the ritual by the younger men who objected to Ekuntjarinja's decision. By 1950, after Ekuntjarinja had died and the younger men had themselves become Elders, the then current Elders agreed to perform the entire *utnitjia* cycle so that Strehlow could film the ceremonies in colour and, as Strehlow (1971a: 316) explains, 'record them by means of a wire recorder'.

The kangaroo increase ceremonies Strehlow filmed in 1950 were not performed publicly, as had occurred in 1933 in Alice Springs, but they were staged at Strehlow's request as part of research he was conducting under a grant from the Australian National University. The *utnitjia* cycle was performed for Strehlow near Jay Creek, where Strehlow had lived when he was serving as the Northern Territory Patrol Officer in the 1930s. In his biography of Strehlow, Barry Hill (2003: 432) reports that Strehlow set up three 'stages' on clearings in the rocky hills located around three miles north of Jay Creek. Hill calls them 'the sets for the shooting', which he likens to 'an open-air theatre' (Hill 2003: 433). This meant that the location where the ceremonies were enacted and the context in which they were performed clearly violated the rigid rule that, according to tradition, they should be conducted only at the sacred ceremonial site where the kangaroo ancestor first emerged from beneath the surface of the earth. By 1950, Strehlow strongly believed that these traditional protocols were rapidly being forgotten or ignored, and thus justified filming the cycle of secret rituals as a means of preserving for future Arrernte leaders, and for academic researchers, knowledge of how they were performed and the songs that accompanied them.

In both cases that Strehlow documents, that of 1933 in Alice Springs and the contrasting circumstances of 1950 near Jay Creek, it is clear that the Elders decided what Strehlow was allowed to observe, describe, photograph, film and record. That the Elders deliberately selected what they revealed to Strehlow is confirmed by what Strehlow calls 'a strong veil of secrecy' that 'shrouds the most sacred ritual mysteries' (Strehlow 1971a: 313). For this reason, it was quite common for 'false versions of ceremonial explanations' to be provided to outsiders by the Elders (Strehlow 1971a: 313). This fact leads Strehlow to observe in *Songs of Central Australia* 'that it was little wonder' that the most secret act involving the symbolic fertilization of the water soak out of which the original kangaroo ancestors emerged 'was omitted from public performance at the Alice Springs festival in 1933' (Strehlow 1971a: 313). Because it was a public performance, Strehlow (1971a: 313) suggests that 'it could have been intended only as a symbolical and reverent representation of the original union between male and female fertility, from which all life was supposed to have originated at Krantji'. Strehlow admits that to have questioned his informants further about the meaning of the closing ritual that was omitted at Alice Springs 'would have been worse than useless', not because the Elders lacked an understanding of its meaning nor because 'they were incapable of abstract thinking', but precisely because the 'religious reverence of their descendants has silenced both logical questionings and loquacious explanations' (Strehlow 1971a: 313).

That Strehlow acknowledged Indigenous agency is evidenced further by the agreement he made with the Elders before they consented to allow him to film and record the kangaroo increase ceremonies in 1950. In his report to the Australian National University on his research in Central Australia, which the ANU had funded, Strehlow admitted: 'I had to give my personal word of honour to the ceremonial leaders that these films would not be shown publicly' (cited by Hill 2003: 433). The complex negotiations and the contrasting contexts of the *utnitjia* kangaroo increase ceremonies held at Alice Springs and Jay Creek nearly twenty years apart, which I have discussed in detail, confirm in equal measure Angeles's concluding remark that he made at the event commemorating the twenty-fifth anniversary of the Strehlow Research Centre, when he attested that senior Arrernte Elders demonstrated agency by choosing what and what not to disclose to Strehlow, and it was the same Elders who did this for the intentional purpose of preserving 'the deepest aspects of Aboriginal men's culture in Central Australia for the benefit of their future generations' (Finnane 2016).

The active role of elders as agents in the repatriation programme

Indigenous agency not only applies to the activities and decisions of the Elders with whom Strehlow worked over a period of thirty years, but it also defines how contemporary Arrernte Elders are using material that Strehlow collected and that now is housed in the Strehlow Research Centre. As Angeles argued in his address during the twenty-fifth anniversary commemoration, agency suggests that the material comprising the Strehlow Collection cannot by itself restore the memory of traditional Arrernte ways of life, but requires consultation 'with our present Elders to realise the collection's true potential' (Finnane 2016). Angeles, who himself forms part of the younger generation, contended that the Elders are 'the only ones … who understand its content and are able to enrich it and enrich the lives of our young men who are coming through the ranks' (Finnane 2016). He added that the Collection, which 'for the past 25 years … has been like a sleeping giant' can achieve its true potential only by identifying 'innovative cultural ways' whereby it can achieve its 'power throughout Central Australia' (Finnane 2016). Angeles concluded his speech by underscoring the fundamental importance of involving the current generation of Arrernte people in unlocking the potential of the Strehlow Collection. He referred to the Collection as 'living' and 'breathing' and insisted that as a dynamic source of information about Arrernte culture and religion, it 'needs Aboriginal custodians interacting with it'. The most important 'stakeholders' in T. G. H. Strehlow's Collection, he asserted, 'are the Indigenous people' whom he called 'the custodians and owners of the material' (Finnane 2016).

By emphasizing the current power of Indigenous agency as Elders interact with the Strehlow Collection, Angeles was arguing that the present Elders must interpret the data contained in the Strehlow Centre in terms of the contemporary situation. This assumes that the Elders possess at least some knowledge of the traditions, particularly with respect to the land, the stories connected to the land and the kinship system that had been taught to them by their Elders. Nonetheless, if Strehlow was correct, many ceremonies he originally documented in the 1930s will no longer be performed today, or they will have been altered substantially in critical ways either because the traditions have been forgotten or because they were suppressed by outside forces. Strehlow (1971a: xlv) confirmed this judgement when he wrote in the Introduction to *Songs of Central Australia* that 'virtually all the old Aranda pmara kutata are dead and forgotten now' and 'are today only geographical points in the Central Australian landscape'. He claimed that 'it would be unfair to the younger aboriginal generation of Central Australia to accuse them of having lightly discarded the ancient traditions of their forefathers without making any struggle to preserve them' (Strehlow 1971a: xlv). Rather, he laid the blame squarely on 'the white population' which inflicted 'shocking casualties' on Indigenous peoples, through 'the unsympathetic older Mission policies, the many acts of interference by the early white cattle-owners, and, in recent years, a number of repressive administrative acts carried out in the name of the governmental assimilation policy' (Strehlow 1971a: xlv). To regain such knowledge, the present Elders will need to consult Strehlow's vast collection of songs, ceremonies and genealogical records, but it is assumed that they will be able to understand this material because their language, which they have maintained, and their cultural traditions are closely intertwined and because they are able to interpret Strehlow's detailed genealogical records onto which they can place their own lineage and totemic identities.

The active role of the current generation of Elders in using the Strehlow Collection as a source of knowledge for contemporary Arrernte young people is demonstrated in a documentary film entitled 'Ntaria Heroes', which was made in 2015 and released in 2016 by Hart Cohen and Juan Salazar (https://www.youtube.com/watch?v=k-64qnmkvsI). The film features the role of the Strehlow Collection as a teaching tool for contemporary young Arrernte people. It begins by documenting a trip made in October 2014 by a group of young men and senior girls from Ntaria School, who travelled from Hermannsburg to the Strehlow Research Centre in Alice Springs. They were shown genealogical records and old photographs by two key Elders as a means for instructing them in their traditional ways of life, including kinship and marriage rules, conception sites and totemic ancestors. The young men were tutored by Mark Inkamala, one of the Indigenous Researchers at the Strehlow Research Centre, and the senior girls were taught by Mavis Malbunka, a woman Elder and a Traditional Owner in Western Arrernte country. The film also shows interviews with Adam Macfie, Shaun Angeles and Wendy Cowan. In his interview, Macfie observed that during their visit the young people were shown 'evidence that there is a connection between what is recorded in this archive and ... what they are taught about by their Elders'. He added that the 'unifying theme' within the Strehlow Collection, that which 'brings it all together, ... is its tie to country'. This is made evident by the Collection's extensive genealogical records that Strehlow so carefully documented, which Macfie explains, include the family trees showing conception sites. He adds that the 'language itself comes from the landscape'.

In the film, Mavis Malbunka is shown teaching the senior girls about how the family trees indicate kinship relations and thus demonstrate proper marriage regulations according to traditional norms. She tells the girls that the family trees show how the 'old people' got married according to 'the right marriage kinship'. She says in an interview, 'that is what young people should learn', adding that they 'can't marry just whoever' because 'their children will have wrong kinship'. She is shown in the film telling the girls that the family trees trace conception sites and personal totemic ancestors, adding that she is from the 'caterpillar' totem. She says: 'I have seen the caterpillar. We knew what animal dreaming we have, what land we belong to.' She emphasizes in an interview: 'We have to teach the children.' The knowledge of conception sites that Mavis Malbunka displays conforms to the traditional role of women in Arrernte society. In *Songs of Central Australia*, Strehlow (1971a: 648) observed that 'since the personal totem of the child depended on the mother's story of its conception-site, the native women were inevitably aware of *all* the landscape features associated with the various totems located in their area of residence'.

Mark Inkamala is shown in the film teaching the boys about their family trees and hence their totemic identities. He discusses their 'skin name' and tells the boys how they can be traced along a lineage to particular ancestors following Strehlow's genealogical records. Skin name refers to the kinship system of classes and subclasses, or sections or subsections. On its website, the Central Land Council explains that a child takes the skin name of his or her parents, which in turn indicates to which section or subsection the child belongs (Central Land Council: http://www.clc.org.au/articles/info/aboriginal-kinship). In the film, Inkamala stresses the importance of language and its relation to culture. He asserts: 'Without no language, without no culture, you are nothing.' In his interview on the film, Shaun Angeles states that for the young people 'looking at genealogies, looking at old photographs ... has been powerful for them and even also for us'. Angeles adds that instructing the young people in the traditions of the people 'needs to be done very soon because we are running out of Elders quickly'. He concludes: 'We need to do as much with these young people while these Elders are still alive.'

In a statement read on his behalf before a public lecture I delivered at Western Sydney University on 9 September 2016, the co-producer of 'Ntaria Heroes', Hart Cohen (private correspondence, Cohen to Cox, 8 September 2016), explained that the intent of the film 'is to foster a relationship between the community and the Strehlow Research Centre where their collection of cultural materials and relevant cultural information could be offered as a resource for learning about cultural traditions, genealogical information and the ancestors to whom the students are related'. Cohen refers to the process I have called the 'repatriation of Indigenous knowledge' as the 'Indigenous reclamation of its valued heritage' and suggests that the Collection of cultural material accumulated by T. G. H. Strehlow 'has the potential to communicate with, and educate the next generation of Indigenous leaders whose authority will rest on their ability to know their cultural heritage'.

In an interview with Shaun Angeles, uploaded on YouTube on 6 October 2015 by the National Film and Sound Archive of Australia, Angeles confirmed that Arrernte Elders currently are using the Strehlow Collection as a way of restoring knowledge of ancient traditions that have been forgotten and fallen into disuse. Angeles observed: 'Arrernte men are able to access this Collection and revisit the knowledge of our old people and revitalize all cultural practices that have been lost.' He explained that 'collections like this are able to fill us up spiritually ... and change people's lives'. Since he had been working at the Strehlow Research Centre, Angeles confirmed that 'men have come in, got a ceremonial film, got the song that goes with it and gone out and taught their young people about it' (Angeles 2015: https://www.youtube.com/watch?v=eUsv2dISgqs).

That Strehlow's records are being used today by Arrernte Elders was confirmed to me in an interview I held with a traditional Elder near Alice Springs on 13 October 2015. The Elder asked that his identity not be revealed and thus I will simply refer to him by a pseudonym as Phillip. Phillip appeared to be approximately sixty-five years old. The interview took place at his homestead. I was introduced to Phillip by Steve Bevis, an independent researcher living in Alice Springs, who attended the interview. Phillip told me that he had been consulting the Strehlow Research Centre to find out things exclusively about his people, his family and was not intruding into the business of other families. By family, he explained, he meant extended family – aunts, uncles, cousins – 'a large mob'. He then repeated what Adam Possamai and I (Cox and Possamai 2016: 182–8) discovered during our research in the Utopia region in 2013: 'The younger generation need to know about their traditions. They are forgetting them.' Then he referred to the importance of the Strehlow Research Centre as a source for preserving knowledge of the traditions: 'At the Strehlow Centre there are pictures, stories, songs, genealogies, sacred objects. I am taking pictures of some of these and using them to teach the younger generation of my family.' He added that his 'mob' were using the Strehlow material in ceremonies, particularly initiation and increase ceremonies. About Strehlow himself, Phillip commented: 'A lot of people say he wasn't good, but I think he did good. He preserved the records of people from all over. That was good. He helped us keep our tradition, our knowledge' (Interview James Cox with 'Phillip', Arrernte Elder, 13 October 2015, Alice Springs). After the interview concluded, Steve Bevis confided to me privately: 'The man was open. He is a good source of knowledge, but his kind are dying out. In ten years, this kind of thing will be gone' (Interview James Cox with Steve Bevis, 13 October 2015, Alice Springs).

Bevis was underscoring the fact, as was confirmed graphically in the film *Ntaria Heroes*, that the present members of the younger generation lack knowledge of Indigenous ways of life and, without the mediation of living Elders, are in danger of losing it altogether. The Strehlow Collection becomes critical at just this point precisely because the present Elders, whose own knowledge of songs and ceremonies has been disrupted, are relying on it as a source for the revival of tradition and are using it as a critical tool in maintaining generational continuity. Of course, the Strehlow Collection cannot be regarded naively as a means for restoring the past by returning to the time when Strehlow recorded his data, since the Collection, as Angeles noted, is 'living' and 'breathing'. This means it does not function as a static record of the past, but must be treated as a dynamic source whereby the next generation of Arrernte men and women can respond to the contemporary world with integrity, pride and innovation in accordance with their age-old cultural values. In this sense, repatriation of knowledge does not imply that ancient traditions can be resurrected, but it suggests that traditional knowledge can and should be returned to its rightful owners. This is consistent with the concept, 'Indigenous agency', which reminds us that local communities use Indigenous knowledge that has been recovered to engage intentionally and productively with changes confronting traditional society by outside forces, such as Western education, modern forms of communication, laws imposed by the national and territorial governments, commercial interests, ease of travel and the dissemination of family ties through processes of urbanization.

Conclusion

From the above cases describing the current repatriation project developing at the Strehlow Research Centre, it has become clear that since 2009, when Adam Macfie was appointed Repatriation Anthropologist, and prominently since 2013, when Mark Inkamala and Shawn Angeles were contracted as Indigenous Repatriation Researchers, the involvement of Arrernte Elders in accessing and using the Strehlow Collection has increased. Hart Cohen drew attention to this when he observed that 'for some time, little interest was shown in the potential for repatriating parts of the collection given the sensitivities and complexities relating to provenance and ownership' (private correspondence, Cohen to Cox, 8 September 2016). Recently, he explains, 'repatriation has been taken on with new earnestness albeit with a changing focus as more material comes to light and more traditional owners express an interest in their materials' (private correspondence, Cohen to Cox, 8 September 2016). The interviews and cases I have highlighted in this chapter demonstrate that Elders are accessing Strehlow's notes and records to confirm their own kinship links and to establish their relationship to the land as traditional owners. We have also seen how this information is being used by current Elders, both men and women, to instruct young people in traditional knowledge, without which they fear it will die out completely.

These developments confirm that Strehlow was correct in his judgement that it was through his notes, diaries and collected data that knowledge of Arrernte traditions would be preserved and passed on to the next generation. With the active involvement of Arrernte researchers, the importance of transmitting knowledge of the traditions has been made evident to the present generation of Elders with the result that Strehlow's diverse Collection is now serving his original purpose as a means not only of restoring to the current generation knowledge of songs, ceremonies, stories and traditions that had been forgotten and gone into disuse, but also as a living source for interpreting them in new and creative ways that will affect future generations.

Conclusion

PHENOMENOLOGY AT THE CUTTING EDGE: AFFIRMING LOCAL AGENCY

At the conclusion of this book, 'local agency' has emerged as an essential concept requisite for identifying new directions in the academic field of Indigenous Religions, and, quite possibly, for the study of all religions. By privileging local agency, academics are acknowledging that the communities they are researching own the knowledge that is being investigated; it is their communal intellectual property. Religious adherents must be involved throughout the development and implementation of a research project in full recognition that they are in control of what they choose to reveal to outside researchers. Academics are enabled to conduct research only by invitation, as Graham Harvey (2003: 125–46) has suggested, as 'guests' of the communities to which they are invited. Once invited, researchers are confronted with increasingly complicated issues resulting from questions about what they do with the knowledge acquired according to academic principles, while still respecting the property of those being investigated.

Theories supporting the concept 'local agency' are consistent with key ideas articulated by scholars of religion I have cited in the chapters of this book, particularly Van der Leeuw, Kristensen, Bleeker, Eliade, W. C. Smith and Smart, each of whom, in his own way, applied the phenomenological maxim that scholarly interpretations that offend the religious communities being studied are illegitimate because they distort the data on which the interpretations are based. In general, phenomenologists agreed that if religious adherents cannot recognize themselves in academic interpretations of their beliefs and practices, they are not being described accurately, nor are scientific principles being observed. This is because the final arbiter of the truth of interpretations must be believing communities themselves, without which there would be no data on which to build academic theories.

This conviction developed and honed within the phenomenological tradition, rather than hiding a theological agenda, is echoed increasingly in other non-theological disciplines in which scholars are putting into practice the dictum that knowledge in the first instance always belongs to those being studied. For example, Marcia Langton, an Indigenous scholar at the University of Melbourne, argues that the most important innovation introduced by current approaches in Indigenous Studies is 'its restitution of the agency of Indigenous people' through which the scholar brings 'the voice of the Indigenous protagonists into their own history' and explains 'events by reference to the perspectives and theories that they themselves exerted on their affairs' (Langton 2012: 173). Interpretative power is transferred on this model from being the sole prerogative of the researcher into a shared, dialogical task developed between the researcher and the researched. A case suggesting how the disciplines of heritage studies, archaeology, Indigenous studies and anthropology are employing this fundamental principle is exemplified by the current struggle of the Ngadjuri people of South Australia to recover data relevant to their cultural history and by their persistent effort to regain knowledge that they assert rightfully belongs to them.

The case of the Ngadjuri Elders of South Australia and the anthropologist Ronald Berndt

An important book in the fields of heritage studies and archaeology, edited by V. Apaydin (2018) of the Institute of Archaeology at University College London, entitled *Shared Knowledge, Shared Power*, explores new theories and methods in the study of human communities based on revised understandings of intellectual property rights. Chapter 2, written by Claire Smith, an archaeological anthropologist at Flinders University, in Adelaide, Australia, her colleague at Flinders, Gary Jackson, and Vincent Copley Sr, Chair of the Ngadjuri Elders Heritage and Landcare Council, suggests a method for reformulating approaches to Indigenous knowledge (Smith, Copley Sr and Jackson 2018: 9–28). Smith, Copley and Jackson describe the relationship of Copley's grandfather, the Ngadjuri Elder, Barney Warria, with the well-known Australian anthropologist Ronald Berndt. When he was a young researcher, between 1939 and 1944, Berndt worked closely with Warria compiling detailed field notes describing Ngadjuri culture, traditions, genealogies and ceremonies (Nicholas and Smith 2020: 149). After Berndt's death in 1990, a thirty-year embargo was placed on access to Berndt's field notes by his widow and co-researcher, Catherine Berndt, who died in 1994. Vincent Copley contends that much of the cultural knowledge that was contained in Ronald Berndt's records had been lost to or forgotten by the present generation. The data compiled by Berndt was needed in the early 1990s, not only to support cultural renewal projects, but to supply information based on genealogical charts relevant to land claims that were being adjudicated with the Australian government (Smith, Copley Sr and Jackson 2018: 9).

Smith, Copley and Jackson (2018: 10) argue that Catherine Berndt imposed the embargo on her husband's early field notes because 'she felt that the material might be used by government agencies to damage Aboriginal causes'. They suggest that her fears may have been justified because the Mabo decision overturning the legal doctrine that Australian land belonged to no one prior to British colonization (*terra nullius*) was not imposed by the Australian courts until 1992 (Brennan 1993: 22–3). A further reason confirming Catherine Berndt's distrust of how her husband's field notes would be used, according to Smith, Copley and Jackson, was based on the commonly maintained Western understanding that intellectual property rights belong to individuals and primarily reflect commercial interests. Little attention would have been given to the rights of communities with respect to knowledge that they possessed and which they had shared with academic researchers (Smith, Copley Sr and Jackson 2018: 10). Finally, the Berndts both knew that it was widely held by academics and government representatives that the Ngadjuri people had disappeared from their original homelands in South Australia by the early twentieth century and had been absorbed into the urban population of Adelaide, thereby excusing any interested parties from entering into negotiations with their descendants on the use of traditional Ngadjuri land and the appropriation of Indigenous cultural knowledge (Smith, Copley Sr and Jackson 2018: 11).

In a separate publication, George Nicholas and Claire Smith explain that the embargo on Berndt's field notes, which was included as a clause in Catherine Berndt's will, is currently being enforced by the University of Western Australia, which houses the notes in the University's Berndt Museum in Perth. Nicholas and Smith call maintaining the embargo by a major Australian academic institution a denigration of 'the rights of Indigenous people' (Nicholas and Smith 2020: 149–50). Ngadjuri Elders have attempted to gain access to the field notes for nearly thirty years arguing that, in the words of Nicholas and Smith (2020: 149), 'there is no legal basis for the current embargo' as the field notes were rightfully the shared intellectual property of Ronald Berndt and Barney Warria. Vincent Copley has made the case that the knowledge Warria conveyed to Berndt was recorded 'verbatim' by Berndt (Nicholas and Smith 2020: 150). He argues that this confirms his contention that the field notes were shared property, Warria providing the details of Ngadjuri culture while Berndt recorded the knowledge that Warria conveyed to him. According to Nicholas and Smith, Western Australia University has consistently rejected Ngadjuri Elders' requests to consult Berndt's material and will continue do so until 2024, according to Catherine Berndt's stated wishes (Nicholas and Smith 2020: 150). The thirty-year ban on Berndt's notes imposed by his wife for interests aimed at protecting Aboriginal rights and traditional knowledge, as Nicholas and Smith confirm, in effect obstructed efforts by Ngadjuri Elders to regain knowledge of their ancient cultural traditions and inhibited them from making a case for the return of their original homelands (Nicholas and Smith 2020: 149–50).

The central issue for Ngadjuri Elders clearly is not restricted to the prohibition of access placed on her husband's early research among the Ngadjuri people by Catherine Berndt, but more broadly relates to intellectual property rights, asking who actually owns the knowledge that Berndt obtained in the 1930s from Barney Warria. Catherine Berndt, despite her altruistic motives, interpreted her husband's research notes as his (and her) private property, something that Vincent Copley slowly challenged as he and his fellow Ngadjuri Elders began the arduous task of reconstructing and repatriating the knowledge that originally belonged to their forebears. For Claire Smith and Gary Jackson, as staff members of a major Australian university, the problem encountered by the Ngadjuri Elders brought to the surface critical issues surrounding the relationship between the aims of academic research and the interests of the communities that constitute the subjects of the research, particularly around questions of communal ownership of knowledge. Smith, Copley and Jackson explain:

> Controversies over cultural and intellectual property have emerged in the form of questions over ownership or access to the results of research and the many claims that descendant communities (including Indigenous peoples) and others make on cultural knowledge and information .... Concerns about claims to the ownership and use of cultural and intellectual property rights are rapidly emerging in all research disciplines and in many policy contexts, as the economic, scientific and cultural uses and values of traditional and Indigenous knowledge demand mounting attention.
>
> (Smith, Copley Sr and Jackson 2018: 13)

Repatriation, ownership and dissemination of knowledge: The analogy of 'Intellectual Soup'

As I noted in Chapter 14 in the case of the Arrernte of Central Australia, repatriation frequently has been associated with the return of material objects often held in museums in Europe or the United States, but Smith, Copley and Jackson, writing from the perspectives of archaeology, heritage studies and Indigenous studies, confirm my contention that repatriation refers equally, or even more importantly, to returning knowledge of religious/cultural traditions that were taken or stolen from Indigenous groups. They write: 'Markedly less attention has been given to the intangible intellectual aspects of archaeological research or cultural knowledge, although this promises to have as great, or greater, an influence on research and policy in the coming decades' (Smith, Copley Sr and Jackson 2018: 14).

Using the analogy of preparing soup, Smith, Copley and Jackson outline the various ingredients and stages when an 'intellectual' soup is concocted by a group of interested cooks. In the case of research into local communities, as demonstrated in the example of Berndt and Warria, at least two cooks are required: 'one to provide the essential ingredients of Aboriginal knowledge (Barney Warria) and the other (Ronald Berndt) to provide essential ingredients relating to the method of production and the tastes of intended consumers' (Smith, Copley Sr and Jackson 2018: 15). The ingredients used in making the intellectual soup also suggest two essential elements: Indigenous knowledge and theoretical frameworks. The recipe that is followed is largely developed by academics, but Indigenous people can use their own knowledge to alter the recipe. The kitchen and the cooking implements reflect practical instruments: the research environment, including the context in which the research is envisaged (usually universities) and the local environment in which the data is collected and recorded. The consumers of the soup, those interested in and affected by the results of the research, include the scholarly community, the general public, and sometimes governmental policy makers and commercial agents. Primarily, however, Smith, Copley and

Jackson (2018: 17) argue, 'Aboriginal people … now expect knowledge to be returned to their communities and to participate in the dissemination of the knowledge'. Once the intellectual soup is completed and ready to be consumed, the final and most important question is asked: 'Who owns the soup?' (Smith, Copley Sr and Jackson 2018: 17). The answer is clear: it is owned jointly by those who participated in its preparation.

The analogy of 'intellectual soup', as Smith, Copley and Jackson contend, demonstrates that researchers and the communities being researched each can claim equal rights of ownership in every aspect of a research project. This means that the knowledge acquired from academic investigations, including the analysis and dissemination of findings that researchers often guard as comprising their academic freedom, must be repatriated to the community that supplied the information in the first place. This is because knowledge that was obtained from past generations can play important roles in contemporary local projects that empower communities to restore cultural pride, solidify their identities and enable them to negotiate with policy makers over issues related to life in the modern world, including business interests, dialogue on religious beliefs and ritual performances, tourism, land claims and re-interpretations of historical records.

Towards a radical phenomenology of Indigenous Religions

By emphasizing the central place of local agency at all stages in a research project, a potential conflict between academic and community interests becomes evident. If adherents must recognize themselves in the academic interpretations offered about them, and if they have a shared role in developing theories about themselves, a line appears to have been crossed between presenting insider knowledge as if it is outsider knowledge. It is at this point that insights obtained from the phenomenology of religion become most relevant. As I discussed in Chapter 6, where I considered the social responsibility of the scholar of religion, according to phenomenological assumptions, any interpretation of the data that offends the belief system of religious communities, even if true, would appear to be prohibited from the outset. As I have shown in Chapters 1 and 7, strong objections to this interpretation of phenomenology have been made based on the argument that this would severely limit academic freedom and critical analysis. In response, I have argued that by employing the *epoché* as a technique for promoting self-awareness or reflexivity and by applying the procedure I have called empathetic interpolation to see as a believer sees, scholars in the phenomenological tradition challenge the widely assumed right of academics to extract knowledge from religious communities and, instead, they engage in dialogue with those who traditionally have constituted the 'objects' of academic research. If students of religion reflect on their role as researchers critically, these conclusions, based on phenomenological principles, must at the very least lead them to take seriously the complaint that by excluding believers from active participation in what is said about them, power is being exercised unfairly and knowledge that belongs to the communities is being exploited for the scholar's own ends.

This precise point was made by Smith, Copley and Jackson, who argued that determining who owns Indigenous knowledge translates into deciding who has the right to exercise interpretative power over the knowledge obtained. They assert that if 'intellectual property is jointly owned, it follows that it should be subject to joint control' (Smith, Copley Sr and Jackson 2018: 18). They admit that in the discipline of archaeology (and arguably in religious studies) this concession is highly controversial because it raises 'the spectre of potential censorship' over what an academic can or cannot say about the contents of the research conducted (Smith, Copley Sr and Jackson 2018: 18). The prospect that the community being researched has a right to veto what is being said about it offends many academics who would contend that this restricts the researcher from employing critical analysis of the data obtained. Smith, Copley and Jackson agree that difficulties for academics and university research schemes are created by acknowledging the right of local groups to claim ownership of their tangible and intangible intellectual property, but they counter objections to this by arguing that all research is subject to limitations: 'Indigenous control is simply another limitation that needs to be acknowledged' (Smith, Copley Sr and Jackson 2018: 18). The fact that this potentially biases the results of research is true but, if we accept the notion that pure objectivity is an illusion, all intellectual analyses are similarly biased.

I introduced this book by admitting that my intention was to present my interpretation of *a* phenomenology of Indigenous Religions rather than prescribing what constitutes *the* phenomenology of Indigenous Religions. In Chapter 9, I also indicated that my limited definition of Indigenous Religions was indicative, or operated as a working definition that should be tested in empirical studies. I have maintained throughout the twenty years represented by the contents of this book that academic work is a heuristic process, sometimes operating by trial and error, but always remaining open to fresh insights and new findings. The present volume provides a balanced picture of how I have interpreted phenomenology while considering different issues within a variety of contexts. The chapters of this book also demonstrate how my thinking has progressed in accordance with my conviction that one's ideas become increasingly credible when they respond to interactions with critics and when they change creatively through exposure to new sources of knowledge.

As I contended in the Introduction to this volume, the phenomenology of religion represents both a theoretical and practical approach that is extremely useful for studying Indigenous societies. I maintain that insofar as phenomenology poses questions about knowledge and offers resolutions to epistemological problems, it provides ways to analyse relationships between the self and the other, between the researcher and the researched, between the insider and the outsider. Through what I have outlined in Chapter 2 as the attitudinal, descriptive and interpretative phases within the phenomenology of religion, philosophical reflection on how we know what we know is put into practice in concrete field situations. This process results in interpretations of those being studied that promote understanding among outsiders and, at the same time, reflect what adherents would be able to affirm as accurately depicting their customary ways of life. In light of what I have written about 'local agency' as the key to empowering Indigenous peoples in their relationships with academic researchers, theories grounded in phenomenological principles and the practical methods that follow from them, if taken seriously, could threaten long-standing scholarly assumptions about the aims of research while, at the same time, altering radically how academic projects among living communities are envisaged and implemented.

NOTES

Chapter 3

1 Peter McKenzie, who died in 2011, wrote a rejoinder to this article, which appeared in the *Journal of Religion in Africa* under the title, '"Hail Orisha" Defended: A Response to James Cox' (2002: 110–9).

Chapter 6

1 The National Aids Council of Zimbabwe reports that as of December 2012 an estimated 15 per cent of the Zimbabwean population, or nearly 1,250,000 people, were infected with the HIV virus. The annual death rate attributed to AIDS was estimated at nearly 46,000. At the time of my research in 2004, the percentage of the population infected was higher having reached a peak of 25 per cent in 1999 (National Aids Council of Zimbabwe, www.nac.org.zw).

Chapter 13

1 Howitt's source for this is: James Manning. Royal Society of New South Wales. 'Notes on the Aborigines of New Holland', 1 November 1882.

REFERENCES

Ackermann, Andreas (2012), 'Cultural Hybridity: Between Metaphor and Empiricism', in P. W. Stockhammer (ed.), *Conceptualizing Cultural Hybridization: A Transdisciplinary Approach*, 5–25, Heidelberg: Springer.

Ajayi, J. F. A. (1965), *Christian Mission in Nigeria 1841–1891: The Making of a New Elite*, London: Longman.

Allman, Jean and John Parker (2005), *Tongnaab: The History of a West African God*, Bloomington and Indianapolis: Indiana University Press.

Alphen, E. van (1991), 'The Other Within', in R. Corbey and J. Th. Leerssen (eds), *Alterity, Identity, Image: Selves and Others in Society and Scholarship*, 1–16, Amsterdam: Rodopi B.V.

Angeles, Shaun (2015), 'Preservation of Remote Indigenous Collections'. Available online: https://www.youtube.com/watch?v=eUsv2dISgqs (accessed 26 March 2021).

Apaydin, Veysel, ed. (2018), *Shared Knowledge, Shared Power: Engaging Local and Indigenous Heritage*, New York: Springer.

Arnold, Robert D., ed. (1976), *Alaska Native Land Claims*, Anchorage: The Alaska Native Foundation.

Austin, J. L. (1963), 'Performative-Constative', in C. E. Caton (ed.), *Philosophy and Ordinary Language*, 18–31, Urbana, Chicago and London: University of Illinois Press.

Australian Bureau of Statistics (ABS) 1266.0 (2011), *Australian Standard Classification of Religious Groups*. Available online: http://abs.gov.au/AUSSTATS/abs@.nsf/Lookup/126 6.0Main+Features12011?OpenDocument (accessed 15 October 2013).

Australian Bureau of Statistics (ABS). Available online: https://www.abs.gov.au/census/find-census-data/historical (accessed 26 March 2021).

Australian Government, Department of Communication and the Arts, 'Return of Indigenous Cultural Property (RICP) Program: National Principles'. Available online: http://arts.gov.au/sites/default/files/pdfs/rics_principles.pdf (accessed 18 August 2016).

Australian Government, Department of Communication and the Arts, 'Indigenous Repatriation'. Available online: http://arts.gov.au/indigenous/repatriation (accessed 12 March 2021).

Australian Law Reform Commission, 'Legal Definitions of Aboriginality', Sections 36:30, 36: 32. Available online: https://www.alrc.gov.au/publication/essentially-yours-the-protection-of-human-genetic-information-in-australia-alrc-report-96/36-kinship-and-identity/legal-definitions-of-aboriginality (accessed 26 March 2021).

Baal, J. van (1971), *Symbols for Communication: An Introduction to the Anthropological Study of Religion*, Assen: Van Gorcum and Comp. N.V.

Bakhtin, Mikhail M. (1981), *The Dialogic Imagination: Four Essays*, trans. C. Emerson and M. Holquist, Austin: University of Texas Press.

Banana, Canaan S. (1991), *Come and Share: An Introduction to Christian Theology*, Gweru, Zimbabwe: Mambo Press.

Barnard, Alan and Justin Kenrick (2001), 'Preface', in A. Barnard and J. Kenrick (eds), *Africa's Indigenous Peoples: 'First Peoples' or 'Marginalized Minorities'?*, vii–xv, Edinburgh: Centre of African Studies, University of Edinburgh.

Batchelor, Stephen (1998), 'The Other Enlightenment Project', in U. King (ed.), *Faith and Praxis in a Postmodern Age*, 113–27, London: Cassell.

Bauman, Zygmunt (1993), *Postmodern Ethics*, Oxford: Blackwell.

Baylis, Philippa (1988), *An Introduction to Primal Religions*, Edinburgh: Traditional Cosmology Society.

Beek, Walter E. A. van and Thomas D. Blakely (1994), 'Introduction', in T. D. Blakely, W. E. A. Van Beek and D. L. Thomson (eds), *Religion in Africa*, 1–20, London: James Currey.

Bell, Diane (2001), 'Living the Dreaming: Aboriginal Ancestors Past and Present', in S. J. Friesen (ed.), *Ancestors in Post-Contact Religion: Roots, Ruptures, and Modernity's Memory*, 177–92, Cambridge, MA: Center for the Study of World Religions, Harvard Divinity School, Harvard University Press.

Belton, T. (2009), 'The Dawn of the "Chaotic Account": Horatio Hale's Australia Notebook and the Development of Anthropologists' Field Notes', *Libraries and the Cultural Record*, 44 (1): 138–52.

Berens, Denis, ed. (1987), *A Concise Encyclopedia of Zimbabwe*, 3rd edn, Gweru, Zimbabwe: Mambo Press.

Bergen, Penelope (2010), 'Repatriation of Sacred Items High on Strehlow's Agenda. ABC Rural'. Available online: http://www.abc.net.au/site-archive/rural/nt/content/201002/s2821494.htm (accessed 10 August 2016).

Berger, Thomas R. (1985), *Village Journey: The Report of the Alaska Native Review Commission*, New York: Hill and Wang.

Berner, Ulrich (2013), 'Religious Traditions – Kinship-based and/or Universal?', in J. L. Cox (ed.), *Critical Reflections on Indigenous Religions*, 49–62, Farnham, Surrey: Ashgate.

Bleeker, C. J. (1963), *The Sacred Bridge: Researches into the Nature and Structure of Religion*, Leiden: E. J. Brill.

Bleeker, C. J. (1972), 'The Contribution of the Phenomenology of Religion to the Study of the History of Religions', in U. Bianchi, C. J. Bleeker and A. Bausani (eds), *Problems and Methods of the History of Religions*, 35–54, Leiden: E. J. Brill.

Bleeker, C. J. (1975), *The Rainbow: A Collection of Studies in the Science of Religion*, Leiden: E. J. Brill.

Bleeker, C. J. (1979), 'Evaluation of Previous Methods: Commentary', in L. Honko (ed.), *Science of Religion: Studies in Methodology. Proceedings of the Study Conference of the International Association for the Study of Religions, Held in Turku, Finland, August 27–31, 1973*, 173–77, The Hague, Paris and New York: Mouton Publishers.

Bourdillon, M. F. C. (1987), *The Shona Peoples. An Ethnography of the Contemporary Shona, with Special Reference to Their Religion*, 3rd edn, Gweru, Zimbabwe: Mambo Press.

Bourdillon, M. F. C. (1996), 'Anthropological Approaches to the Study of African Religion', in J. Platvoet, J. Cox and J. Olupona (eds), *The Study of Religions in Africa: Past, Present and Prospects*, 139–54, Cambridge: Roots and Branches.

Bowker, John, ed. (1997), 'Judaism', in *The Oxford Dictionary of World Religions*, 512–14, Oxford: Oxford University Press.

Brennan, Frank (1993), *Land Rights: The Religious Factor*, Adelaide: Charles Strong Memorial Trust.

Bullivant, Stephen (2008), 'Introducing Irreligious Experience', *Implicit Religion*, 11 (1): 7–24.

Bullivant, Stephen (2010), 'The New Atheism and Sociology. Why Here? Why Now? What Next?', in M. Amarasingam (ed.), *Religion and the New Atheism: A Critical Appraisal*, 109–24, Leiden and Boston: Brill.

Bullivant, Stephen and Lois Lee (2012), 'Interdisciplinary Studies of Non-religion and
    Secularity: The State of the Nation', *Journal of Contemporary Religion*, 27 (1): 19–27.
Burch, Ernest S., Jr. (1998), *The Iñupiaq Eskimo Nations of Northwest Alaska*, Fairbanks:
    University of Alaska Press.
Campbell, Colin (2013 [1971]), *Toward a Sociology of Irreligion*, London: Alcuin
    Academics.
Capps, Walter H. (1995), *Religious Studies: The Making of a Discipline*, Minneapolis:
    Fortress Press.
Case, David S. and David A. Voluck (2002), *Alaska Natives and American Laws*, 2nd edn,
    Fairbanks: University of Alaska Press.
Central Land Council, 'Kinship and Skin Names'. Available online: http://www.clc.org.au/
    articles/info/aboriginal-kinship (accessed 21 July 2017).
Chance, Norman A. (1990), *The Inupiat and Arctic Alaska: An Ethnography of
    Development*, Chicago: Holt, Rinehart and Winston.
Chidester, David (1996), *Savage Systems: Colonialism and Comparative Religion in
    Southern Africa*, Charlottesville and London: University Press of Virginia.
Cohen, Hart and Juan Salazar (co-producers) (n.d.), *Ntaria Heroes*. Available online:
    https://www.youtube.com/watch?v=k64qnmkvsl (accessed 21 August 2016).
Cohen, Hart, Juan Salazar and Wendy Cowan (2015), 'ICS Abstract. Cultural Mediation
    of the Visual: Knowledge Resources for Remote Indigenous Communities'. Available
    online: https://tinyurl.com/ics-seminar-2015 (accessed 21 August 2016).
Cook Inlet Region, Inc. (2003), *Annual Report 2002*, Anchorage: CIRI.
Corbey, Raymond and J. Th. Leerssen (1991), 'Studying Alterity: Backgrounds and
    Perspectives', in R. Corbey and J. Th. Leerssen (eds), *Alterity, Identity, Image: Selves and
    Others in Society and Scholarship*, vi–xviii, Amsterdam: Rodopi B.V.
Cox, James L. (1991), *The Impact of Christian Missions on Indigenous Cultures: The 'Real
    People' and the Unreal Gospel*, Lewiston, NY: Edwin Mellen Press.
Cox, James L. (1993), 'Not a New Bible but a New Hermeneutics: An Approach from
    within the Science of Religion', in I. Mukonyora, J. L. Cox and F. J. Verstraelen (eds),
    'Re-writing' the Bible: The Real Issues, 103–23, Gweru, Zimbabwe: Mambo Press.
Cox, James L. (1995), 'Ancestors, the Sacred and God: Reflections on the Meaning of the
    Sacred in Zimbabwean Death Rituals', *Religion*, 25 (4): 339–55.
Cox, James L. (1996a), 'Methodological Considerations Relevant to Understanding African
    Indigenous Religions', in J. Platvoet, J. Cox and J. Olupona (eds), *The Study of Religions
    in Africa: Past, Present, and Prospects*, 162–70, Cambridge: Roots and Branches.
Cox, James L. (1996b), *Expressing the Sacred: An Introduction to the Phenomenology of
    Religion*, 2nd edn, Harare: University of Zimbabwe Publications.
Cox, James L. (1996c), 'The Classification "Primal Religions" as a Non-empirical Christian
    Theological Construct', *Studies in World Christianity*, 2 (1): 35–56.
Cox, James L. (1998a), *Rational Ancestors: Scientific Rationality and African Indigenous
    Religions*, Cardiff: Cardiff Academic Press.
Cox, James L. (1998b), 'Introduction: Ritual, Rites of Passage and the Interaction between
    Christian and Traditional Religion', in J. L. Cox (ed.), *Rites of Passage in Contemporary
    Africa*, viii–xix, Cardiff: Cardiff Academic Press.
Cox, James L. (1998c), 'Religious Typologies and the Postmodern Critique', *Method and
    Theory in the Study of Religion*, 10: 241–62.
Cox, James L. (1999), 'Intuiting Religion: A Case for Preliminary Definitions', in J. G.
    Platvoet and A. L. Molendijk (eds), *The Pragmatics of Defining Religion: Contexts,
    Concepts and Contests*, 267–84, Leiden: E. J. Brill.

Cox, James L. (2003), 'Contemporary Shamanism in Global Contexts: "Religious" Appeals to an Archaic Tradition?', *Studies in World Christianity*, 9 (1): 69–87.

Cox, James L. (2004), 'Separating Religion from the "Sacred": Methodological Agnosticism and the Future of Religious Studies', in S. J. Sutcliffe (ed.), *Religion: Empirical Studies*, 259–64, Aldershot: Ashgate.

Cox, James L. (2006), *A Guide to the Phenomenology of Religion: Key Figures, Formative Influences and Subsequent Debates*, London: T & T Clark (Continuum).

Cox, James L. (2007a), *From Primitive to Indigenous. The Academic Study of Indigenous Religions*, Aldershot: Ashgate.

Cox, James L. (2007b), 'Secularizing the Land: The Impact of the Alaska Native Claims Settlement Act on Indigenous Understandings of Land', in T. Fitzgerald (ed.), *Religion and the Secular: Historical and Colonial Formations*, 71–92, London: Equinox.

Cox, James L. (2008), 'Religious Studies *Sui Generis*: The Debate between Theological and Scientific Approaches to the Study of Religion', in M. Warrier and S. Oliver (eds), *Theology and Religious Studies: Exploring Disciplinary Boundaries*, 48–57, London and New York: T & T Clark (Continuum).

Cox, James L. (2009), 'Towards a Socio-cultural, Non-theological Definition of Religion', in D. L. Bird and S. G. Smith (eds), *Theology and Religious Studies in Higher Education: Global Perspectives*, 99–116, London and New York: Continuum.

Cox, James L. (2010), *An Introduction to the Phenomenology of Religion*, London and New York: Continuum.

Cox, James L. (2013a), 'The Transmission of an Authoritative Tradition. That without Which Religion Is Not Religion', in A. Adogame, M. Echtler and O. Freiberger (eds), *Alternative Voices: A Plurality Approach for Religious Studies*, 308–23, Göttingen: Vandenhoeck and Ruprecht.

Cox, James L. (2013b), 'Reflecting Critically on Indigenous Religions', in J. L. Cox (ed.), *Critical Reflections on Indigenous Religions*, 3–18, Farnham, Surrey: Ashgate.

Cox, James L. (2014a), *The Invention of God in Indigenous Societies*, Durham, England: Acumen (Routledge).

Cox, James L. (2014b), 'Can Christianity Take New Forms? Christianity in New Cultural Contexts', in P. Hedges (ed.), *Controversies in Contemporary Religion III. Education, Law, Politics, Society, and Spirituality*, 195–222, Santa Barbara, CA: Praeger.

Cox, James L. (2016), 'Kinship and Location: In Defence of a Narrow Definition of Indigenous Religions', in Christopher Hartney and Daniel J. Tower (eds), *Religious Categories and the Construction of the Indigenous*, 38–57, Leiden and Boston: Brill.

Cox, James L. (2018), *Restoring the Chain of Memory: T. G. H. Strehlow and the Repatriation of Australian Indigenous Knowledge*, Sheffield, UK and Bristol, CT,: Equinox.

Cox, James L. and Steven Sutcliffe (2006), 'Religious Studies in Scotland: A Persistent Tension with Divinity', *Religion*, 36 (1): 1–28.

Cox, James L. and Adam Possamai (2016), 'Religion, Cultural Hybridity and Chains of Memory', in J. L. Cox and A. Possamai (eds), *Religion and Non-religion among Australian Aboriginal Peoples*, 179–203, London and New York: Routledge.

Danquah, J. B. (1944), *The Akan Doctrine of God*, London: Lutterworth Press.

Davidsen, Markus Altena (2021), '"There Was No Dutch Phenomenology of Religion". Academic Implacability and Historical Accidents – An Interview with Jan G. Platvoet (The Netherlands)', in S. Fujiwara, D. Thurfjell and S. Engler (eds), *Global Phenomenologies of Religion: An Oral History in Interviews*, 245–76, Sheffield and Bristol, CT: Equinox.

Dickson, Kwesi (1984), *Theology in Africa*, Maryknoll: Orbis.

Docherty, Thomas (1993), 'Postmodernism: An Introduction', in T. Docherty (ed.), *Postmodernism: A Reader*, 1–31, London: Harvester Wheatsheaf.

Dupre, Wilhelm (1975), *Religion in Primitive Cultures*, The Hague: Mouton.

Durkheim, Émile (1915), *The Elementary Forms of Religious Life*, trans. J. W. Swain, London: George Allen and Unwin Ltd.

Eliade, Mircea (1969), *The Quest: History and Meaning in Religion*, Chicago: University of Chicago Press.

Eliade, Mircea (1973), *Australian Religions: An Introduction*, Ithaca and London: Cornell University Press.

Eliade, Mircea (1975), *Myth and Reality*, New York: Harper Torchbooks.

Eliade, Mircea (1987 [1959]), *The Sacred and the Profane. The Nature of Religion*, trans. Willard R. Trask, San Diego, New York and London: Harcourt.

Eliade, Mircea (1996 [1958]), *Patterns in Comparative Religion*, trans. Rosemary Sheed, Lincoln and London: University of Nebraska Press.

Elkin, A. P. (1930), 'Rock-Paintings of North-West Australia', *Oceania*, 1 (3): 257–79.

Evans-Pritchard, E. E. (1965), *Theories of Primitive Religion*, Oxford: Oxford University Press.

Evans-Pritchard, E. E. (1976), *Witchcraft, Oracles, and Magic among the Azande*, abridged with introduction by Eva Gillies, Oxford: Clarendon Press.

Fienup-Riordan, Ann (1990), *Eskimo Essays: Yup'ik Lives and How We See Them*, New Brunswick: Rutgers University Press.

Fienup-Riordan, Ann (1994), *Boundaries and Passages: Rule and Ritual in Yup'ik Eskimo Oral Tradition*, Norman: University of Oklahoma Press.

Fienup-Riordan, Ann (2000), *Hunting Tradition in a Changing World: Yup'ik Lives in Alaska Today*, New Brunswick: Rutgers University Press.

Finnane, Kieran (2016), '"This Beautiful Body of Knowledge" at the Strehlow Centre', *Alice Spring News*, 23 (8): 30 September 2016.

Fitzgerald, Timothy (2000), *The Ideology of Religious Studies*, New York and Oxford: Oxford University Press.

Flood, Gavin (1999), *Beyond Phenomenology: Rethinking the Study of Religion*, London and New York: Cassell.

Frazer, James G. (1911–1915), *The Golden Bough. 12 Volumes*, 3rd edn, London: Macmillan.

Freud, Sigmund (1949), *An Outline of Psycho-analysis*, trans. J. Strachey, London: The Hogarth Press.

Fujiwara, Satoko, David Thurfjell and Steven Engler (2021), 'Introduction: The Contested Legacies of Phenomenologies of Religion', in S. Fujiwara, D. Thurfjell and S. Engler (eds), *Global Phenomenologies of Religion: An Oral History in Interviews*, 1–27, Sheffield and Bristol, CT: Equinox.

Geertz, Armin W. and Russell T. McCutcheon (2000), 'The Role of Method and Theory in the IAHR', in A. W. Geertz and R. I. McCutcheon (eds), *Perspectives on Method and Theory in the Study of Religion*, 3–37, Leiden: Brill.

Gennep, Arnold van (1960), *The Rites of Passage*, trans. Monika B. Vizedom and Gabrielle L. Caffee, Chicago: University of Chicago Press.

Glatzer, N. M. (1962), 'Introduction', in M. Guyau, *The Non-Religion of the Future: A Sociological Study*, 11–20, New York: Schocken Books.

Grenz, Stanley (1996), *A Primer on Postmodernism*, Grand Rapids: William B. Eerdmans.

Guyau, M. (Jean-Marie) (1962 [1897]), *The Non-Religion of the Future: A Sociological Study*, New York: Schocken Books.

Haar, Gerrie ter, Ambrose Moyo and S. J. Nondo (1992), 'Introduction', in G. ter Haar, A. Moyo and S.J. Nondo (eds), *African Traditional Religions in Religious Education: A Resource Book with Special Reference to Zimbabwe*, 3–10, Utrecht: Utrecht University.

Habel, Norman (2007), 'Preface', in Rainbow Spirit Elders, *Rainbow Spirit Theology: Towards an Australian Aboriginal Theology*, 2nd edn, vii–xii, Hindmarsh, Australia: ATF Press.

Hadden, Jeffrey K. (1987), 'Toward Desacralizing Secularization Theory', *Social Forces*, 65: 587–611.

Hall, T. W., R. B. Pilgrim and R. R. Cavanagh (1985), *Religion: An Introduction*, San Francisco: Harper and Row.

Hansson, Gurli (1995), 'Religious Innovation in Zimbabwe. Mbuya Juliana Movement', in T. Negash and L. Redebeck (eds), *Dimensions of Development with Emphasis on Africa*, 91–114, Uppsala: Nordiska Afrikainstitutet.

Harvey, Graham, ed. (2000), *Indigenous Religions: A Companion*, London and New York: Cassell.

Harvey, Graham (2003), 'Guesthood as Ethical Decolonising Research Method', *Numen*, 50 (2): 125–46.

Harvey, Graham (2013a), 'Why Study Indigenous Religions?', in J. L. Cox (ed.), *Critical Reflections on Indigenous Religions*, 19–28, Farnham, Surrey: Ashgate.

Harvey, Graham (2013b), *Food, Sex and Strangers: Understanding Religion as Everyday Life*, Durham, England: Acumen (Routledge).

Heiler, Friedrich (1979 [1949]), *Erscheinungsformen und Wesen der Religion*, Stuttgart: Verlag W. Kohlhammer.

Hawley, Janet (1987), 'The Strehlow Collection Preserved in Vitriol', *Good Weekend*, 29 August: 28–34.

Hedges, Paul (2014), 'Why Are There So Many Gods? Religious Diversity and Its Challenges', in P. Hedges (ed.), *Controversies in Contemporary Religion, Vol. 1: Education, Law, Politics, Society, and Spirituality*, 191–218, Santa Barbara, CA: Praeger.

Hervieu-Léger, Danièle (1999), 'Religion as Memory: Reference to Tradition and the Constitution of a Heritage of Belief in Modern Societies', in J. G. Platvoet and A. L. Molendijk (eds), *The Pragmatics of Defining Religion: Contexts, Concepts and Contests*, 73–92, Leiden: Brill.

Hervieu-Léger, Danièle (2000), *Religion as a Chain of Memory*, Cambridge: Polity Press.

Hiatt, L. R. (1996), *Arguments about Aborigines: Australia and the Evolution of Social Anthropology*, Cambridge: Cambridge University Press.

Hick, John (1989), *An Interpretation of Religion: Human Responses to the Transcendent*, London: Macmillan.

Hill, Barry (2003), *Broken Song: T. G.H. Strehlow and Aboriginal Possession*, Milsons Point, NSW: Vintage Books.

Hinnells, John R. (1984), *The Penguin Dictionary of Religions*, Harmondsworth: Penguin Books.

Hobson, Marian (1987), 'History Traces', in D. Attridge, G. Bennington, and R. Young (eds), *Post-structuralism and the Question of History*, 105–15, Cambridge: Cambridge University Press.

Horton, Robin (1975), 'On the Rationality of Conversion', *Africa*, 45 (3): 219–35.

Howitt, A. W. (1904), *The Native Tribes of South-East Australia*, London: Macmillan and Co.

Husserl, Edmund (1931), *Ideas. General Introduction to a Pure Phenomenology*, trans. W. R. G. Gibson, London: George Allen and Unwin Ltd.

Husserl, Edmund (1969 [1929]), *Forma₁ and Transcendental Logic*, trans. D. Cairns, the Hague: Martinus Nijhoff.

Husserl, Edmund (1977), *Cartesian Meditations: An Introduction to Phenomenology*, trans. D. Cairns, The Hague: Martinus Nijhoff.

Idowu, E. Bolaji (1962), *Olódumare: God in Yoruba Belief*, London: Longman.

Idowu, E. Bolaji (1973), *African Religion: A Definition*, London: SCM Press.

Ifa Foundation International, 'Who We Are'. Available online: http://www.ifafoundation .org (accessed 18 March 2021).

International Association for the Cognitive and Evolutionary Sciences of Religion. Available online: www.iacesr.com (accessed 26 March 2021)

International Labour Organization (1989), *Indigenous and Tribal Peoples Convention (No. 169)*, Part 1 General Policy: 1 (2). Available online: https://www.ilo.org/dyn/normlex/ en/f?p=NORMLEXPUB:12100:0::NO::P12100_ILO_CODE:C169 (accessed 26 March 2021).

Irwin, James (1984), *An Introduction to Maori Religion*, Bedford Park: Australian Association for the Study of Religions.

Jakobsen, Merete D. (1999), *Shamanism: Traditional and Contemporary Approaches to the Mastery of Spirits and Healing*, Oxford and New York: Berghahn Books.

James, George A. (1995), *Interpreting Religion: The Phenomenological Approaches of Pierre Daniel Chantepie de la Saussaye, W. Brede Kristensen, and Gerardus van der Leeuw*, Washington, DC: The Catholic University of America Press.

Johnson, Christopher D. L. (2010), *The Globalization of Hesychasm and the Jesus Prayer: Contesting Contemplation*, London and New York: Continuum.

Juergensmeyer, Mark (2001), *Terror in the Mind of God*, 2nd edn, Berkeley: University of California Press.

Kenny, Anna (2005), 'A Sketch Portrait: Carl Strehlow's German Editor Baron Moritz von Leonhardi', in A. Kenny and S. Mitchell (eds), *Collaboration and Language, Strehlow Research Centre, Occasional Paper Number 4*, 54–70, Alice Springs: Strehlow Research Centre.

Kolig, E. and G. Petri-Odermann (1992), 'Religious Power and the All-Father in the Sky. Monotheism in Australian Aboriginal Culture Reconsidered', *Anthropos*, 87 (1): 9–32.

Krieger, David J. (1991), *The New Universalism: Foundations for a Global Theology*, Maryknoll, NY: Orbis Books.

Kristensen, W. Brede (1960), *The Meaning of Religion: Lectures in the Phenomenology of Religion*, trans. John Carman, The Hague: Martinus Nijhoff.

Krmpotich, Cara (2012), 'Post-Colonial or Pre-Colonial: Indigenous Values and Repatriation', in J. Hendry and L. Fitznor (eds), *Anthropologists, Indigenous Scholars and the Research Endeavour: Seeking Bridges towards Mutual Respect*, 162–70, London: Routledge.

Lang, Andrew (1884), *Custom and Myth*, London: Longmans, Green and Co.

Lang, Andrew (1887), *Myth, Ritual and Religion. Two Volumes*, London: Longmans, Green and Co.

Lang, Andrew (1898), *The Making of Religion*, London: Longmans, Green and Co.

Lang, Andrew (1907a), 'Edward Burnett Tylor', in W. H. R. Rivers, R. R. Marett and N. W. Thomas (eds), *Anthropological Essays Presented to Edward Burnett Tylor in Honour of His 75th Birthday Oct. 2 1907*, 1–16, Oxford: The Clarendon Press.

Lang, Andrew (1907b), 'Australian Problems', in W. H. R. Rivers, R. R. Marett and N. W. Thomas (eds), *Anthropological Essays Presented to Edward Burnett Tylor in Honour of His 75th Birthday Oct. 2, 1907*, 203–18, Oxford: The Clarendon Press.

Lang, Andrew (1908), *The Origins of Religion and Other Essays*, London: Watts and Co.

Langdon, Steve J. (2002), *The Native People of Alaska: Traditional Living in a Northern Land*, Anchorage: Greatland Graphics.

Langton, Marcia (2012), 'The Diaspora and the Return: History and Memory in Cape York Peninsula, Australia', in J. Hendry and L. Fitznor (eds), *Anthropologists, Indigenous Scholars and the Research Endeavour. Seeking Bridges towards Mutual Respect*, 171–84, London and New York: Routledge.

Lee, Lois (2012), 'Research Note. Talking about a Revolution: Terminology for the New Field of Non-religion Studies', *Journal of Contemporary Religion*, 27 (1): 129–39.

Lee, Lois (2013), 'Introduction: Resuming a Sociology of Irreligion', in C. Campbell, *Toward a Sociology of Irreligion*, xiv–xxxvi, London: Alcuin Academics.

Leeuw, Gerardus van der (1938), *Religion in Essence and Manifestation: A Study in Phenomenology*, trans. J. E. Turner, London: George Allen and Unwin Ltd.

Luckmann, Thomas (1967), *The Invisible Religion: The Problem of Religion in Modern Society*, New York: Collier-Macmillan.

Lynch, Gordon (2020), 'Sacred', in A. Possamai and A. J. Blasi (eds), *The Sage Encyclopedia of the Sociology of Religion*, vol. 2, 715–18, Thousand Oaks, CA and London: Sage Publications.

Lyotard, Jean-François (1991), *Phenomenology*, trans. B. Beakley, Albany: State University of New York Press.

Lyotard, Jean-François (1993), 'Answering the Question: What Is Postmodernism?' in T. Docherty (ed.), *Postmodernism: A Reader*, 38–46, London: Harvester Wheatsheaf.

McCutcheon, Russell T. (1997), *Manufacturing Religion: The Discourse on Sui Generis Religion and the Politics of Nostalgia*, Oxford and New York: Oxford University Press.

McCutcheon, Russell T. (2001), *Critics Not Caretakers: Redescribing the Public Study of Religion*, Albany: State University of New York Press.

Macfie, Adam, Mark Inkamala and Shaun Angeles (2014), 'Abstract: Cultural Mapping Interactive Workshop: Strehlow Conference, 24 September 2014'. Available online: http://www.strehlow.co.uk/conference_2014.html (accessed 21 August 2016).

McKenzie, Peter R. (1976), *Inter-Religious Encounters in West Africa: Samuel Ajayi Crowther's Attitude to African Traditional Religion and Islam*, Leicester: Study of Religion Sub-department, University of Leicester.

McKenzie, Peter R. (1990), 'Phenomenology and "the Centre" – the Leicester Years', in A. F. Walls and W. R. Shenk (eds), *Exploring New Religious Movements: Essays in Honour of Harold W. Turner*, 29–33, Elkhart, IN: Mission Focus.

McKenzie, Peter R. (1997), *Hail Orisha! A Phenomenology of a West African Religion in the Mid-Nineteenth Century*, Leiden: Brill.

McKenzie, Peter R. (2002), '"Hail Orisha!" Defended: A Response to James Cox', *Journal of Religion in Africa*, 32 (1): 110–19.

Mafu, Hezekiel (1995), 'The 1991–92 Zimbabwean Drought and Some Religious Reactions', *Journal of Religion in Africa*, 25 (3): 288–308.

Magesa, Laurenti. (1997), *African Religion: The Moral Traditions of Abundant Life*, Maryknoll: Orbis.

Malik, Kenan (2007), 'Who Owns Knowledge?', *Index on Censorship*, 36 (3): 156–67.

Marks, Sarah (2012), 'Cognitive Behaviour Therapies in Britain: The Historical Context and Present Situation', in W. Dryden (ed.), *Cognitive Behaviour Therapies*, 1–24, London: Sage Publications.

Mawere, Abraham and Ken Wilson (1995), 'Socio-religious Movements, the State and Community Change: Some Reflections on the Ambuya Juliana Cult of Southern Zimbabwe', *Journal of Religion in Africa*, 25 (3): 252–87.

Mbiti, John S. (1969), *African Religions and Philosophy*, London: Heinemann.

Mbiti, John S. (1970), *Concepts of God in Africa*, London: S.P.C.K.

Mellor, Phillip A. and Chris Shilling (1994), 'Reflexive Modernity and the Religious Body', *Religion*, 24 (l): 23–42.

Mitchell, Donald Craig (2001), *Take My Land, Take My Life: The Story of Congress's Historic Settlement of Alaska Native Land Claims, 1960–1971*, Fairbanks: University of Alaska Press.

Mitchell, Robert C. (1977), *African Primal Religions*, Niles, IL: Argus Communications.

Morton, John (n.d.), 'Central Land Council. The Strehlow Collection of Sacred Objects', 1–12. Available online: http://www.clc.org.au/articles/info/strehlow (accessed: 10 August 2016).

Müller, F. Max (1898), *Theosophy or Psychological Religion*, London: Longmans, Green and Co.

Nagel, Thomas (1986), *The View from Nowhere*, New York: Oxford University Press.

National AIDS Council of Zimbabwe. Available online: www.nac.org.zw (accessed 25 March 2021).

Nelson-Pallmeyer, Jack (2003), *Is Religion Killing Us? Violence in the Bible and the Quran*, Harrisburg, PA: Trinity Press International.

Nicholas, George and Claire Smith (2020), 'Considering the Denigration and Destruction of Indigenous Heritage as Violence', in V. Apaydin (ed.), *Critical Perspectives on Cultural Memory and Heritage: Construction, Transformation and Destruction*, 131–54, London: UCL Press.

Nonreligion and Secularity Research Network (NRSN). Available online: https://thensrn.org (accessed 26 March 2021).

Norris, Christopher (1995), 'Structuralism', in T. Honderich (ed.), *The Oxford Companion to Philosophy*, 855, Oxford: Oxford University Press.

Nthoi, Leslie S. (1998), 'Wosana Rite of Passage: Reflections on the Initiation of Wosana in the Cult of Mwali in Zimbabwe', in J. L. Cox (ed.), *Rites of Passage in Contemporary Africa*, 63–92, Cardiff: Cardiff Academic Press.

Olupona, Jacob K. (2000), 'Introduction', in J. K. Olupona (ed.), *African Spirituality: Forms, Meanings, and Expressions*, xv–xxi, New York: Crossroad.

O'Reilly, Karen (2009), *Key Concepts in Ethnography*, Los Angeles: Sage.

Ormiston, G. L. (1991), 'Foreword', in Jean-François Lyotard, *Phenomenology*, 1–25, Albany: State University of New York Press.

Oswalt, Wendell H. (1999), *Eskimos and Explorers*, 2nd edn, Lincoln: University of Nebraska Press.

Panikkar, Raimundo (1979), *Myth, Faith and Hermeneutics*, New York: Paulist Press.

Parrinder, Geoffrey (1974), *African Traditional Religion*, 3rd edn, London: Sheldon Press.

Parrinder, Geoffrey (1976), *Africa's Three Religions*, London: Sheldon Press.

Parker, K. L. (1905), *The Euahlayi Tribe: A Study of Aboriginal Life in Australia, with an Introduction by Andrew Lang*, London: A. Constable and Company.

P'Bitek, Okot (1990), *African Religions in European Scholarship*, New York: ECA Associates. Originally published as *African Religions in Western Scholarship*, Kampala: East African Literature Bureau, 1970.

Peel, J. D. Y. (2000), 'Review. McKenzie, Peter, *Hail Orisha!*', *Journal of Religion in Africa*, 30 (3): 401–3.

Platvoet, J. G. (1990), *African Traditional Religion: A Reader*, Harare: University of Zimbabwe, Department of Religious Studies, Classics and Philosophy.

Platvoet, J. G. (1992), 'African Traditional Religions in the Religious History of Humankind', in G. ter Haar, A. Moyo and S. J. Nondo (eds), *African Traditional Religions in Religious Education. A Resource Book with Special Reference to Zimbabwe*, 11–28, Utrecht: Utrecht University Press.

Platvoet, J. G. (1993), 'African Traditional Religions in the Religious History of Humankind', *Journal for the Study of Religion*, 6 (2): 29–48.

Platvoet, J. G. (1996), 'The Religions of Africa in Their Historical Order', in J. Platvoet, J. Cox, and J. Olupona (eds), *The Study of Religions in Africa: Past, Present and Prospects*, 46–102, Cambridge: Roots and Branches.

Platvoet, J. G. and Arie L. Molendijk, eds (1999), *The Pragmatics of Defining Religion: Contexts, Concepts and Contests*, Leiden: Brill.

Platvoet, J. G. (2002), 'Pillars, Pluralism and Secularisation: A Social History of Dutch Sciences of Religions', in G. Wiegers (ed.), *Modern Societies and the Science of Religions*, 83–148, Leiden: E.J. Brill.

Popkin, Richard H. and Avrum Stroll (1986), *Philosophy. Made Simple*, 2nd edn, London: Heinemann.

Quack, Johannes (2014), 'Outline of a Relational Approach to "Nonreligion"', *Method and Theory in the Study of Religion*, 26 (4–5): 439–69.

Radcliffe-Brown, A.R. (1926), 'The Rainbow-Serpent Myth of Australia', *Journal of the Royal Anthropological Institute*, 56 (1): 19–25.

Radcliffe-Brown, A. R. (1930), 'The Rainbow-Serpent Myth in South-East Australia', *Oceania*, 1 (3): 342–7.

Rainbow Spirit Elders (2007), *Rainbow Spirit Theology: Towards an Australian Aboriginal Theology*, 2nd edn, Hindmarsh, Australia: ATF Press.

Ralls-Macleod, Karen and Graham Harvey (2000), 'Introduction', in K. Ralls-macleod and G. Harvey (eds), *Indigenous Religious Musics*, 1–21, Aldershot: Ashgate.

Ranger, Terence (1995), 'Religious Pluralism in Zimbabwe. A Report on the Britain-Zimbabwe Society Research Day, St Antony's College, Oxford, 23 April 1994', *Journal of Religion in Africa*, 25 (3): 226–51.

Ranger, Terence O. (1996), 'Postscript: Colonial and Postcolonial Identities', in R. P. Werbner and T.O. Ranger (eds), *Postcolonial Identities in Africa*, 271–80, London: Zed Books.

Ranger, Terence and M. Ncube (1996), 'Religion in the Guerrilla War: The Case of Southern Matabeleland', in N. Bhebe and T. Ranger (eds), *Society in Zimbabwe's Liberation War*, 35–57, Oxford: James Currey.

Rice, Jesse (2009), *The Church of Facebook: How the Hyperconnected Are Redefining Community*, Colorado Springs: David C. Cook.

Róheim, Géza (1934), *The Riddle of the Sphinx, or, Human Origins*, New York: Harper and Row.

Rosendale, George (2004), 'Aboriginal Theology', in D. Thomson (ed.), *Milbi Dabaar: A Resource Book from Wontulp-Bi-Buya College in Queensland*, 4–13, Cairns: Wontulp-Bi-Buya College.

Sainsbury, M. (1995), 'Accidental', in T. Honderich (ed.), *The Oxford Companion to Philosophy*, 4, Oxford and New York: Oxford University Press.

Schmidt, Roger (1988), *Exploring Religion*, 2nd edn, Belmont, CA: Wadsworth Publishing Company.

Schmidt, Wilhelm (1931), *The Origin and Growth of Religion: Facts and Theories*, trans. H. J. Rose, London: Methuen and Co.

Segal, Robert (1999), 'In Defense of Reductionism', in R. McCutcheon (ed.), *The Insider/Outsider Problem in the Study of Religion: A Reader*, 139–63, London and New York: Cassell.

Sharpe, Eric. J. (1965), *Not to Destroy but to Fulfil: The Contribution of J. N. Farquhar to Protestant Missionary Thought in India before 1914*, Uppsala: Swedish Institute of Missionary Research.

Sharpe, Eric J. (1986), *Comparative Religion: A History*, 2nd edn, London: Duckworth.

Shaw, Rosalind (1990), 'The Invention of "African Traditional Religion"', *Religion*, 20 (4): 339–53.

Shoko, Tabona (2007), *Karanga Indigenous Religion in Zimbabwe: Health and Well-Being*, Aldershot: Ashgate.

Shorter, A. (1997), 'African Religions', in J. R. Hinnells (ed.), *A New Handbook of Living Religions*, 562–80, London: Penguin.

Smart, Ninian (1973a), *The Phenomenon of Religion*, New York: Seabury Press.

Smart, Ninian (1973b), *The Science of Religion and the Sociology of Knowledge*, Princeton: Princeton University Press.

Smart, Ninian (1981), *Beyond Ideology: Religion and the Future of Western Civilization*, London: Collins.

Smart, Ninian (1984a), *The Religious Experience of Mankind*, 3rd edn, New York: Charles Scribner's Sons.

Smart, Ninian (1984b), 'Scientific Phenomenology and Wilfred Cantwell Smith's Misgivings', in F. Whaling (ed.), *The World's Religious Traditions: Current Perspectives in Religious Studies*, 257–69, Edinburgh: T. and T. Clark.

Smart, Ninian (1995), *Choosing a Faith*, London: Bowerdean Publishing Company, Ltd.

Smart, Ninian (1996), *Dimensions of the Sacred: An Anatomy of the World's Beliefs*, London: HarperCollins.

Smart, Ninian (1999), *World Philosophies*, London: Routledge.

Smith, Claire, Vincent Copley Sr and Gary Jackson (2018), 'Intellectual Soup: On the Reformulation and Repatriation of Indigenous Knowledge', in V. Apaydin (ed.), *Shared Knowledge, Shared Power: Engaging Local and Indigenous Heritage*, 9–28, New York: Springer.

Smith, Edwin W. (1950), 'Introduction', in E.W. Smith (ed.), *African Ideas of God: A Symposium*, 1–35, London: Edinburgh House Press.

Smith, Huston (1992), *Beyond the Postmodern Mind*, Wheaton: Theosophical Publishing House.

Smith, Jonathan Z. (1990), *Drudgery Divine: On the Comparison of Early Christianities and the Religions of Late Antiquity*, London and Chicago: The University of Chicago Press.

Smith, Linda Tuhiwai (1999), *Decolonizing Methodologies: Research and Indigenous Peoples*, London and New York: Zed Books Ltd.

Smith, Wilfred Cantwell (1964), *The Meaning and End of Religion: A New Approach to the Religious Traditions of Mankind*, New York: Mentor Books.

Smith, Wilfred Cantwell (1972), *The Faith of Other Men*, San Francisco: Harper and Row.

Smith, Wilfred Cantwell (1998), *Patterns of Faith around the World*, Oxford and Boston: Oneworld Publications.

Smyth, R. B. (1878), *The Aborigines of Victoria, Vol. I*, London: Trübner and Co.

Spencer, Baldwin (1896), *Report on the Work of the Horn Scientific Expedition to Central Australia*, 4 vols, Melbourne: Melville, Mullen and Slade.

Spencer, Baldwin and F. J. Gillen (1899), *The Native Tribes of Central Australia*, Melbourne: Macmillan.

Spencer, Baldwin and F. J. Gillen (1927), *The Arunta. A Study of a Stone Age People. In Two Volumes*, London: Macmillan and Co, Limited.

Stanner, W. E. H. (2009), *The Dreaming and Other Essays*, Melbourne: Black Inc. Agenda.

Strehlow, T. G. H. (1947), *Aranda Traditions*, Melbourne: Melbourne University Press.

Strehlow, T. G. H. (1963), 'Commentary', in W. E. H. Stanner and H. Sheils (eds), *Australian Aboriginal Studies. A Symposium of Papers Presented at the 1961 Research Conference of the Australian Institute of Aboriginal Studies*, 248–51, Melbourne: Oxford University Press.

Strehlow, T. G. H. (1966), *The Sustaining Ideals of Aboriginal Societies of South Australia*, Adelaide: Aborigines Advancement League Inc. of South Australia.

Strehlow, T. G. H. (1971a), *Songs of Central Australia*, Sydney: Angus and Robertson.

Strehlow, T. G. H. (1971b), 'Religions of Illiterate People: Australia', in C. J. Bleeker and G. Widengren (eds), *Historia Religionum, vol. II*, 609–28, Leiden: Brill.

Strehlow, T. G. H. (1978a), *Central Australian Religion. Personal Monototemism in a Polytotemic Community*, Bedford Park, South Australia: Flinders University.

Strehlow, T. G. H. (1978b), *Aboriginal Religion*. Adelaide: The Strehlow Research Foundation (pamphlet no. 4, vol. 1, June 1978). (Now held at the Strehlow Research Centre, Alice Springs, Box A: T.G.H. Strehlow. Articles by Title.)

Strenski, Ivan (1993), *Religion in Relation: Method, Application and Moral Location*, London: Macmillan.

Swain, Tony (1985), *On 'Understanding' Australian Aboriginal Religion*, Bedford Park, South Australia: Australian Association for the Study of Religions for the Charles Strong Memorial Trust.

Swain, Tony (1993), *A Place for Strangers. Towards a History of Australian Aboriginal Being*, Cambridge: Cambridge University Press.

Tafjord, Bjørn Ola (2013), 'Indigenous Religion(s) as an Analytical Category', *Method and Theory in the Study of Religion*, 25 (3): 221–43.

Tafjord, Bjørn Ola (2016), 'Scales, Translations, and Siding Effects: Uses of *indígena* and *religion* in Talamanca and beyond', in C. Hartney and D. J. Tower (eds), *Religious Categories and the Construction of the Indigenous*, 138–77, Leiden and Boston: Brill.

Taylor, John B, (1976), *Primal World Views: Christian Involvement in Dialogue with Traditional Thought Forms*, Ibadan: Daystar Press.

Thrower, James (1999), *Religion: The Classical Theories*, Edinburgh: Edinburgh University Press.

Thurfjell, David (2021), 'Semantic Confusions and the Mysteries of Life: An Interview with Ulf Drobin (Sweden)', in S. Fujiwara, D. Thurfjell and S. Engler (eds), *Global Phenomenologies of Religion: An Oral History in Interviews*, 29–49, Sheffield and Bristol, CT: Equinox.

Tremlett, Paul-François (2007), 'The Ethics of Suspicion in the Study of Religions', *DISKUS* 8: 1–16. Available online: http://www.basr.ac.uk/diskus/diskus8/tremlett.htm (accessed 24 February 2021).

Tremlett, Paul-François (2008), *Religion and the Discourse on Modernity*, London and New York: Continuum.

Troeltsch, Ernst (1991), *Religion in History: Essays*, trans. J. L. Adams and W. F. Bense, with an introduction by James Luther Adams, Edinburgh: T & T Clark.

Trompf, Garry W. (2016), 'Reflections on Indigeneity and Religion', in C. Hartney and D. J. Tower (eds), *Religious Categories and the Construction of the Indigenous*, 8–37, Leiden and Boston: Brill.

Tsonis, Jack (2016), 'Against "Indigenous Religions": A Problematic Category That Reinforces the World Religions Paradigm', in C. Hartney and D. J. Tower (eds),

Religious Categories and the Construction of the Indigenous, 58–73, Leiden and Boston: Brill.

Turner, Harold (1971), *Living Tribal Religions*, London: Ward Lock Educational.

Turner, Victor W. (1985), 'Liminality, Kabbalah and Media', *Religion*, 15: 205–17.

Tylor, E. B. (1892), 'On the Limits of Savage Religion', *Journal of the Anthropological Institute*, 21: 283–301.

Tylor, E. B. (1903 [1871]), *Primitive Culture: Researches into the Development of Mythology, Philosophy, Religion, Language, Art, and Custom*, 2 vol, 4th edn, London: John Murray.

UiT Arctic University of Norway, 'Indigenous Studies Master'. Available online: https://uit.no/utdanning/program/270446/indigenous_studies_-_master (accessed 17 March 2021).

UNESCO, 'Text of the Convention for the Safeguarding of the Intangible Cultural Heritage'. Available online: http://www.unesco.org/culture/ich/en/convention (accessed 21 August 2016).

Waardenburg, J. (1978), *Reflections on the Study of Religion*, The Hague, Paris and New York: Mouton Publishers.

Walls, Andrew F. (1980), 'A Bag of Needments for the Road: Geoffrey Parrinder and the Study of Religion in Britain', *Religion*, 10 (2): 141–50.

Walls, Andrew F. (1987), 'Primal Religious Traditions in Today's World', in F. Whaling (ed.), *Religion in Today's World: The Religious Situation of the World from 1945 to the Present Day*, 250–78, Edinburgh: T & T Clark.

Walls, Andrew F. (1988), 'Foreword', in Philippa Baylis, *An Introduction to Primal Religions*, v, Edinburgh: Traditional Cosmology Society.

Walls, Andrew F. (1996), 'African Christianity in the History of Religions', *Studies in World Christianity*, 2 (2): 183–203.

Walls, Andrew F. (1998), 'Christianity', in J. R. Hinnells (ed.), *A New Handbook of Living Religions*, 55–161, London: Penguin Books.

Walls, Andrew F. (2004), 'Geoffrey Parrinder (*1910) and the Study of Religion in West Africa', in F. Ludwig and A. Adogame (eds), *European Traditions in the Study of Religion in Africa*, 207–15, Wiesbaden: Harrassowitz Verlag.

Westerlund, David (2006), *African Indigenous Religions and Disease Causation: From Spiritual Beings to Living Humans*, Leiden: Brill.

Wiebe, Donald (1999), *The Politics of Religious Studies: The Continuing Conflict with Theology in the Academy*, London: Macmillan.

Worby, Eric (2003), 'The End of Modernity in Zimbabwe? Passages from Development to Sovereignty', in A. Hammar, B. Raftopoulos and S. Jensen (eds), *Zimbabwe's Unfinished Business: Rethinking Land, State and Nation in the Context of Crisis*, 49–81, Harare: Weaver Press.

INDEX

Hubert, H. 143
Husserl, E.
  eidos 15
  epistemological framework 3
  epoché 12, 13, 15
  'fact world' 15
  intentionality 13, 45
  'natural attitude' 24
  phenomenology 2
  philosophy 69
hybridity 74, 203
  intentional 190, 200, 201, 203
  organic 201
hybridization 201

identifiable community 100, 124, 127–9,
  168, 169, 175
identity 79
  and alterity 79–81
  Elders 217
  implications of 80–1
  totemic 215, 216
Ideology of Religious Studies, The
  (Fitzgerald) 5, 97–8
Idowu, E. B. 21, 24, 44, 110, 163, 164, 175
illocutionary speech 79
'indigenous' 113, 115, 117–23, 128, 130–3,
  138, 177
Indigenous Australia 173–4
Indigenous populations 93, 109, 118, 119,
  133, 135, 141, 142, 163, 173, 199, 205
Indigenous Religions 123
  academic study of 109–13
  African 21–6, 43, 44, 55
  Arrernte 37, 39
  characteristics of 115, 116, 129, 141
  Christianity 111–13, 132
  competing theories of 117–20
  contemporary studies of 200–3
  definition of 5–6, 28, 38, 113–17, 121,
    123, 127–9, 131, 132, 134, 177, 226
  global study of 27, 28
  Hervieu-Léger and 123–7
  international study of 29
  kinship relations 128, 130
  and 'mutating structures of believing'
    137–8
  narrow and restricted definition 127–9
  Primal Religions 110–15, 136
  problems in 117–20

quasi-legendary myths 128
radical phenomenology of 225–7
restricted use of 132–7
scholarly opinion 33
Strehlow's contribution 29–32, 38–41
Tafjord and 129–32
theory 117–20
types of material 191
of Zimbabwe 22, 101
individual consciousness 17, 18
individualism 170–2, 175
Inkamala, M. 209, 216–18
'insider' discourse 8, 11, 13, 20, 21, 24, 25,
  74, 75, 77, 79, 81, 122, 225, 226
Institute for the Study of Secularism in
  Society and Culture (ISSSC) 164
intellectual climate 74, 170
intellectual soup 224–5
intentional hybridity 190, 200, 201, 203
intentionality 12, 13, 45, 61
interlocutionary situation 81
internalization 63
International Association for the History
  of Religions (IAHR) 86
International Convention of Intangible
  Cultural Heritage 209
interpolation 14, 17–18, 21, 24, 25, 30, 35,
  36, 61, 85, 225
Interpretation of Religion, An (Hick) 76
interpretative phase 29–31
Interpreting Religion (James) 4
interreligious dialogue 78, 81
Introduction to Maori Religion, An (Irwin)
  163
Introduction to Primal Religions (Baylis)
  113, 163
Irwin, J. 163
Isambert, F. -A. 143
Islam 22, 24, 44, 45, 50, 51, 53, 83–6, 98,
  110, 111, 114, 126, 129, 133, 136, 145,
  174, 190, 191
Is Religion Killing Us? (Nelson-Pallmeyer)
  83

Jackson, G. 222–6
James, G. 4
Jedism 125
Jesus Christ 22, 112, 132, 173, 180, 181,
  183, 185, 202, 203
Johnson, C. 168

www.ingramcontent.com/pod-product-compliance
Lightning Source LLC
Chambersburg PA
CBHW050413280326
41932CB00013BA/1847